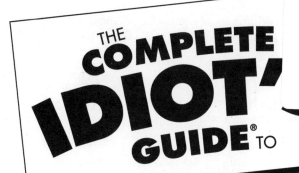

THE
COMPLETE
IDIOT'S
GUIDE® TO

CW00919865

Hebrew Scripture

by Rabbi Aaron Parry

ALPHA

A member of Penguin Group (USA) Inc.

This work is dedicated to my dear wife, Mindy, who epitomizes the astute insight of King Solomon
"The wisdom of women builds her house ...." (Proverbs 14:1)

ALPHA BOOKS

Published by the Penguin Group

Penguin Group (USA) Inc., 375 Hudson Street, New York, New York 10014, U.S.A.

Penguin Group (Canada), 10 Alcorn Avenue, Toronto, Ontario, Canada M4V 3B2 (a division of Pearson Penguin Canada Inc.)

Penguin Books Ltd, 80 Strand, London WC2R 0RL, England

Penguin Ireland, 25 St Stephen's Green, Dublin 2, Ireland (a division of Penguin Books Ltd)

Penguin Group (Australia), 250 Camberwell Road, Camberwell, Victoria 3124, Australia (a division of Pearson Australia Group Pty Ltd)

Penguin Books India Pvt Ltd, 11 Community Centre, Panchsheel Park, New Delhi—110 017, India

Penguin Group (NZ), cnr Airborne and Rosedale Roads, Albany, Auckland 1310, New Zealand (a division of Pearson New Zealand Ltd)

Penguin Books (South Africa) (Pty) Ltd, 24 Sturdee Avenue, Rosebank, Johannesburg 2196, South Africa

Penguin Books Ltd, Registered Offices: 80 Strand, London WC2R 0RL, England

Copyright © 2005 by Rabbi Aaron Parry

International Standard Book Number: 1-59257-354-1
Library of Congress Catalog Card Number: 2005925416

07   06   05   8   7   6   5   4   3   2   1

Interpretation of the printing code: The rightmost number of the first series of numbers is the year of the book's printing; the rightmost number of the second series of numbers is the number of the book's printing. For example, a printing code of 05-1 shows that the first printing occurred in 2005.

Printed in the United States of America

Note: This publication contains the opinions and ideas of its author. It is intended to provide helpful and informative material on the subject matter covered. It is sold with the understanding that the author and publisher are not engaged in rendering professional services in the book. If the reader requires personal assistance or advice, a competent professional should be consulted.

The author and publisher specifically disclaim any responsibility for any liability, loss, or risk, personal or otherwise, which is incurred as a consequence, directly or indirectly, of the use and application of any of the contents of this book.

Most Alpha books are available at special quantity discounts for bulk purchases for sales promotions, premiums, fundraising, or educational use. Special books, or book excerpts, can also be created to fit specific needs.

For details, write: Special Markets, Alpha Books, 375 Hudson Street, New York, NY 10014.

Publisher: *Marie Butler-Knight*
Product Manager: *Phil Kitchel*
Senior Managing Editor: *Jennifer Bowles*
Senior Acquisitions Editor: *Randy Ladenheim-Gil*
Development Editor: *Nancy D. Lewis*
Production Editor: *Janette Lynn*

Copy Editor: *Tricia Liebig*
Cartoonist: *Shannon Wheeler*
Cover/Book Designer: *Trina Wurst*
Indexer: *Tonya Heard*
Layout: *Angela Calvert*
Proofreading: *John Etchison*

Contents at a Glance

Contents

Appendixes

Foreword

Although he preferred to concentrate on the grammar and literal meaning of biblical texts, the great eleventh-century Sephardic Jewish scholar, poet, astrologer, scientist, and Hebrew grammarian Abraham Ibn Ezra also reminded readers in the introduction to his commentary on the Book of Genesis that *shivim panim la'torah*—"the Torah has seventy facets." By that he, and all those who over the ages have used this phrase to describe the intellectual wealth that is implanted in the Hebrew Scriptures, meant to tell us that, in terms the following pages might use, only a "complete idiot" would approach these texts with a simplistic and brittle reading of them. Those fundamentalists who diminish these texts with such an approach rob them of most of their meaning. That is why the Talmud urged that Scripture be studied and not just read.

In the pages that follow, Aaron Parry offers those who have for whatever reason been unable to gain access to these Scriptures such an opportunity for study. For those who are literalists and see only the simplest truths, or those who can only make selective sense out of a few of the ideas in Hebrew Scripture, this "Idiot's Guide" should offer help.

Informed readers have always understood that these texts have complex meanings that cannot be understood without interpretation. After all, what for example is one to make of the words, repeated three times (Exodus 23:19, 34:26, and Deuteronomy 14:21): "Thou shalt not boil a kid in its mother's milk"? The words and the fact of their repetition clearly needs interpretation, and indeed the sages puzzled over it as they did over almost all the others in the Tanach. Some saw the words as an injunction against eating meat and milk together in a single meal; others saw the repetition as expressing a prohibition against eating, cooking, and enjoying meat and milk together. The interpretations are many. Those who studied these words understood, as readers of these pages will, that the Scriptures need interpreters and guides. How else could so ancient a set of writings continue to speak to readers for countless generations?

There are those who will argue that only those who believe in God need open these books. God is surely a major actor here, but the sages understood that the "Torah is not in heaven." The insights and ideas, messages and perspectives offered in the sacred texts are human. As the Talmud put it, "the Torah speaks in the language of human beings." If, as Parry tells us, that language and style at first "seems foreign to contemporary living and thinking," this guide demonstrates that once one penetrates its ideas, there is much here that can offer meaning and guidance. When it came to the Torah, Rabbi Yochanan ben Bag Bag, one of a select group of converts to Judaism who became a Talmudic sage, rightly urged *hafoch bah ve hafoch bah de kula bah*—"turn it this way and that for all that there is is in it."

Samuel Heilman

Samuel Heilman is Distinguished Professor of Sociology and holder of the Harold Proshansky Chair in Jewish Studies at Queens College and the Graduate Center of the City University of New York. He is the author of nine books, including most recently *When a Jew Dies* and *Sliding to the Right: The Contest for the Future of American Jewish Orthodoxy.*

Introduction

The Jewish people have made their impact on civilization felt louder than any other nation that has walked this earth. Curiously, it has not been through monumental buildings, political supremacy, or the visual arts. They have no Taj Mahal, Great Wall of China, Coliseum, great Pyramids, or Eiffel Tower. The modest Knesset structure housing Israel's seat of government cannot compare to Buckingham Palace or the White House.

Perhaps no greater writer than that famous American author and humorist, Mark Twain, could capture the essence of that contribution. He made this observation about the Jewish people in his article "Concerning The Jews," published in *Harper's Magazine*, March 1898:

"If the statistics are right, the Jews constitute but one percent of the human race. It suggests a nebulous dim puff of stardust lost in the blaze of the Milky Way. Properly the Jew ought hardly to be heard of; but he is heard of, has always been heard of. He is as prominent on the planet as any other people, and his commercial importance is extravagantly out of proportion to the smallness of his bulk. His contributions to the world's list of great names in literature, science, art, music, finance, medicine, and abstruse learning are also away out of proportion to the weakness of his numbers.

He has made a marvelous fight in this world, in all the ages; and has done it with his hands tied behind him. He could be vain of himself, and be excused for it. The Egyptian, the Babylonian, and the Persian rose, filled the planet with sound and splendor, then faded to dream-stuff and passed away; the Greek and the Roman followed, and made a vast noise, and they are gone; other peoples have sprung up and held their torch high for a time, but it burned out, and they sit in twilight now, or have vanished.

The Jew saw them all, beat them all, and is now what he always was, exhibiting no decadence, no infirmities of age, no weakening of his parts, no slowing of his energies, no dulling of his alert and aggressive mind. All things are mortal but the Jew; all other forces pass, but he remains. What is the secret of his immortality?"

Samuel Clemens might have only to look at the one truly unique and exceptional contribution Jews have made—their contribution to religious thought—to discover the secret of his immortality. Of course, I am referring to the Jewish Scriptures or the Bible. In these pages we discover not only the history of one of the longest-surviving ethnic groups—but also tap into the origins of their singularly profound religious outlook, the spiritual matrix that makes them tick, and how Scripture has shaped their culture for more than 4,000 years.

How to Use This Book

Part 1, "All About the Jewish Scriptures." Like any discipline, studying Jewish Scripture has its unique principles, rhythm, and cadence. While it is impossible to give you a complete lesson on the entire body of teachings, you'll get a good taste. This part also explores the historical origins and provides a basic understanding of what the Hebrew Bible is all about.

Part 2, "In the Beginning: The Torah." God's revelation at Mount Sinai to the Jewish people and to Moses, their most influential leader, revolutionized the world. The written account of that communication is contained in the Five Books of Moses, which you'll explore in this section.

Part 3, "The Major Prophets." Much of the books of the Major Prophets is devoted to relating accounts of ancient Israelite history. You will also see how the prophets, more than predicting history, actually shaped it. They also contain profound prophetic messages that have both inspired and intrigued millions of people, and continue to do so today.

Part 4, "The Minor Prophets." The books of the *Trei Asar* (Maker's Dozen) are distinguished from the Major Prophets primarily by their shorter length. However, their content is just as valuable and significant to Judaism and the Jewish people. In this part, you'll also sample several passages that contain predictions that many believe are unfolding in contemporary times.

Part 5, "Writings Part I: The Poetical Books." Books like Psalms, Proverbs, and Job contain stirring verse and prose that have guided many through times of trials, tribulations, and suffering. The Jewish people have consistently turned to these works to seek advice and inspiration in the challenges that life deals them.

Part 6, "Writings Part II: The Five Scrolls." The Five Scrolls (in Hebrew, the Five Megillot), contain historical accounts of significant events in Jewish history. Whether the content is joy and miraculous deliverance, as found in the Book of Esther, or commemorates national Jewish tragedies, as recorded in the Book of Lamentations, these scrolls evoke very strong sentiments. Each is so unique that its public recital has become central to the observance of five special days in the Jewish calendar.

Part 7, "Writings Part III: The End of Prophecy." The Historical Books of Daniel, Ezra/Nehemiah, and Chronicles were the last to be incorporated into the Jewish canon of Scriptures. These books contain some of the most esoteric and profound passages found in the bible. The coming of the Messiah, tribulations at the end of days, and Armageddon (the war to end all wars)—you'll get a glimpse of all of these themes in this part.

Things to Help You Out Along the Way

Here's a guide to the different types of sidebars you'll see throughout the pages that follow.

Tower of Babel

Hebrew Scripture was written in Biblical Hebrew and Aramaic. Many such words are taken from these dialects to spice this guide for you. Look to these for approximate translations and meanings.

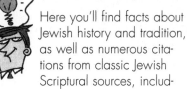

The Sages Say

The Hebrew written text is not complete without the comments of the greatest Jewish scholars of antiquity. You'll find words of wisdom from these important individuals here.

Lord Knows

These contain further insights and details of Judaism and Jewish life to enrich your study of Hebrew Scripture.

It Is Written

Here you'll find facts about Jewish history and tradition, as well as numerous citations from classic Jewish Scriptural sources, including the Talmud.

Acknowledgments

A production of this scope necessitates the efforts of a devoted team. I am particularly grateful to the profound skills of the good people at Alpha Books who worked with me on this project. First, warmest thanks to Randy Ladenheim-Gil, senior acquisitions editor, for her professional wisdom and patience in seeing this project to fruition. Special kudos are also in order to development editor Nancy D. Lewis for her keen eye and creative editing. Her requests for my clarifications and deeper explanations of the material greatly influenced the final product.

Many thanks to copy editor Tricia Liebig for keeping the text grammatically consistent. Production editor Janette Lynn, with her timely suggestions and assistance, is likewise noted. Finally, I wish to extend a most hearty thanks to Sonia Weiss, who has again come through masterfully with her editorial insights and brilliant literary instincts that enhanced the overall structure and organization of the text. May you all be abundantly blessed!

There is a Talmudic saying that "I learned much from my colleagues, more from my teachers, and most from my students." A good portion of this book was written while teaching Jewish students of my 11th grade Talmud class at Shalhevet High School in Los Angeles. Sharing some of the ideas found in this book with them help crystallize their expression—and we all benefit from that. While space doesn't permit me to mention them all, particular acknowledgment goes to Allan Azra, Sara Leah Cogan, Jonathan and Jordan Denitz, Erica Fensten, Alex Fox, Amanda Gelb, Talya Gold-finger, David Hanasab, and Seth Samuels. Keep up the good work.

As for colleagues, my brother Rabbi Moshe Parry is warmly recognized for his scholarly insights and suggestions to Chapter 20 on the Book of Psalms.

I wish to share eternal gratitude to the most influential person in my life—my dear wife Mindy. Her patience, forbearance, humility, charm, and grace have infused every page of this book. Concerning her, King Solomon spoke, "With all forms of wisdom did she build her house …." (Proverbs 9:1)

"Trust in the Lord with all your heart, and lean not on your own understanding; in all your ways acknowledge Him, and He shall direct your paths." (Proverbs 3:5–6) I pray that the Almighty finds favor in this work and thank Him for blessing the fruit of our labor.

Trademarks

Part 1

All About the Jewish Scriptures

God's commandments, genealogical rolls, wondrous and sometimes bizarre stories that reflect the world in its infancy—all this and more is what Jewish Scriptures, and in particular, the Hebrew Bible—are all about. Not only are these writings integral to Jewish life, they have influenced billions of other people in many ways.

1

What Is Jewish Scripture?

In This Chapter

- ◆ Discovering the Tanakh
- ◆ Teaching me
- ◆ Learning about Moses' five books
- ◆ Reading about life and literature

God's commandments, ancestral rolls, wondrous (and sometimes bizarre) stories that reflect the world in its infancy—all this and more are part and parcel of Jewish Scripture.

For more than 3,000 years, Jewish Scripture has played an integral role in Jewish life. But the unique nature of this important work has influenced billions of people in many different ways.

In this chapter, I set the tone and give you some background and context to prepare you for your journey through Jewish Scripture.

One Bible, Many Names

You might know the Jewish Bible, which is the cornerstone of Jewish Scripture, as the Hebrew Bible or the Old Testament. The last name is the one that many Christians use, but is not generally preferred by Jews. Regardless of the name, the content is the same. Or, as you'll soon see, pretty much the same.

Tanakh When a Jewish person hears the words Hebrew Bible or Jewish Scriptures, he or she invariably thinks of the word Tanakh, which stands for the acronym formed from the first letters of the Hebrew words for the three sections of the Hebrew Bible:

- ◆ Torah = Five Books of Moses
- ◆ Ne'viim = Prophets
- ◆ Ketuvim = Holy Writings

This acronym is seen in writings from the time of the Second Temple (ending 70 C.E.) and in Talmudic and Rabbinic literature.

Mikra Before the term Tanakh was invented, Jewish Scripture was often referred to as Mikra (plural Mikraot, readings), or reading. This term also connotes the entire body of the Jewish Bible, and is used to this day when referring to Jewish Scripture.

Tower of Babel

The literal meaning of **Pentateuch** is five cases, which refers to the sheaths or boxes in which the separate rolls or volumes of the ancient Bible are believed to have been originally stored.

Hebrew Bible Because the books comprising the Tanakh were largely written in Hebrew, the name Hebrew Bible is quite appropriate. This term is also preferred by some scholars who wish to avoid sectarian bias.

Torah The Torah, or the *Pentateuch*, is the first five books of the Bible: Genesis, Exodus, Leviticus, Numbers, and Deuteronomy. The word Torah is typically used to describe these first five books, but it can also be used to refer to the entire Jewish Bible. Some people apply the term even more broadly to the entire body of Jewish law and teachings.

Meet the Hebrew Bible

To start our study off on the right foot, let's tackle some of the basics about the Hebrew Bible by taking a closer look at how it's structured and what it contains. If you've never looked through a Jewish Bible, you might be surprised to find some basic differences between it and the Christian Old Testament. If you're familiar with the Christian Old Testament, you'll also see some obvious differences in order and number. For starters, there are fewer books. You'll find 24 books in a Jewish Bible; 39 in the Christian Old Testament.

Why the discrepancy in numbers? Because some books of the Jewish Bible, such as Samuel, Kings, and Chronicles, were simply too big to be issued as single volumes in the first printed versions.

The second major difference between the Jewish Bible and the Christian Old Testament is how the books are ordered. The 24 books of the Hebrew Bible are divided into three sections:

◆ Torah, the first section, contains five books: Genesis, Exodus, Leviticus, Numbers, and Deuteronomy. It's the same in the Christian Old Testament. According to Jewish tradition, God dictated the entire Torah to Moses.

◆ Prophets contains eight books: Joshua, Judges, Samuel, Kings, Isaiah, Jeremiah, Ezekiel, and The Twelve (Minor Prophets). The books in Prophets, as the name of this section implies, were revealed prophetically.

◆ Writings contains eleven books: Psalms, Proverbs, Job, Song of Songs, Ruth, Lamentations, Ecclesiastes, Esther, Daniel, Ezra/Nehemiah, and Chronicles. Tradition holds that these writings were conveyed by divine inspiration without prophetic revelation.

In this book, I follow the Jewish convention unless otherwise indicated.

Part 1: God's Commandments

As you now know, the Jewish Bible is divided into three parts. In the first part is found the repository and sum total of the communication between God and Moses on Mount Sinai. However, to the Jewish people, it's not merely a written collection of commandments. In Hebrew, commandment has a deeper meaning.

The Hebrew counterpart for commandment is *mitzvah*. The conventional translation of this word indeed is commandment. However, mitzvah contains the root *tzav*, and means "connection." Hence, the word mitzvah connotes a connection with God.

Commanding someone to do something sounds dictatorial, while connecting with someone (or in this case with an omniscient being) is inviting.

To millions of people who live their lives structured around these commandments contained in the Five Books of Moses, that is precisely how they feel. God is inviting them to make a personal connection with Him, and the vehicles with which they do so are the mitzvahs contained in the first five books of the Bible.

What you might not know is that the commandments or mitzvahs contained in the Torah only comprise less than two percent of God's divine legislation. There are many more commandments—in fact, 613 in all—covering subjects ranging from dietary laws to civil codes. They're contained in another set of Jewish Scripture called the Talmud, in which the great teachers of the Jewish faith explain how all these mitzvahs are inferred from verses in the Five Books of Moses.

> **Lord Knows**
>
> The Torah, or Written Law, is somewhat like crib notes to the actual lecture, while the Talmud, or Oral Law, is the actual lecture.

All 613 commandments are considered to be of equal importance and are the sacred and binding word of God. Of them, 248 are positive commandments, or suggest how one should act or behave, and 365 are negative, and warn against various acts or behaviors. We won't go into the Talmud much in this book, but it's important to know that the two are greatly intertwined, and, for that matter, can't exist without each other. As such, you will find some commentary from the Talmudic sages along the way. You'll also learn more about the Talmud in Chapter 3, and you'll find some sources for additional information on the Talmud in Appendix B.

Part 2: Seers and Leaders

The second part of the Jewish Bible contains writings from Jewish prophets. They were men and women of great virtue and sterling character who served as role models for the Jewish people.

These prophets were the real deal, whose exhortations, predictions, and teachings have stood the test of time. More than just a microphone for the Almighty, these prophets were profoundly enlightened human beings with unique personalities.

Each prophet wrote in a style exclusively his own and therefore quite original. Moreover, throughout Jewish history, these leaders stood up to deliver God's message and unite their people closer to God, even when their vision was unpopular among the masses—and even at risk to their own lives.

There have been prophecies and prognostications about every type of event, some of which happened, and some which didn't. We have all heard of these things in some form or another.

So what set the Prophets of Israel apart from the masses in this regard?

These individuals did not come to introduce new practices or laws to the people. Rather, they were appointed by God to reprove the nation when they strayed from the golden path—the Law of Moses.

The gist of all the teachings of the prophets was to encourage and instill within the Jewish people a greater conscientiousness toward upholding God's Will as presented in the Torah.

These prophets vigilantly followed in Moses' footsteps, took the basic themes that Moses conveyed, and gave clear illustrations on how these concepts could be manifested. But they never added or subtracted from the law Moses had given.

Although they often railed against the shortcomings of the nation, their words were never spoken as personal vendettas or deliberate retaliations.

It is a maxim of Jewish thought that, although many words of prophecy were uttered and transcribed, only those that contained teachings for future generations were recorded.

The eight books of prophets are divided into two parts:

- ◆ Ne'viim Rishonim (Early Prophets)   These books include Joshua, Judges, Samuel, Kings.

- ◆ Ne'viim Achronim (Later Prophets)   They consist of Isaiah, Jeremiah, and Ezekiel as well as what is called the Trei-Assar, or The Twelve, also referenced as the Minor Prophets.

The main objective of a prophet was to serve as a conduit between God and man. More than seeing the future, a prophet's purpose was to relay a divine message of an impending retribution or punishment from above unless the people mended their ways.

In short, the role of a prophet was more to shape history than to predict it. Our definition of the role of a prophet as shaper rather than predictor of the future is bolstered by the fact that most of the books of the Early Prophets were written after the events took place. As an example, the prophets Samuel and Jeremiah wrote the books of Judges and Kings respectively. They lived at the tail end of the time periods they wrote about. Read the books of Joshua and Samuel and you'll strain your eyes looking for even a hint of prediction about the future.

Part 3: The Writings

As mentioned earlier, the Ketuvim (the plural form of Ketav), means Writings, which makes up the third part of the Hebrew Bible. The Ketuvim are subdivided into three major parts.

◆ Wisdom literature (or Poetical Books): Psalms, Proverbs, and Job.

◆ Megillot (scrolls): Ruth, Esther, Lamentations, Ecclesiastes, and Song of Songs.

◆ Histories: Daniel, Ezra, Nehemiah, 1 and 2 Chronicles.

The Torah is a distinctively multifaceted document. Its components are simultaneously legal, ethical, mystical, religious custom, historical, advisory, and deeply spiritual. Let's take a closer look at some of these components.

A Book of History

When we study the Hebrew Bible we are studying the history of Israel. The entire Tanakh is a chronicle of history and the greatest repository of accurate historical information the world has ever known. This history is placed in the context of theology, because God has used the Jewish people and their history to reveal Himself to mankind. The Bible is much more than a history book; the events that occurred in the ancient past are a key to understanding our relationship to God.

How can we use this history?

Millions utilize these immortal, timeless words to learn from the triumphs and failures of biblical heroes to modify their lives to live in harmony with God's Will. However, as mentioned earlier in this chapter, chronicling history was not the main focus of its writers. Even the Book of Chronicles, while relating significant names and events of biblical history, is better known in Jewish literature as Sefer HaYuchasim (Book of Lineages).

> **Lord Knows**
>
> The Bible has been critically analyzed by scholars for both its literary style and historicity. The vast majority of departments of religion and Bible studies believe and teach that the Bible is a concoction of myths—ancient Israelite campfire legends that comprise a pseudo-history put together as a political document after the Jewish exile in Babylonia.

The Torah records the history of humankind's struggle to come to grips with the implications of its very creation. There is but one story to tell here, the story about how a created being was given the freedom to choose whether or not to confront the humbling fact of his/her being created with all its implications. And will that being, the only other one in existence besides God, utilize that freedom toward the betterment of society, drawing closer to his/her Creator, or delude himself into thinking he is the "end all" of creation and beholden to no one? In a nutshell, that is the history taught by the Torah. All else is superfluous.

In terms of historical events, developments, and personalities—the way we usually conceive of history—the Torah is an insufficient manuscript begging for the gaps to be filled in. But that's okay. "For my thoughts are not your thoughts, neither are your ways my ways, declared the Lord. As the heavens are higher than the earth, so are my ways higher than your ways and my thoughts higher than your thoughts." (Isaiah 55:8–9) Rather, God reveals history in its most influential and complete sense.

Archeological studies over the last 150 years have done much to independently confirm the accuracy of the events mentioned in the Bible. As an example, in 1828, the Leiden Museum in the Netherlands acquired a 16-page papyrus containing the words of an Egyptian scribe named Ipuwer. It gathered dust until 1909 when Oxford scholar Alan Gardiner translated the papyrus.

As he did, he saw some amazing parallels between events described in the document and those found in the book of Exodus, including the following:

Ipuwer Papyrus	Bible Verse (Exodus)
"Plague is throughout the land. Blood is everywhere." 2:5–6	"All the water of the Nile was turned to blood and the fish in the Nile died." 7:20
"The river is blood. Men shrink from tasting—human beings, and thirst after water." 2:10	"The Nile stank so that the Egyptians could not drink water from it and there was blood throughout the land." 7:21
"Behold cattle are left to stray, and there is none to gather them together." 5:5	"Then the hand of the Lord will strike your livestock in the fields … a very severe pestilence." 9:3
"He who places his brother in the ground is everywhere." 2:13	"For there was not a house where one was not dead." 12:30

Hebrew University professor Immanuel Velikovsky reported Gardiner's find in his book *Ages in Chaos* (Doubleday, 1952). He also concluded that from the style of the papyrus, it was evident that Ipuwer wasn't merely penning wild prognostications of future events. Velikovsky's dating approach placed the papyrus very close to 1250 B.C.E., which made Ipuwer a probable eyewitness to the events recorded in the Book of Exodus.

Teach Me

Unlike any other work of literature, the Tanakh conveys its message and transmits its instruction (another translation of the word Torah) in virtually unlimited ways. How are things such as animal sacrifice, idolatrous pyres used to consume Canaanite babies, trembling mountains, splitting seas, and talking donkeys relevant today?

The sages of Israel teach that there are 70 faces to a scriptural verse. What this means is that a verse might be interpreted in 70 different ways. What's more, none of them are wrong in the conventional sense. Each one may be perfectly intelligible within their given context.

It's important to know, however, that this doesn't mean that any and all interpretations of the text are correct. Nor does it give anyone license to manipulate the passage to conform to his or her assumptions about a biblical teaching.

What it does mean, in a sense, is that within context—and following certain rules—there is no "right" or "wrong" way to interpret a scriptural verse. However, some interpretations are more plausible than others and there are usually measurable criteria for making such determinations.

Another important concept commonly expressed throughout Rabbinic literature is "Dibberah Torah ke-lashon beney adam." Translated, this asserts that the "Bible speaks in a human tongue," as opposed to some sort of mystical code. This means that biblical discourse displays the same ambiguities of meaning that everyday speech both reveals and conceals.

It can also mean that the Torah will present a subject using the most common scenario, although application to other situations is implied. For instance, the Torah commands one to refrain from "cooking a kid goat in its mother's milk" (Exodus 23:19), although the prohibition of cooking meat and milk together is applicable to all lactating kosher mammals.

Lord Knows

A good portion of Jewish Scripture is written in a way that seems very foreign to contemporary living and thinking. However, it has a divine author and it contains an eternal message. As such, it also speaks to today's reader. It is relevant to every generation and to every individual.

The Legal Torah

Another translation of Torah is law. Truth be told, there is a very "do this, don't do that" element to divine legislation. So how does it work?

The greatest challenge the rabbis faced, starting with Moses, was to guide the people's will in conforming to that of a higher source. And what guided them in this? The Torah. They examined the Torah and tried to figure out what its take would be concerning a problem or question at hand. In so doing, they would try to negate their own ego, personal outlook, and prejudicial notions. To them, there were no values other than Torah values. As such, the study and analysis of Torah is a process of tremendous self-discipline—bending one's will and beliefs to conform to the contour of Torah's demands—not the other way around.

This is the major objective of the Torah legal system—where a rabbi or scholar attempts to hone in on the best solution and fit himself and his world into the Torah's structure. The only weapons in his quiver are his skill and focused training in the techniques of proper rendition of Biblical passages.

Visions of the Future

Does the Tanakh contain passages predicting events that are unfolding before our very eyes? Does the enmity of the Arab world for the West and toward America in particular have something to do with the miraculous rebirth of the Jewish homeland and America's embrace of it?

There is probably no greater religio-political issue facing Bible believers, Jew and non-Jew alike, than whether or not the re-establishment of the State of Israel is portentous in light of Scripture.

The hostility of Islamic fundamentalists toward Israel cannot be easily explained. Is there a Biblical source for this centuries-old conflict? How far will it go and how will it be resolved? These questions and many more are grist for the prophetic mill.

How America fits into Biblical prophecy is a huge hot button as well. American history seems to be saturated with Jewish influence and disproportionate attention seems to be given to this significant minority.

Does the Bible also forecast this phenomenon? As God said to Abraham, "I will bless those who bless you, and whoever curses you I will curse." (Genesis 12:3)

The second president of the United States, John Adams, declared toward the end of his life, "For I really wish the Jews again in Judea an independent nation." Harry Truman, the "Buck Stops Here" president, made good on Adams's best wishes by influencing his administration and the United Nations to approve the establishment of the Jewish State in 1948. Was the moral vision and clarity of these statesmen likewise predicted by Scripture? Or was it simply an issue of free choice?

In this book we will share with you several fascinating passages that uncannily portend many historical events that have transpired and seem to loom heavily in the future.

The Least You Need to Know

- ◆ The Jewish Scriptures are composed of 24 books and are also known by the acronym Tanakh, which is formed from the first letters of the Hebrew words for the three sections of the Hebrew Bible: Torah (Five Books of Moses), Ne'viim (Prophets), and Ketuvim (Holy Writings).

- ◆ Although clearly not its major objective, Jewish Scriptures are the most accurate historical documents of antiquity.

- ◆ Certain books of Scripture were so esoteric that the sages wanted to suppress them, lest the masses misinterpret them.

- ◆ There are various levels of divine inspiration that could settle upon a person to achieve a prophetic vision.

- ◆ There is tremendous interest among both scholars and laymen in what the Scriptures have to say about the modern State of Israel, America's relationship with it, and other contemporary issues.

Chapter 2

The World of the Hebrew Bible

In This Chapter

- ◆ Putting things into perspective
- ◆ Discovering life with the first patriarch
- ◆ Living everyday life in the Fertile Crescent
- ◆ Moving from many gods to one God

As mentioned, the Hebrew Bible is by, about, and for the people of Israel from their origins as a single family in Canaan through their partial return as a nation from exile in Babylonia.

To better understand how this all came about, and to put the good book into relevance, it's helpful to know a little more about the history of the people of Israel.

First Civilization

About 5,500 years ago in the Middle East, humanity evolved from hunting and gathering their food to farming it. Instead of spending most of their energy looking for food, they raised animals to eat, to use for clothing, and to plow the land so they could grow crops.

After this occurred, there was a surplus of food. This led to population growth and to civilization—sophisticated arrangements of people living together, not just simple agrarian settlements of a few people living in a few huts. People started specializing in types of labor. They became craftsmen, scribes, priests, and warriors. This, in turn, led to the growth of cities.

In cities, people of similar social, philosophical, and ethnic backgrounds lived together. The greatest unifying elements of these early civilizations were their religious principles and practices. Which brings us to a fundamental question: How did early humankind worship a power greater than themselves?

The Origins of Idol Worship

Adam and Eve had experienced God firsthand. As such, it wasn't difficult for them to acknowledge the presence of their Creator. Even after their slip up in the Garden of Eden, they didn't have a hard time following God's wishes, and they imparted a good level of devotion to their Creator.

Other early people didn't have the benefit of Adam and Eve's firsthand experiences. They found it difficult to find the Creator Himself. So they decided instead to serve and honor His great celestial servants. They reasoned that because God created the sun, the moon, and the stars (as well as placed them into the heavens above, thereby giving them prominence), it would only be proper to praise them and honor them as well. The flaw in the thinking of early people was they believed God wanted mankind to revere His closest servants in the same way a king wants his subjects to honor his princes, ministers, and servants.

Many, such as the Aztecs and others, believed they should honor and serve the sun because the sun seemed to be the most significant and the biggest player in their lives, without which the world could not exist. Great temples were erected in its honor. They began worshipping images of the sun in the belief that they would not only show homage to its Creator, but also be able to understand His Will.

Although early civilizations didn't believe that these images were actually God, they were under the false impression that it was somehow pleasing to God that they honored His mighty servants. It did not take long before even this concept was forgotten and people began to address these images in godly terms—"Then (God's name) became profaned as people began calling (humans and images) by the name of the

Lord." (Genesis 4:26) This really means they began to attribute godly powers to these graven images.

If the sun didn't do it for some people, water attracted their attention. Life couldn't exist without water either. They began to honor and later worship the mighty power of water in the same way the sun-worshippers did. The Pharaohs, in fact, claimed they were also gods, and duped people into believing that they wielded control over the Nile River, which was rain-bereft Egypt's main source of water. The Pharaohs, in collusion with their sorcerers, convinced the masses that anytime they approached the water it miraculously flowed in their direction. With this trick all Pharaohs laid claim to godly powers. Being the *pantheists* they were, the Egyptians also chose to worship sheep, as the huge statues at Karnak indicate, because they supplied the all-important product of wool.

Tower of Babel

Pantheists are people who believe that God and the material world are one and the same, and that God is present in everything. As such, they believe in many deities.

In time, people actually became convinced that when they directed their prayers to the god of water, the Pharaoh, or whomever, and soon thereafter it began to rain, it proved that the god of rain had actually answered their prayers. It did not occur to them that a master being was really manipulating the clouds.

The absurdity of this belief can be illustrated by someone praying to the "gods" of the electric company to turn the electricity back on during a blackout. A moment later, when the electricity comes back on, the person deludes himself into thinking that it was his prayers to the electric company that did the trick. Chances are no one at the electric company heard a word of this forlorn soul's supplications. Putting the lights back on had absolutely nothing to do with his prayers. Yet these clever priests and sorcerers fooled the masses into believing this nonsense. It was a good business that brought in lots of gold and silver and made them look powerful, so why not scam the people if there was big money to be made?

People would bring their sacrifices along with a delicious meal to these idols. The priest would lock the door and tell the person to come back tomorrow. After all, idols only eat their food in private, right? The gods wouldn't be pleased with people staring into their faces while they ate their meals. During the night the priests would of course go into the room through some trapdoor and enjoy a good meal of steak and wine. The next day when the person came back to see if his sacrifice had been eaten, he was happy to discover that it was eaten to the very last drop.

The priests also made absurd healing claims of every sort. They used their clever conjuring skills to get people to believe that they could make the blind see, the deaf hear, the lame walk, and even cure every incurable disease. The priests were very good at compelling individuals to serve a particular star or planet, with the claim that their god had instructed them so. Even today there are certain religious movements and religious leaders who employ some type of manipulation that preys on the ignorance and desperation of the masses in the name of "healing."

Life in the Fertile Crescent

The Fertile Crescent includes a huge swath of land incorporating the area bordering the Nile River in Egypt, the Levant (that middle section where the land of Israel is located), and the area where the Euphrates and Tigris rivers flow.

It Is Written

The three great rivers contribute mightily to the fertility and consequent desirability of this area. The Nile is an incredible river; the largest river in the world and the only one that actually flows backward. Without it, Egypt would be the Sudan, with its parched Sahara relying solely on rainfall. Egypt has been 97 percent desert since ancient times. The other two mighty rivers mentioned in the account of the Garden of Eden are the Euphrates and the Tigris rivers; they flow through what historians coined Mesopotamia, or "in the middle of two rivers," in Greek.

Whether civilization first sprang up in Egypt or in Mesopotamia (specifically in the section of Mesopotamia called Sumer as in Sumeria) is up for debate. However, we do know that the Fertile Crescent was where writing began, which is arguably the single greatest human innovation.

The written word gave civilization the opportunity to add one more dimension to its oral system of handing down traditions and legends about its culture and beliefs. How did it begin? With pictographs. When tribal elders convened, someone probably drew a stick figure and decided it should stand for "man." Someone else drew a figure with four legs and placed a tail on it; "beast."

One can imagine that these rudimentary drawings evolved into more abstract symbols that stood for phonetic sounds. Finally, there developed a system of two or three "letters," each representing a sound. These were combined to form a word that represented an idea or entity. Biblical Hebrew, for instance, is based on a two-consonant root system.

The Fertile Crescent was home to a great confluence of culture. Ur, the major city in southern Mesopotamia during the Neo-Sumerian period, contained a culture unlike anything that had ever existed before in human history. In Ur, there were great skilled craftsmen of all kinds, people who could read and write, an elite cosmopolitan class, and of course an elaborate religious structure.

It Is Written

Biblical critics in the late nineteenth century doubted that a city called Ur ever existed. However, in the late 1920s, Sir Charles Woolley led an expedition that excavated the ruins of Ur near the Euphrates River in Mesopotamia. They indicated that Ur was quite a well-developed city heavily steeped in idol worship, agreeing with the Biblical account. Ur is now referred to as Tall al-Muqayyar (or Mughair), about 200 miles (300 km) from Baghdad.

In about 1960 B.C.E., the strong third dynasty of Ur, which had ruled for more than 100 years, came to an end and was replaced by the rival dynasties of Isin and Larsa. Ur then declined somewhat in importance as a political center in the Mesopotamian valley.

During the next 75 years or so, Ur was under the domination of Sumerian rulers, although the Amorites, who had already taken over most of Syria and Palestine, were already pouring into Mesopotamia. By 1830 B.C.E., they founded the powerful first dynasty of Babylon, whose sixth king, Hammurabi (c. 1728–1686 B.C.E.), became the strongest ruler. Some scholars identify him with Nimrod, who is mentioned in Genesis (10:8–9). It seems that Nimrod initiated the building of the Tower of Babel, which you'll read more about in Chapter 4.

Up to this point, everyone spoke one language. The building of the Tower of Babel was yet another unifying effort to install the Babylonian demigod Nimrod "on top."

The Babylonians were not the only ones who were beginning to place faith in one deity. A small nomadic tribe that had wondered the Fertile Crescent for some time had entered into a covenant with their god Adonai. Adonai, the God of the Hebrews, was a mighty Leader, Creator, and Judge. Among the tribe was one

The Sages Say

The sages of Israel believed that Nimrod planned to build this tower ascending to the heavens to wage war against the One God. True, the actual verses do not reveal the true intentions of this plot—however, tradition instructs that Nimrod's machinations were intended to consolidate all forms of worship in the Fertile Crescent into one—him!

person who wanted to enlighten mankind that Adonai was more powerful than all their other false gods. He also wanted to convince them that He stood apart from the others because He needed no pantheon of lesser gods to accompany Him.

This person was Abram, who as Abraham is considered the first Hebrew. Of all things Mesopotamian, Abram just couldn't buy its religious beliefs. Despite the fact that he had been raised in a society that knew nothing other than polytheism, it all seemed like nonsense to him. Now that Nimrod had seduced his countrymen with his glib tongue and oration to worship, Abram was equally appalled. In time, Abram did more than reject the belief system of his family, friends, and society—he came to a novel and utterly unique conclusion about life:

> "I Am the Lord Your God"

Today we call that conclusion monotheism, the belief in one supreme God who is the sole source of all existence and upon whom everything remains totally dependent. It is at this point of radical departure that the Bible tells us that God appeared to Abram, confirmed his convictions, told him to pack his bags, and sent him on his first trip to Israel, known then as Canaan.

The Least You Need to Know

- Humanity evolved from hunting and gathering to farming about 5,500 years ago in the Middle East.

- Early people found it difficult to find the Creator Himself, and instead chose to serve and honor His great celestial servants.

- The Fertile Crescent is where writing began. It was also known as Mesopotamia, "the land between the rivers," for the very fertile land located in the triangular area between the Tigris and Euphrates rivers.

- Monotheism, which is the belief in one God, is what set the Hebrews apart from the other occupants of the Fertile Crescent.

Chapter 3

Reading Jewish Scripture

In This Chapter

- ◆ Reading front to back
- ◆ Learning it's all in the translation
- ◆ Keeping things in context
- ◆ Showing the way

To get a feel for what Jewish Scripture is really all about, you would have to read the real deal—a Hebrew Bible, not the Christian Old Testament. Ideally, you'd learn biblical Hebrew so that you can read the text in the language in which it was written. And, you'd follow the advice of the Talmudic sages and "provide thyself with a teacher and get thee a friend" to help you along your journey.

Although this approach may be ideal, it's simply not practical for many people. But here's the good news: It is possible to study Jewish Scripture without knowing Hebrew, and you can do it on your own. You learn how to go about it in this chapter.

Different, Yet Similar

As you now know, the Hebrew Bible is different from the Christian Old Testament. Some of the differences are cosmetic, such as the order and number of chapters. Other differences go deeper. One of the biggest differences lies in how the words themselves got onto the pages.

If you know anything at all about the Bible, you know there are different versions, or translations. (In scholarly writing, ancient translations are frequently referred to as *versions*. The term *translation* is typically reserved for medieval or modern translations.)

Jewish Scripture was, of course, originally written in Hebrew, the holy tongue. Some portions, such as parts of the books of Daniel and Ezra, were written in Aramaic, which was the language of the indigenous people of Babylonia, and later translated into Hebrew.

> **The Sages Say**
>
> The author of the Zohar, Rabbi Shimon bar Yochai, said "Just as the Torah was given in the Holy Tongue so was the world created with the Holy Tongue." The sages of the Talmud likewise teach that Hebrew was the language originally spoken by Adam and Eve and all human beings until the time of the Great Dispersion. Hebrew was often thought to be the language of the angels.

Early Christians translated the Hebrew Bible into several languages, including Syriac, Coptic, and Latin. Their source was a biblical text called the Septuagint, written in about the second century B.C.E. The Latin translations were historically the most important to the church in the West. The Greek-speaking East continued to use the Septuagint translation. However, the Old Latin translation was far from ideal so the church authorized another translation. This translation, known as the Vulgate, is based on Hebrew rather than Septuagint.

There are also a wide range of English translations of Jewish Scripture. Some, such as the King James Version (KJV), not only sorely missed the finer rules of Hebrew grammar and interpretation, it was written with a bias that seemed more interested in proving the divinity of Jesus than sticking to the context of the verse.

In 1917, the Jewish Publication Society (JPS) produced the first true English translation of the Tanakh. Although it was a great improvement over the KJV, it also had its flaws. One of the biggest flaws was that the divine name was sometimes spelled out as though it were meant to be pronounced by the reader, which is a strict no-no, as Jewish tradition forbids such pronunciation until the Temple is rebuilt in Jerusalem.

Over the years, some fine translations have been done of Jewish Scripture. You'll find several of them listed in Appendix B, "References." Any of the ones listed there are worth using as you explore the world of Jewish Scripture.

It Is Written

Unless you are a fan of the ancient Greek language, Latin, or even Hebrew, starting your study with any of these original texts or versions is not recommended.

Reading the Jewish Bible

Hold a Jewish Bible in your hands and you'll notice that things seem, well, a little backward. If you've never read a Jewish Bible before, you're in for some surprises. One of the biggest is that you'll probably feel like you're starting from the back of the book and working forward.

Jewish Bibles might seem like they're printed backward, but they aren't. The book is read from back to front instead of front to back, which is what we're most accustomed to. They do this because Hebrew script is written from left to right. As such, most English translations of Hebrew writings follow this format.

It Is Written

Jews first used chapter divisions in a 1330 manuscript and for a printed edition in 1516. For the past generation most Hebrew/English Jewish editions of the complete Tanakh have made a systematic effort to relegate chapter and verse numbers to the margins of the text.

Jewish Bibles do follow some conventions that Christian readers find familiar, including chapter divisions. This is not a Jewish division; rather, it was introduced by Stephen Langton, the thirteenth-century Archbishop of Canterbury. The Jews adopted them so they could quote chapter and verse in disputes with Christian clergy.

As for the traditional Jewish arrangement of the Five Books of Moses, there is a deliberate system that is organically related to the text. When God transmitted the Torah to Moses, He would dictate a paragraph at a time and give Moses a "break" in order to contemplate.

These breaks are preserved in the Torah in the form of spacings. They divide the text into what are called *parshiot*, or paragraphs. The Hebrew Bible and the Christian Bible sometimes differ on how verses are numbered. For example, the creation story in chapter 1 is artificially interrupted at verse 31, leaving the final three verses of the story to begin chapter 2.

The Importance of Context

Although it's typically best to study Scripture with the help of a learned and wise teacher—as I mentioned at the beginning of this chapter—it is possible to do it on your own. This is true of Jewish Scripture as well. However, should you decide to embark on this journey by yourself, it's important to keep a few things in mind. One very important precept is the significance of context.

It Is Written

When studying Jewish Scripture on your own, it's a good idea to keep in mind that the nuances of Hebrew language make an exact translation of the text from Hebrew to English almost impossible. Even the best translations can't tell the whole picture, as many passages were written metaphorically, not literally. In addition, most English commentaries only touch the surface or completely ignore the oral tradition that complements the text.

For Jewish people, studying the Tanakh in "Bible roulette" fashion is a no-no. There are no shortcuts. One needs to sit and carefully learn through an entire book. Simply parachuting into the middle of a passage without understanding the context of the chapter is foolish. It is popular among certain church circles to skip around from verse to verse and passage to passage to try to prove a theological assumption. This haphazard approach does not really give a true understanding of Scripture.

As an example, fundamentalist Christians base a major tenet of their belief system on the following verse: "For the life of the flesh [is] in the blood: and I have given it to you upon the altar to make atonement for your souls: for it [is] the blood [that] maketh atonement for the soul." (Leviticus 17:11, KJV)

They take this to mean that there is no forgiveness without the shedding of blood. Those who find this compelling proof should examine the verse more carefully, as it has been taken out of context. Although this verse does illustrate an aspect of importance in blood sacrifice, nowhere does it say that blood is the exclusive means for atonement. It's not even the main theme of this passage, for it appears in a section of Leviticus devoted to dietary laws.

"And whatsoever man [there be] of the house of Israel, or of the strangers that sojourn among you, that eateth any manner of blood; I will even set my face against that soul that eateth blood, and will cut him off from among his people. For the life of the flesh [is] in the blood: and I have given it to you upon the altar to make atonement for your souls: for it [is] the blood [that] maketh atonement for the soul. Therefore I said unto the children of Israel, No soul of you shall eat blood, neither shall any stranger that sojourneth among you eat blood." (Leviticus 17:10–12, KJV)

It's the blood that makes atonement, as opposed to the brains, kidneys, or lungs—just the blood. God simply instructs, "don't consume it." That's all. In no way do these verses suggest that blood is the only ticket to atonement from sin.

It should also be noted that these verses are spoken to the Jewish people. The sacrificial atonement system of the Mosaic Law was given exclusively to the Jewish people. Non-Jews could find remission of sin through sincere, confessionary repentant prayer.

The moral here: Don't use Scripture to prove theological assumptions. Read verses in context and base your learning as they are read.

Guiding the Way

The Bible contains wisdom from God, which is very different from worldly wisdom. As mentioned earlier, we aren't merely talking about a collection of entertaining prose or historical accounts. God's word communicated through Moses and a host of other prophets was intended to teach the Jewish people lessons on life.

We know that context is a very important rule in any form of writing and interpretation. Likewise, we have to know who, what, where, and when the writers of Tanakh were referring to when they spoke to the people. What did their words mean? Who were the prophets addressing? What were they trying to say?

Looking at Scripture kind of makes one scratch his head and wonder what it's all about. Do we take these things literally, allegorically, or as a combination of both? How do we correctly translate a verse? These issues are what make studying the Hebrew Bible so fascinating. They're also what make reading Jewish Scripture almost impossible without something to guide the way.

The Wisdom of the Talmud

It's customary to read the Hebrew Bible with study aids. For the Jewish people, the greatest study aid of all is the Talmud.

The Talmud records historical facts, homilies about how to live a righteous life, mystical teachings, medical advice, philosophy, and much more. It was written by the sages of Israel and is the main repository for commentary and historical context of Biblical verses.

The Talmudic sages of Israel were part of an unbroken chain of transmission going back to Moses at Mount Sinai. As integral links of this chain, they were the spiritual heirs of the prophets, disciples of their teachings, and charged with conveying the message of these holy men to subsequent generations. Some gave biblical texts a new reading remote from the plain meaning. They interpreted them in strange and marvelous ways based on the legends of natural impossibilities, perhaps intended as allegory. Others adhered closely to the literal meaning of texts.

> **Lord Knows**
>
> The first book to be printed in Hebrew was not the Bible but the Torah with the commentary of Rashi, one of the greatest Talmudic sages.

Jewish tradition holds that the Talmud is the Oral Torah, or a verbal explanation of the laws that God gave to Moses on Mount Sinai, and that Moses taught to others. It was maintained orally for nearly 1,500 years until persecutions and exiles at the hands of the Romans made it necessary to commit them to writing. The sages Ravina and Rav Ashi completed the 2,711 pages of the Talmud around the year 500.

Many Jews feel that it is impossible to truly understand Jewish Scripture without the guidance of the Talmudic sages. Studying Jewish Scripture, especially with these learned teachers, is a joy as it shows what questions can be asked of a text. "Look here!" Is this a contradiction? "Look here!" This can have two opposite meanings. Which is right? Why does the Torah not tell us this piece of information needed to understand the text? Why does it give us a fact that seems to be of no significance at first glance?

Depending on the version of the Tanakh you choose to read, you might see some Talmudic commentaries sprinkled throughout. You'll also meet a number of them in the pages ahead, as it's virtually impossible to have a meaningful discussion of Jewish Scripture without relying on them. Let's take a quick look at who they are.

Rabbenu Shlomo ben Yitzchaki (Rashi) 1040-1105

The outstanding Biblical commentator of the Middle Ages, Rashi was born in Troyes, France. He survived the massacres of the First Crusade through Europe. He was a fantastic scholar who, although he had no sons, fathered three daughters who became exemplary scholars in their own right. He studied with the greatest student of Rabbenu Gershom of Mainz.

Rashi's commentary was unique. His concern was for every word in the text that needed elaboration or explanation. Thus he used the fewest words possible in his commentaries. Ironically, he did not write most of his explanations. Tradition has it that his students would ask him questions about the text, or he would ask questions about specific words, and a student would write his short, lucid answers in the margin of the parchment text. These answers more or less comprise Rashi's commentary.

Nachman ben Moshe (Nahmanides) 1194-1270

Nahmanides was a mere 16 when he penned his first Talmud commentary. He wrote prolifically on every imaginable religious topic.

His commentary on the Torah was his last work, and his best known. He was prompted to write it by three motives: (1) to satisfy the minds of students of the Law and stimulate their interest by a critical examination of the text; (2) to justify the ways of God and discover the hidden meanings of the words of Scripture, "for in the Torah are hidden every wonder and every mystery, and in her treasures is sealed every beauty of wisdom"; (3) to soothe the minds of the students of the Law by simple explanations and pleasant words when they read the appointed sections of the Pentateuch on Sabbaths and festivals.

Nahmanides wove homiletic and mystical interpretations throughout his writings, which were based on careful philology and original study of the Bible. He was a vocal critic of the Greek philosophers, especially Aristotle, and even criticized Maimonides' biblical interpretations.

Abraham ben Meir Ibn Ezra (also known as Ibn Ezra or Abenezra) 1092-1167

One of the most distinguished Jewish men of letters and commentators on Hebrew Scripture of the Middle Ages, Ibn Ezra lived in Spain and wrote extensively on Tanakh. He also produced the first significant work on Biblical Hebrew grammar.

Contemporary Commentary

Recent commentaries for laypersons are different. They have been written as introductory notes to help explain the text and are often composite collections of comments from scholars of the past and from current biblical scholars.

There are too many to enumerate. Here are a couple of the most significant:

♦ Rabbi Shimshon Rafael Hirsch (1808–1888, Germany) was a prolific writer whose many works included "Horeb," a basic explanation of many Judaic principles. His greatest achievement was his commentary on the Bible. An English translation of the original German is widely disseminated today. He was famous for his mastery of Hebrew grammar and for explaining Biblical concepts in rational contemporary terms. He is credited with saving Torah observance in Germany during the nineteenth century.

♦ Rabbi Meir Leibish Malbim (1809–1879, Eastern Europe) is famous for his commentary on the entire Bible. He also wrote a significant monumental work on biblical grammar called "Ayelet HaShachar." All his writings are in a lucid style; his original comments pay close attention to the detailed nuances and derivations of words. His commentary of the Early Prophets is considered a modern classic in many circles.

These classic "modern" commentaries, among many others, are not restricted to explaining Scripture according to its simple meaning. As mentioned earlier, there are many levels of understanding.

Tower of Babel

The word **Pardes** (literally meaning orchard) is an acronym that developed in the Middle Ages to refer to four levels of biblical analysis or exploration. Some authorities believe that within each of these levels there are 70 faces of interpretation, thus yielding 280 ways of understanding.

Levels of Understanding

Traditional study of Jewish Scripture encompasses four levels of biblical understanding or exploration of the text. This is known as the system of *Pardes*, which stands for the following:

♦ Pshat: Simple, plain, intended meaning.

♦ Remez: Alluded meaning (reading between the lines). Traditionally, remez referred to methods such as gematria, or Jewish numerology. In modern Hebrew, remez means "hint."

- ◆ Drash: Literally means "to seek or draw out." The interpretative meaning. Drash is the opposite of pshat.

- ◆ Sod: Literally means "secret." The mystical or esoteric meaning.

Some commentaries concentrate exclusively on the Pshat, or simple meaning of the text. Others delve deeper into the more esoteric and hidden meanings of the text. The most famous, Rashi, for instance, concentrates mostly on this level, although he liberally ventured into Remez and Drash, with a little Sod sprinkled in on occasion.

Although it's not really possible to work through everything that Pardes is about in a book like this, you will get a taste for the deeper meaning behind some Scripture in the pages ahead.

Studying Versus Reading

Most people can study the Tanakh without knowledge of Hebrew, using English-language translations and scholarly commentaries. The key word here, however, is study. There's a difference between reading Scripture and studying it.

As mentioned, the sages of the Talmud teach "Provide thyself with a teacher and get thee a friend." (Ethics of The Fathers 1:6).

Lord Knows

The Jewish people have a time-honored system of completing the Five Books of Moses annually. The name for this is *Parshat HaShavua* (in Hebrew, portion of the week), which is the name given to the weekly portion of the Pentateuch that is read publicly in the synagogue each week of the Jewish calendar year. The public reading of the Torah dates all the way back to Moses and was done to ensure that the Jewish people would not go three days without hearing words of Torah.

If you're serious about studying Jewish Scripture, as opposed to reading it, it's best to do so in a scholarly setting. Fairly common sources of Biblical Hebrew instructions are classes at synagogues, colleges, and universities (including associated Hillel organizations and recommended private tutors) as well as Jewish and Christian seminaries.

There's also online instruction. Such organizations as The National Jewish Outreach Program (NJOP) provide a free crash course in reading Hebrew. Their website is www.NJOP.com and they are constantly opening new sites around the country where qualified teachers are sharing their wisdom with eager pupils.

One can choose to jump right in and locate a synagogue where this weekly study is conducted or follow your own pace. If you're not Jewish, you might feel uncomfortable simply walking into a synagogue. If so, an online resource or private tutoring center might be more to your taste.

The Least You Need to Know

♦ Although not essential to the process, learning Hebrew can greatly enhance the study and understanding of the original Hebrew Scriptures.

♦ Context means everything when reading a passage of Hebrew Scripture correctly. It is a bad practice to cut and paste a verse by lifting it from its context to advance some belief or agenda.

♦ Translating a verse or word correctly is an art. The traditions of how to do this were diligently passed down by the sages of Israel.

♦ Many Jews follow an ancient custom of public Torah and other Scripture readings each week. This allows each person to complete the cycle of the Five Books of Moses each year.

Part 2

In the Beginning: The Torah

The Five Books of Moses (the "T" of Tanakh) contain both the early history of the Jewish people and the wondrous communication that took place between God and Moses on Mount Sinai. There are lots of do's and don'ts here, but the writings go beyond mere commandments.

Chapter 4

From Nothing, Something: The Book of Genesis Part I

In This Chapter

- ◆ Letting there be light
- ◆ Creating the world
- ◆ Living in the Garden
- ◆ Floating away

Although the Book of Genesis is most familiar as the book that describes how the world was created, it's much more than that. It's not just the story of what happened, it also foretells what will happen. For this reason, Nahmanides, who you learned about in the previous chapter, called it the Book of Signs, for it reflects the destiny of the Jewish people. The Book of Genesis also reveals the exemplary deeds of the patriarchs and matriarchs—the righteous individuals who formed the very foundation of Judaism.

In this chapter, we explore the first half of Genesis, from the creation of the world and humankind through its near destruction.

In the Beginning ...

Genesis begins, of course, with the creation of the universe. It is an axiom of faith that this came about *ex-nihilo*, meaning "from nothing." Before it, nothing existed, not even the basic elements of nitrogen, helium, carbon, and hydrogen. Call it the Big Bang, Cosmological Cataclysm, or Nuclear Nascence; at God's command, miraculously, everything came into being at once. No other event holds a candle to this one. Nor can anyone explain it. Nor does the Bible attempt to explain it.

> **Tower of Babel**
>
> **Genesis** is a Greek word meaning origin, beginning, source, or generation. The original Hebrew title of this book, Bereshith, means in the beginning.

Although there are schools of thought that try to reconcile the first chapter of Genesis with the best scientific inquiry has to offer, the fact remains that we will never know exactly how this miraculous event came about.

Although there is no direct mention of the author anywhere in the book of Genesis, tradition holds that Moses penned this work, as well as the rest of the first five books of the Bible.

Let There Be Light

One of the first things God did was to throw a little light on the subject. He then divided the light from the darkness and created the first day.

> **The Sages Say**
>
> According to Rabbi Moshe Chaim Luzzatto, the seventeenth-century Italian scholar and mystic, God did not create the world because He *needed* to do so. Nor did He bring the world into existence out of being indebted to anyone; rather, He created the world purely as an act of kindness with no other motive. The orderliness of a pristine world, perfect in all its wondrous systems, speaks of design and purpose.

There is great disagreement over what actually constitutes a creation *day*. Some scholars believe that they were 24-hour days just like we know them today. Others believe they were periods of undetermined length. Here, as is the case in many parts of the Bible, it's best not to take things too literally or to strive for a perfect understanding. Perhaps the best take on these words of Scripture is to see them as a reflection of God's creating the world in an orderly fashion, as part of His plan—and on His terms.

Let There Be Earth and Water

"God said, 'Let the waters beneath the heaven be gathered into one area, and let the dry land appear.'

God called to the dry land: 'Earth,' and to the gathering of waters He called: 'Seas.' And God saw that it was good." (Genesis 1:9–10)

God then creates earth and water from that which was "without form, and void." (Genesis 1:2)

As noted, He gathers the water into one area at first, then calls for dry land to appear. This separates the one body of water into seas.

The Sages Say

Mystical teachings indicate that God commanded the waters that they should not move from their place; and He set the sand as the boundary of the seas as a warning of sorts that they should go no further. Thus we see that when there is a storm, the great waves rage, and it seems as if they are about to destroy the world. But when they reach the sand, they back down submissively in deference to God's command.

Let There Be Flora and Fauna

"And the earth brought forth vegetation; herbage yielding seed after its kind, and trees yielding fruit each containing after its kind. And God saw that it was good." (Genesis 1:12)

So now there's the earth, and it's bursting with flora and fauna. Or is it? In chapter 1, it sure seems to be. In chapter 2, however, we read "Now all the trees of the field were not yet on the earth and all herb of the field had not yet sprouted, for the Lord God had not sent rain upon the earth and there was no man to work the soil." (Genesis 2–5)

What are we to make of this? There are at least a couple of ways to look at it. One is to follow the wisdom of the sages who teach that not until man was created did all herbage sprout above the earth. It was ready to go, but it lacked one thing—rain.

God had not sent rain because there was no man to work the soil, thus no one to properly acknowledge its usefulness. When the rain eventually falls, in answer to Adam's prayer, the trees and vegetation that were poised just beneath the earth, sprout out in all their majesty. There's a simple, profound lesson here: God provides exactly what mankind needs.

A more analytical approach would hold that the first two chapters of Genesis actually contain fragments of two creation stories. Either way, they get us to the same place, so it's probably not necessary to come to a complete reconciliation here, either.

So now there's a world. But God isn't done yet. It's now time for His greatest creation.

Man Oh Man!

Adam was God's handiwork and created as perfect as they come. His majestic countenance was so radiant that even after his death, it's said the cave he was buried in shone like the sun. It's also said that the angels were bedazzled by his brilliance, clamored over him and bowed to him as he strolled through the Garden. Only after God caused Adam to sleep did the angels realize that he was only human and recognized their error.

All this, and more, is implied when on the sixth day of creation God proclaims "Let Us make man in Our image, according to Our likeness." (Genesis 1:26)

Our image? Our likeness? But Jews only believe in one God. What's with that?

God's words here have been the subject of great debate throughout the centuries. Trinitarian Christians maintain they are Biblical evidence of a triune god. Jews don't see it this way, and, in fact, find this claim erroneous. This inference is also refuted by the subsequent verse, which relates the creation of man to a singular God, "And God created man in **His** image." (Genesis 1:27)

Why, then, did God choose to convey the creation of man in this ambiguous fashion? The answer to this question requires understanding the spiritual context of Scripture. Here, God allows the plural usage to manifest His humility.

God addresses the angels and says to them, "Let us make man in our image." It is not that He needs or invites their help, but He does this as a matter of modesty and courtesy. God associates them with the creation of man.

Because the Torah is foremost a document of instruction on living a proper life, it teaches us that a great person should act humbly and consult with those lower than him.

Lord Knows

It is not unusual for God to refer to His heavenly court (angels) as "us." We find in Isaiah 6:8, "And I heard the voice of the Lord, saying, 'Whom shall I send, and who will go for us?'" Although God is perfectly capable of acting without assistance, He makes His intentions known to His servants. Thus, we find "Shall I conceal from Abraham that which I am doing?" (Genesis 18:17) Likewise; "For the Lord God will do nothing without revealing His counsel to His servants the prophets." (Amos 3:7)

One additional thought, advanced by the founder of the Chassidic movement, Rabbi Yisrael Bal Shem Tov (1698–1760), goes like this. Following the concept that the Torah is foremost a book of divine instruction, God's words here directly address readers, beckon them to recognize their potential, and encourage them to fashion themselves into the best they can be. What better image could there be?

In the Garden

God made two perfect creatures and placed them in the Garden of Eden, paradise on earth. He did, however, give them one condition: that they not eat from the Tree of Knowledge.

Why did God command them not to eat from this tree? Why didn't He make life easier for them and not put that temptation there in the first place?

The answer is that God created Adam and Eve so they would do well and perfect the world. If they did not have the opportunity to perform evil, then they would not have the opportunity to perform good. They would have become robots.

> **It Is Written**
>
> God's first commandment in Scripture is also a dietary one. His directive to Adam and Eve serves as a valuable lesson in setting boundaries and reflects humankind's challenge to subdue its own interest in favor of a higher voice. Restraint and conquering one's evil inclination so that humankind should enjoy complete reward for its freewill decisions is what God created the world for.

A Cunning Snake

But Eve falls prey to the seductive reasoning of a snake, which Scripture notes was "more cunning than any beast of the field which the Lord God has made." (Genesis 3:1) The snake taunts Eve, telling her that the reason God doesn't want her and Adam to eat the fruit is because "God knows that in the day you eat of it your eyes will be opened, and you will be like God, knowing good and evil." (Genesis 3:5)

The temptation is simply too much for Eve. She eats the fruit and gives a piece to Adam. The rest is … well, history. Adam and Eve hear God as he's taking his customary early evening walk through the Garden, and they hide from him. God asks them what's going on and the answers aren't good. Both Adam and Eve are fearful, aware of their nakedness, and trying to pin the blame on anyone but themselves.

Adam and Eve's simple, serene existence in the Garden is no more. Adam is relegated to a life of hard work. Eve and all the women after her endure painful childbirth. And the serpent literally bites the dust, "and dust shall you eat all the days of your life." (Genesis 3:14) Perhaps his punishment is true poetic justice—he caused mankind to return to dust, so he is made to taste the least desirable product of the earth—dust!

> **Lord Knows**
>
> Jewish tradition has it that when the long-awaited Messiah arrives, he will repair the damage of Adam's mistake. The state of the world will return to a perfected state that existed before the sin.

Leaving the Garden

Adam and Eve were created on the sixth day of the week, they sinned on that day, the holiness of the Sabbath gave them a brief reprieve, and then they were banished immediately after the Sabbath ended.

Among the post-Garden realities concerning Adam and Eve's existence is that life was no longer a "piece of cake." The ready-to-eat delights that beckoned to them in the Garden were no longer available. They would have to toil for their sustenance.

The First Family Feud

After man unleashed the proverbial Pandora's Box on the world, it didn't take long before things spiraled out of control.

In keeping with the new world order of man eking a livelihood from physical labor, the two sons of the first couple chose different forms of work; Abel became a shepherd, and Cain became a farmer. This division eventually spawned jealousy and hatred. God accepted Abel's offering, comprised of sheep (perhaps its shearing), and rejected Cain's, which consisted of flax (the least significant of his crops). It is no wonder that God accepted Abel's offering while rejecting that of his brother.

We don't know how Cain knew how to inflict a mortal wound, as no one had ever killed a human being before. However he did it, God swiftly rebuked him. "Maybe you can hide from your parents but you cannot hide from Me." Then He asked him the famous question, "Where is Abel your brother?" (Genesis 4:9)

Cain bold-facedly replied, "Am I my brother's keeper? How do I know where he went?" (ibid) Even the long-suffering merciful God had enough of such chutzpah.

He decreed that Cain would never again derive benefit from the earth. Whatever he would sow and reap in harvest would leave the earth depleted and less fertile than before. The brazen, over-confident Cain, who thought he would become sole ruler over the world, would become nothing more than a wanderer upon the earth.

Noah and His Ark

Cain's actions, coupled with his parents' indiscretions in the Garden, spawned a series of decadent generations that stooped to new lows. So low, in fact, that God regretted He had made man and decided to destroy his creation. But, as Scripture notes, "Noah found grace in the eyes of the Lord." (Genesis 6:8)

Not much could be done with such a perverse world. God found only one person and family worthy of any virtue to build from. Noah and his small family were the only ones who maintained a semblance of decency.

God wanted to destroy the world outright, but gave His people a 120-year furlough to repent their evil ways. That was the time it would take Noah and his family to build an ark, according to God's commandments.

God told Noah that He was establishing his covenant with Noah and his family, and that they would be spared His wrath. He commanded Noah to bring two of every living thing to the ark to keep them alive.

Unlike the later chosen ones who questioned and debated with God about his plans, ever trying to change His mind, Noah never spoke. He simply "did according to all that the Lord had commanded him." (Genesis 7:5)

Floodwaters rise, the world dies, and locked up in the box God planned for him, he weathers the storm.

It Is Written

Noah's ark was built only to float, not to sail anywhere. Many ark scholars believe that the ark was a barge shape, not a pointed boat shape. It had neither oars nor sails. This greatly increased the cargo capacity and buoyancy.

Lord Knows

The top 3,000 feet of Mount Everest (from 26,000–29,000 feet) is made up of sedimentary rock packed with seashells and other ocean-dwelling animals. Sedimentary rock, which is formed in water, is found all over the world. Petrified clams in the closed position, found in sedimentary rock all over the world, testify to their rapid burial while they were still alive, even on top of Mount Everest.

After the floodwaters recede, God establishes his covenant with Noah, as promised. He tells him that a flood will never destroy the earth and sends a rainbow as a visual sign of the "covenant that I have established between Me and all flesh that is on the earth." (Genesis 9:17)

Back on terra firma, Noah showed no further interest in the sea—he took up farming and planted the world's first vineyard. He also became the world's first drunk—he wanted to forget the gray reality of a world undone and he was soon up and about to direct the new world. Among his accomplishments in that regard, he is credited with being the first one to manufacture, or at least fashion, the world's first farming implements.

Noah's Sons

Scripture notes that Noah had three sons: Shem, Ham, and Japheth. From them, the whole earth was repopulated. Japheth, whose name is synonymous with beauty, represents the European-Asian people who have historically devoted much energy to developing architecture, technology, arts, and science. Ham is associated with the peoples of Africa. Shem represents the Semitic people. From his line comes Abraham, who you'll meet in the next chapter along with the other patriarchs and matriarchs who were the ancestors of Israel.

The Least You Need to Know

- It is an axiom of faith that the world came about ex-nihilo—from nothing. Before it nothing existed, not even the basic elements of nitrogen, helium, carbon, and hydrogen.

- The account of creation is one of the most difficult to comprehend and one of the most controversial topics of the entire Bible.

- As perfect as Adam and Eve's creation and idyllic existence was in the Garden of Eden, they still ate from the Tree of Knowledge and unleashed to the world not only mortality, but the inclination to choose evil over good.

- Humankind continued in a decline from the time of Cain's murder of his brother Abel, until it was so corrupt in Noah's time that it greatly angered God and necessitated its demise through a great flood.

5

The Papas and the Mommas: The Book of Genesis Part II

In This Chapter

- ◆ One God
- ◆ Abraham and Sarah
- ◆ Isaac and Rebecca
- ◆ Jacob and Esau
- ◆ Joseph and his coat

God has wiped the world clean and started things anew with Noah and his small family. However, even with this new start, people quickly reverted to their old ways. But an individual would emerge who would lead the transition from chaos to enlightenment: Abram.

The simple purpose of the second half of Genesis is to reveal the exemplary deeds of this exemplary leader and the other righteous individuals who formed the very foundation of the Jewish people.

Shem's Descendants

Remember Shem, Noah's son? He had many sons and daughters after the flood. One of his descendants is a man named Abram.

Abram hailed from Ur Kasdim, a rich city full of culture and art. His father Terach was a merchant in stone and wood images. As was the custom, Abram also worshipped these images.

Tradition has it that from the time he was a little boy, Abram wondered what powered the great celestial bodies. His intellectual honesty allowed him to notice that some unifying force gave everything in creation its boundaries.

God revealed Himself to Abram through His presence in nature. All Abram did was reason that behind all the plan and purpose there must be some heavenly intelligence. Abram did not have a father or a mentor to teach him these truths. Instead, God imbued him with tremendous wisdom and intellect to understand that this beautiful intricate world must have a creator.

Lord Knows

The nickname for Genesis, Sefer HaYahsar or Book of the Upright, reflects the book's purpose of relating the deeds of the patriarchs and matriarchs, who were its most upright personalities.

So great were Abram's faith and courage that he transformed the generation by his example and teachings.

In chapter 11 of Genesis, we also learn that Abram is married to a woman named Sarai. She, too, will play a key role in the transformation of a generation.

From Many Gods to One God

Although the biblical details are sketchy, God clearly reveals himself to Abram at some point along the way. The first mention of this divine revelation appears in chapter 12: "Now the Lord had said to Abram: Go for yourself from your land, from your relatives, and from your father's house to the land that I will so you." (Genesis 12:1)

For his troubles, God promises Abram that He will "make of you a great nation; I will bless you, and make your name great, and you shall be a blessing." (Genesis 12:2)

Abram receives God's word at the ripe old age of 75. As such, it must have been disheartening to be asked to leave his birthplace and home with the promise that the grass will be greener in some unidentified new pasture. But Abram does as God asks, as he will do throughout this biblical book. He takes Sarai, his wife; Lot, his nephew, and their possessions, and sets out for the land of Canaan.

Abram and his family first settled in a place called Shechem. It is there that God tells Abram "To your seed shall I give this land." (Genesis 13:7) Abram erects an altar to God to acknowledge that every act of divine kindness is an opportunity for people to gather, turn their hearts heavenward, and dedicate the land in the service of God.

It wasn't long before famine forced Abram to seek provisions in another land. He headed south to Egypt, stopping at least once along the way to build another altar to God.

Trouble in Egypt

Despite his growing reputation and following, Abram feared for his life in Egypt. It was an enchanting land, but not known for its virtue. And he had an additional concern. Sarai, his wife, was a fair-skinned beauty. Aware of the decadent morals of the people he was about to encounter, Abram smelled trouble. They would now be at the mercy of the Egyptians who might lust after Sarai and dispose of Abram without hesitation. To circumvent this problem, Abram conjured a ruse—he would identify her as his sister.

Lord Knows
In reality, Sarai was Abram's niece. It was common to refer to a niece as one's sister. Abram further justified his ruse, as Sarai was his niece, being the daughter of his brother Haran. She was called also Iscah (Genesis 11:29), because her beauty attracted general attention and admiration. She was so beautiful that all other persons seemed apes in comparison. (Talmud Baba Batra 58a)

Despite Abram's best efforts to conceal his wife from the Egyptians, the plan backfired. The moment Sarai set foot in Egypt, rumors began flying about the extraordinarily beautiful newcomer. Pharaoh's men saw her and took her to their ruler.

Sarai carried out the ruse when brought before the Pharaoh. The ruler immediately dispatched messengers to shower Abram with lavish gifts and even gave him a parcel of land in Goshen that his descendants would later inhabit.

But God sent a plague on Pharaoh, smiting him and his house with boils. Sarai could not hold back and revealed that Abram was actually her uncle and husband. The king was forced to release Sarai and commanded Abram to leave town immediately, but not before bestowing even more gifts upon him, including his own daughter, Hagar, as a maidservant.

Detour in Sodom and Gomorrah

Abram and his family leave Egypt and travel south once again. Along the way, both Abram and Lot, his disciple and nephew, become so wealthy with livestock that the land can't support both of them. Abram suggests they separate to avoid tension between their shepherds. Abram goes to Canaan and Lot settles close to the city of Sodom in the Jordan Valley.

By all indications, Sodom and its neighbor Gomorrah were where all the evil in the world had settled after the great flood. As it is noted in Scripture "… the men of Sodom were exceedingly wicked and sinful against the Lord." (Genesis 13:13)

A Child Is Born

For his faithfulness, God promises Abram that he will eventually have an heir. But God doesn't stop there. He also tells Abram that his descendants will be more than the man can count: "… count the stars if you are able to number them … so shall your descendants be." (Genesis 15:5)

But Sarai remains childless. As such, she devises a scheme to give Abram an heir and gives him Hagar, her maid, as another wife.

Abram takes Hagar to his bed and she conceives. When Sarai is confronted with the pregnancy, she regrets what she has done and, as Scripture notes, Hagar becomes "despised in her eyes." (Genesis 16:5)

Hagar bears a son. Abram names him Ishmael, which means "God hears."

From Abram to Abraham

Thirteen years after Ishmael's birth, God appears to Abram and asks him to "walk before Me and be blameless." (Genesis 17:1) For doing so, God promises Abram that he will "make My covenant between Me and you, and will multiply you exceedingly." (Genesis 17:2)

Abram falls on his face. God continues: "… My covenant is with you, and you shall be a father of many nations. No longer shall your name be called Abram, but your name shall be Abraham; for I have made you a father of many nations." (Genesis 17:5)

To seal the covenant, God commands Abraham to circumcise himself, and commands that all the male children among Abraham's descendants follow suit. Anyone who is not circumcised "shall be cut off from his people; he has broken My covenant." (Genesis 18:14)

> ### Lord Knows
>
> Circumcision is the first mitzvah, or religious duty or obligation that God gives to the Jewish people, and one still cherished and observed in most circles today.

God also changes Sarai's name to Sarah, and tells Abraham that he will "bless her and also give you a son by her; then I will bless her and she shall be a mother of nations." (Genesis 18:16)

Abraham is 100 years old now and has a hard time believing God. He doesn't voice his reservations, but he does suggest that Ishmael would be the one to "live before You." (Genesis 17:18) God says no, that Sarah will bear a son, and that the boy shall be named Isaac. What's more, God's covenant will be established with Isaac and Isaac's descendants.

But Ishmael won't be forgotten. As for him, God says "I have blessed him, and will make him fruitful, and will multiply him exceedingly. He shall beget 12 princes, and I will make him a great nation." (Genesis 17:20)

Ishmael, being a son of Abraham, possessed profound but latent spiritual qualities. This is reflected in Ishmael's willingness to make sacrifices for the service of God. The Talmud teaches us "Ishmael said to Isaac, 'I am greater than you because you were only 8 days old when you were circumcised (and barely felt the pain). I was 13 years old!'"

Ishmael does indeed serve God with much faith, prayer, and sacrifice. In fact, his very name means that God will listen to his prayers as a result of his suffering and sacrifice. (Genesis 16:11) His descendants are likewise imbued with a desire to express themselves through prayer and sacrifice. Traditional Jewish sources indicate that Ishmael himself, after being cast out of Abraham's household, reconciled himself with his family and made peace.

Sarah finds God's words as incredulous as Abraham does. But she also doesn't voice her concerns to God. As Scripture puts it, "she laughed within herself, saying 'After I have grown old, shall I become fertile, my lord being old also?'" (Genesis 18:12)

God tells her that nothing is too hard for Him, and assures her that she'll bear a son. And she does.

The Destruction of Sodom and Gomorrah

"Because the outcry against Sodom and Gomorrah is great, and because their sin is very grievous, I will go down now and see whether they have done altogether according to the outcry against it has come to Me; and if not, I will know." (Genesis 18:20)

Soon after God's covenant is struck, He decides it's time to do in the sinful cities of Sodom and Gomorrah. But Abraham argues on behalf of the righteous people who might live there "Would You also destroy the righteous with the wicked?" (Genesis 18:23) God tells Abraham that if he can find 50 righteous people, all will be spared. But Abraham isn't sure there are 50, and starts to bargain with the Lord.

"What about 45?" he asks. God says yes.

"What about 40?" he says. God says yes again.

"What about 30?" Again, yes.

"What about 20?" Sure, no problem.

"What about 10?" God again says yes.

Perhaps a bit perturbed at this point, God now departs. Abraham returns home.

God now dispatches two angels, one to save Lot and his family, and the other to overturn the city.

When the angels arrived at Sodom, Lot was at the entrance of the city to greet them. At Lot's urging, the angels stayed at his house. They weren't there for long when the men of Sodom demanded that Lot send out his guests so they can "know them" (in the biblical sense).

Lot pleaded to accept his two virgin daughters instead. This angered the crowd even more. When they eventually broke into his house, the angels stopped them by blinding them.

One angel told Lot to take his family and leave the city immediately, for he was there to destroy it. This angel is identified as Michael, who is often associated with justice and retribution. When Lot told this to the two men who were engaged to marry his daughters, they stayed because they thought he was joking. The next morning, before sunrise, the angels took Lot, his wife, and their daughters safely out of the city. The angels warned them not to look back or they would be destroyed.

When the sun rose, Lot, his wife, and their daughters were safe in the small city of Zoar. Then fire and brimstone literally rain from heaven. As the cities of Sodom and

Gomorrah were being destroyed, Lot's wife looked back and turned into a pillar of salt.

When it was all over, Lot traveled from Zoar and took refuge in a cave in the mountains. Desolation was all they could see for miles. Lot's virgin daughters lost their mother and their husbands to be, and reasoned that they were the only surviving women on the planet. So they hatched a plan to have children by their father. For two nights in a row, they got their father drunk and slept with him.

Their two sons became the fathers of the Moabites and the Ammonites. Lot's ignominy is seen as a direct result of his decision to take residence in proximity to the evil people of Sodom.

After the destruction of Sodom and Gomorrah, God makes good on his promise and visits Sarah. She conceives and bears a son, exactly when God said she would. They name the boy Isaac.

Soon after Isaac's birth, Sarah sees Ishmael laughing about it. She tells Abraham to banish Hagar and her son from their home.

> **The Sages Say**
>
> Sarah's exceptional prophecy and parenting skills were crucial to the development of the Jewish people. It was Sarah, untainted by misplaced love, who ensures that her son would have the purest of influences by having Hagar and Ishmael sent away from her home. This effort ensured that Ishmael would become one of the spiritual pillars of the Jewish people.

A Test of Faith

Abraham was promised that in Isaac his seed would be called and perpetuated. So what does God do? He calls on Abraham to offer up Isaac as a sacrifice.

Abraham was faced with the mother of all dilemmas. Human sacrifice was rampant at the time, but Abraham had spent his entire life preaching about a merciful God who abhorred these abominations. If he carried out God's command here, he would negate all he stood for and nullify his life's work.

Abraham had every justification in the world for reinterpreting God's order or for delaying its execution. But he didn't. In fact, father and son went about this task without question or protest. The two of them walked together confident in their service of God, whatever may come. In fact, Abraham was so ready to do the bidding of his Creator that at the moment he wielded the knife to kill his son, God restrained him with the words, "Do not stretch your hand against the lad, nor do anything to him ...." (Genesis 22:12)

Scripture reveals that God had never intended for Abraham to kill Isaac. If we examine the verse correctly, God said, "bring him up." Not one word about slaughtering the lad. Abraham did just that, and God basically said "Okay, you can bring him down now. You passed the test."

How many of us are ready to essentially toss out our life's work on a command from God? To die as a Jew, in the sanctification of God's name, is something that Jews are unfortunately all too familiar with. That was Isaac's role in this test—one that is a bit easier to comprehend. However, Abraham's was much harder, doing something that would permanently undermine his message—and worse, actually counter what he understood as making God acknowledged throughout the world.

Isaac and Rebecca

Sarah dies not long after Abraham and Isaac's challenge. Soon after, Abraham asks Eliezer, one of his servants, to find Isaac an appropriate wife. But not from the Canaanites, among whom Abraham and Isaac live. He wants the man to go back to his homeland to find the right girl.

Eliezer expresses reservations. He's concerned that the woman he finds won't be willing to accompany him back home, and that he'll have to leave Isaac where he finds the girl.

Abraham tells him not to worry, that God has spoken to him and told him that He will "send His angel before you, and you shall take a wife for my son from there." (Genesis 24:7) Further, if the woman is not willing to come to Canaan, Eliezer's commission would end.

Thus reassured, Eliezer departs, accompanied by 10 of Abraham's camels. He travels to Mesopotamia, where he stops to water the camels. As they tank up, Eliezer offers up a little prayer: "Oh Lord God of my master Abraham, please give me success this day …." (Genesis 24:12) Further, he asks God to send him a sign so he may know the right girl. She would be the one who offers water to Abraham's camels.

Before Eliezer's lips close, the beautiful Rebecca arrives, carrying a pitcher on her shoulder to draw water. She offers water to Eliezer and all his camels.

Eliezer has his girl. He graces her with a gold nose ring and a couple of bracelets and asks her to take him to her father's home. She does so. When there, Eliezer tells Rebecca's family of his quest and tells them that Rebecca is its fulfillment. They ask Rebecca if she's willing to go with him back to Canaan. She says yes and the two depart.

The story continues: "And Rebecca lifted her eyes and saw Isaac, she inclined while upon the camel. And she said to the servant, 'Who is that man walking in the field toward us?' And the servant answered, 'He is my master.' She then took the veil and covered herself (A Jewish custom at a wedding, to this day, is to have the bride veiled by her groom). The servant told Isaac all the things that had transpired. And Isaac brought her into the tent of Sarah his mother, he betrothed her, and he loved her and thus was Isaac consoled after his mother." (Genesis 24:64–67)

Jacob and Esau, Eternal Adversaries

It took a long time for Isaac and Rebecca to conceive. When she did, her pregnancy didn't go well. As Scripture relates, "they struggled together within her." (Genesis 25:22) Rebecca, somewhat alarmed, asks God what's going on. God says "Two nations are in your womb, Two peoples shall be *separated* from your body; One people shall be stronger than the other, and the older shall serve the younger." (Genesis 25:23)

Sure enough, Rebecca has twins. One emerges red and covered with hair. They call him Esau, which means "hairy." The other emerges and grasps Esau's heel. They call him Jacob, which means the "supplanter."

The two boys are vastly different. Esau becomes a skilled hunter; Jacob is described as a "mild man, dwelling in tents." Esau is the apple of Isaac's eye; Rebecca favors Jacob.

A Stolen Birthright

Jacob was jealous of his brother and decided to indulge in some deception to elevate his stature with his father.

As the story unfolds: "Jacob was cooking food when Esau came exhausted from the field. 'Give me some of that red stuff, because I'm exhausted' said Esau. 'Sell me your birth-right today,' replied Jacob. 'I'm going to die (anyway), what do I need a birthright for?'" concluded Esau. (Genesis 25:27–32)

Esau sold his birthright that he believed had only to do with spiritual entitlements for a portion of red lentils. He didn't even give it a second thought.

> **The Sages Say**
>
> A Midrashic source teaches us that Esau thought the whole issue of the birthright was nothing more than a big joke. Esau even brought a group of unruly and crude friends who joined in the fun of belittling the birthright and praised Esau for getting the better end of the deal. "Nah nah, what a loser!" they chided Jacob.

Several years pass and the incident is all but forgotten. Isaac's sight dims. (Some say it was from the tears of the angels who wept when he was bound on the altar about to be sacrificed by Abraham.) Aware of his imminent demise, Isaac decides the time has come to bless Esau, his first-born, unaware that he had long abandoned the path blazed by his illustrious grandfather and father. But first, he sends Esau to hunt game that will be fixed up like he desires and eaten before imparting the blessings.

Rebecca overhears Isaac. She persuades Jacob to disguise himself as Esau and receive the blessing in his stead. The ruse works to perfection, and eventually Isaac even agrees to Jacob being the rightful bearer of his blessings.

Esau returns from a hard day out in the field, and shortly realizes he's been duped: "And Esau cried an extremely great and bitter outcry." (Genesis 27:34) "Bless me as well, father. Don't you have one blessing left, father?" (Genesis 27:36)

Esau can run but he cannot hide from his angst. He has been exposed. He sold the birthright for a bowl of lentils—and he is no longer laughing.

The Sages Say

Rabbi Shimshon R. Hirsch (1808–1888), one of the greatest Bible scholars of the nineteenth century, wrote that when Rebecca told Jacob to impersonate Esau, she sensed this facade was inevitably going to be revealed. Esau would return and Isaac would realize that he had been hoodwinked. But that is precisely what she wanted. Up to this point, she had tried and failed to open Isaac's eyes to Esau's dual life. Only after having Jacob trick Isaac did Isaac realize that if Jacob could masquerade, Esau could masquerade as well. The wise Rebecca worked this ruse to perfection.

Isaac now knows that Esau had deceived him all his life. He immediately proclaimed: "And indeed he shall be blessed," (Genesis 27:33) thus reaffirming the blessing he had just conferred on Jacob.

It was time for Jacob to pack his bags. Rebecca advised him to take refuge with her brother Laban until his brother's wrath abates.

Jacob's Dream

Jacob goes to Charan to find a wife. On the way, he arrives at the place where the Holy Temple in Jerusalem would be built and has a prophetic dream. "And behold, there was a ladder standing on the ground with its head reaching the heavens. And behold, God was standing above him." (Genesis 28:12)

The dream reassures Jacob that God is with him and will guide him so he can someday come back to his father's house. He vows his faithfulness to God and pledges a tenth of all he earns to Him.

Jacob and Rachel

Jacob eventually reaches his mother's homeland. There he meets Rachel, the daughter of Rebecca's brother Laban. He falls in love the second he sees her.

Understanding that Rachel is his soul mate, he offers to work seven long years for her hand in marriage. Laban must have thought this was a steal. He was getting one of the most powerful men he'd ever seen, a husband for his daughter, and seven years of intense labor to boot!

Jacob held to his end of the bargain with diligence and honesty. When the seven years were up, Laban threw a lavish feast to celebrate the wedding. However, instead of bringing Rachel to Jacob, he substitutes with his older daughter Leah. It isn't the first time Laban tried to dupe Jacob, and the younger man is ready for him.

Here is where the dream of the ladder came in handy. Jacob could have crushed Laban and would have been fully justified in doing so. He might have simply grabbed Rachel and fled the scene. But his humanity and vision compelled him to do what was right and he quietly acquiesced to Laban's proposal that he take Rachel as a second wife. The price? Another seven years of work.

Jacob agreed to the offer. How many people, after not being appreciated or compensated properly for their labor, would continue to work like that? Not many. But Jacob not only makes the best of the situation, he absolutely thrives. After 20 years he accumulates a fabulous amount of wealth, four beautiful wives, and twelve mighty sons.

Now Jacob prepares to leave for home. But he is afraid to do so openly, for Laban will certainly protest. Jacob has been too precious an asset in Laban's house and business enterprises to be discarded so easily. Not to mention the fact that Jacob's wives are Laban's daughters and Jacob's children are Laban's grandchildren.

While Jacob prepares for their departure, Rachel takes her father's *teraphim*, or idols, in his absence. When Laban learns of the couple's departure, he sets out in hot pursuit. God appears to Laban in a dream and warns him not to harm Jacob in any way.

When Laban overtakes Jacob he confronts him about the unannounced departure and the missing *teraphim*. Jacob answers in kind, expressing his anger at Laban's repeated attempts to cheat him. As to the *teraphim*, Jacob lets Laban search for them and boldly declares that the one who took them shall not live. Laban fails to find his *teraphim* because Rachel convinces him not to search her personal belongings. Little did Jacob know she had taken them. Later, upon the birth of her son Benjamin, she indeed dies prematurely. Jacob holds his ground and manages to enter into a covenant with Laban that allows him to flee and continue on his journey back to the Land of Israel.

Jacob's next challenge would be meeting Esau again after 20 years. He gets a taste of what he might encounter by a nocturnal wrestling match with an angel, who the sages identify as Esau's guardian angel. (Genesis 32:25–33) After the bout with the angel, Jacob sees that Esau is coming. He divides his camp by placing his wives and sons in order, with his most beloved Rachel and Joseph in the rear. He sends a lavish gift of 550 animals through a messenger to appease his brother. Then he places himself before them to defend his family and prays for the best.

Esau comes forth and meets him; but his spirit of revenge has been somewhat appeased by the gifts. Esau shares some words of conciliation and seems impressed with the large family and possessions that have issued from Jacob. They part ways amicably. Esau moves his family and belongings far to the south of the Promised Land. Jacob settles near Shechem in Samaria.

Joseph the Dreamer

"His brothers saw that it was he Joseph whom their father loved more than all the brothers, and they hated him, and they could not speak with him peaceably." (Genesis 37:4)

Thus begins the concluding drama of the Book of Genesis, the story of the sons of Jacob—Joseph and his 11 brothers.

Joseph is the favored son and acts like it. His father doesn't help matters by giving him a special-colored garment. Joseph dreams and prognosticates that his brothers will eventually bow down to him. His father wants him to keep the dream a secret, but Joseph can't resist sharing it with his brothers.

The brothers have had enough of their upstart brother. They accuse him of a number of serious transgressions and conspire to throw him into a pit. They justify executing him until one brother comes up with the idea to sell him into slavery. They tell their father that a wild animal attacked Joseph. Joseph ends up in Egypt as the servant of Potiphar.

Potiphar's wife subjects Joseph to an extraordinary test by tempting him day after day. He refuses, invoking a powerful teaching he must have learned from his father and grandfather's house "How can I do this great evil and sin against God?" (Genesis 39:9)

When her efforts fail, she turns against him and libels him to her household, "Look, He (her husband) brought us a Hebrew slave to sport with us! He came to lie with me but I called out in a loud scream!" (Genesis 39:14) The bewildered Joseph is thrown into prison, where he ends up interpreting the dreams of Pharaoh's servants. This brings him to Pharaoh's attention.

Joseph successfully interprets Pharaoh's disturbing dreams and is elevated to viceroy, second only to the king himself. He must have been eager to inform his father Jacob of his incredible story and whereabouts, but resisted. He well remembered his dream about his brother's bowing to him and realized it demonstrated that adage "a prophet is the most zealous of his own prophecy—to see its fulfillment."

Joseph was interested in proving his innocence to his brothers and felt that words alone would not suffice. He awaited the famine that he correctly predicted while interpreting Pharaoh's dream. He knew his family would soon descend to Egypt, where there would be plenty.

Joseph declares that God orchestrated the entire ordeal to protect his family from the ravages of the famine. Recognition that God governs the events of man was a hallmark of this blessed family and permeates this final chapter of the Book of Genesis.

One central component of the story of Joseph and his brothers is Genesis 45:1–15, where Joseph reveals his identity to his brothers.

Joseph sends away all the Egyptians for fear of embarrassing them publicly when they discover the cause of his being sold as a slave. He then addresses them, "Concerning this brother you say has died—are you sure he is dead?"

"Absolutely" they respond.

"You are all liars. I know you bartered with his life and sold him to Ishmaelites. I, myself, purchased him as a slave and shortly will send for him."

Joseph then calls out; "Joseph son of Jacob, Joseph son of Jacob!" The flabbergasted brothers turn in all directions but no one enters.

"Gentlemen, what are you looking for?" he inquired, "I am Joseph, your brother, whom you sold to Egypt; is my father still alive?" (Genesis 45:3)

The humbled and mortified brothers do not let out a peep—their tongues are fully tied.

The reassuring Joseph then draws his brothers near, proves his identity and promises them he harbors no ill will, "And now, it was not you who sent me here, but God; He has made me a wise counselor to Pharaoh, a master over his entire household, and ruler over the entire land of Egypt." (Genesis 45:8) He instructs them to summon his father and their families and settle in the choicest land—Goshen—where the Israelites will flourish for many years.

The Least You Need to Know

- The lives, challenges, and deeds of the patriarchs and matriarchs contain valuable lessons about faithfulness and trusting in God that are relevant even today.

- Rebecca had two sons: Jacob and Esau. Only Jacob would continue the ethical teachings and holy work of their forebears.

- Jacob, who fled from his home after exposing his brother Esau's true nature, went on to sire twelve sons who would become the Tribe of Israel.

- The story of Joseph is one of the most amazing "rags to riches" story even known. It is the elevation of a slave boy to the most influential man of the most powerful empire the world had ever seen.

Chapter 6

The Birth of a Nation: The Book of Exodus

In This Chapter

- A man named Moses
- A burning bush
- The Ten Plagues
- The great escape
- A sea-splitting sensation
- Moses and the mountain

The Book of Exodus is the account of how God led the Israelites out of captivity in Egypt. However, this book can actually be viewed as two separate books. The first book is basically a history lesson, telling us about the birth of Moses, the oppression of the Israelites at the hands of the Egyptians, their liberation from slavery, the crossing of the Red Sea, and the revelation at Mount Sinai.

The second half of the book focuses almost entirely on commandments related to atonement for the Israelites' sins, and whether the fallen camp of Israel could experience God's presence after them.

How do these seemingly diverse events and topics enmesh to form one of the most profoundly meaningful books of Jewish Scripture? Let's take a look.

A Pharaoh's Fear

The Book of *Exodus* opens with an account of a newly crowned Pharaoh who fears the Israelites will join his enemies and overthrow him. Pharaoh is also paranoid over the prospect of Jacob's descendents proliferating. There are just too many of them for comfort.

The new monarch established policies that reduced the once proud and independent Israelites to lowly slaves. Ruthless taskmasters compelled the Israelites to build the fortresses and storage cities of Pithom and Rameses.

Pharaoh's real intention was to eventually exterminate the Jews. Yet, despite his genocidal efforts, the Jewish birthrate steadily increases. Alarmed, Pharaoh decrees that Hebrew midwives must kill all their male infants at birth. But the midwives defy Pharaoh, who retaliates by issuing another decree. Now every newborn Jewish male must be drowned in the Nile.

> **Tower of Babel**
>
> *Exodus* is a Latin word from the Greek *Exodos*. *Exodos* is made from two words: *Ex*, meaning "out of" and *hodos* which means "road or way." Thus Exodus means "the way out." Judaism calls the book after the first words in the book *Ve'eleh Shemoth*—"These are the names of"—an allusion to the 70 souls of Jacob's family who emigrated from Canaan to Egypt.

> **It Is Written**
>
> Tradition has it that Moses refused to nurse from any Egyptian wet-nurse. So Yocheved raises her own son in the traditions of his ancestors, but it is Pharaoh's daughter who actually gave Moses his name and is credited with assisting in his development.

Down to the River

Soon after this edict, Amram and Yocheved, leaders of the tribe of Levi, give birth to a son. Not able to keep his birth a secret, they place the baby in a cradle made of rushes and set him loose to float down the Nile.

In one of the Bible's more ironic moments, none other than Pharaoh's daughter, Bithiah, comes to bathe in the Nile. She spots the baby in the basket and sends her maidens to fetch it. She immediately realizes the child is a Hebrew. Against all odds—and her father's edict—she summons the baby's actual mother to nurse him.

The Young Moses

Flying in the face of conventional wisdom and eschewing the life of royalty, Moses goes out among his oppressed Israelite brethren and observes their bitter affliction. While among them, something happens that would forever alter Moses' life and put him on the path of being Israel's redeemer:

"It happened in those days that Moses grew up and went out to his brethren and witnessed their burdens, and he saw an Egyptian overseer striking a Hebrew man. He turned this way and that, and saw that there was no man, then he smote the Egyptian and hid him in the sand." (Exodus 2:11–12)

The very next day, Moses intervenes in a quarrel between two Israelites. One of them asks him "Who appointed you a judge over us?" and cynically inquires if Moses intended to kill them as he killed the overseer. Moses realizes his act is known and that he is in grave danger. He is also troubled that there were slanderers and informers among his people, and flees to Midian (in Sinai's southeastern region).

Providentially, Moses makes it to a well where he protects the seven daughters of Jethro (one of Midian's leaders) from hostile shepherds. Jethro takes a liking to Moses, welcomes him into the clan, and allows him to tend his sheep to earn his keep, so to speak. Moses soon marries Zipporah, one of Jethro's daughters. They have two sons, Gershom and Eliezer.

God Speaks

Pharaoh dies while Moses remains in Midian. His successor intensifies the Israelites' oppression and the Israelites cry out to the Lord for salvation. Moses is minding his own business—and Jethro's sheep—when he witnesses a most amazing sight; a lowly thorn bush that burned intensely but wasn't being consumed.

With his curiosity piqued, Moses gazes in wonder at the apparition. God then speaks to Moses for the first time. He bids Moses to remove his shoes, as the ground he is standing on is holy. God then says something such as, "I need you for a little personal project," and tells Moses that he has been chosen to lead the Israelites out of Egypt.

Moses feels there are better people for the job, and pleads with God to find someone else. God assures him he won't have to go it alone. Moses (or *Moshe*, as he's often called), is still looking for a way out and asks God what he should tell the Israelites, as he figures they'll ask for some sign that he indeed spoke with the Lord Himself and would inquire about his name. (Notwithstanding the backbreaking labor they were subjected to, the Israelites were skeptics at heart and weren't prepared to participate in some suicidal uprising unless the instigator came with good credentials.)

Tower of Babel

Moshe, the Biblical name for Moses, is derived from an Egyptian expression coined by Pharaoh's daughter that means, "From the water he was drawn."

God must have felt this was a reasonable request, as He replied that He could simply be identified by the declaration, "I shall be as I shall be." (Exodus 3:14)

God also commanded Moses to tell the elders of Israel about His appearance, and that they were all to demand the improbable—that Pharaoh was to allow the Israelites to offer sacrifices to their God in the wilderness.

Naturally, Pharaoh would refuse, God predicted. Divine wrath would be swift in the form of horrendous plagues, forcing him to relent and liberate his slaves laden with the riches of Egypt.

Three Miracles

Moses continues to protest that the Israelites would never believe him. God cuts Moses off and empowers him with the ability to perform three miracles to convince the Israelites:

- His rod would turn into a snake and back again to a rod.

- His hand would contract leprosy and then be cured.

- He would turn water from the Nile into blood.

Moses is still reluctant to take on such an awesome task. He takes another tack and protests that he's not the most brilliant orator and lacks the requisite speaking ability for the task. Again the good Lord has an answer, "Is there not Aaron your brother, the Levite? I know that he will surely speak, he is going out to meet you … and he will rejoice in his heart." (Exodus 4:14)

The Dynamic Duo

As instructed, Moses meets Aaron at Mount Sinai and tells him what God has said. Aaron shows little of his brother's trepidations and readily signs on.

Upon reaching Egypt, they address the elders of the people and inform them of God's intentions. After Moses shows his credentials by demonstrating the miracles that God empowered him with, the Israelites affirm their belief that God is indeed responding to their outcry for deliverance and prostrate themselves to worship the Lord. (Exodus 4:29–31)

Moses and Aaron then appear before Pharaoh. They ask him to let the Israelites leave Egypt and worship their god in the wilderness. As anticipated, this demand doesn't sit well with Pharaoh. As a result, he imposes even harsher decrees; specifically, they now have to produce the same number of bricks, but they will no longer be given straw to help fashion them. This is tantamount to being asked to make bagels without water!

The taskmasters mercilessly whip the Hebrew foremen because they are unable to perform this impossible feat. The Israelites, finding no sympathy from Pharaoh, turn against Moses and Aaron for having made a bad situation even worse. God bids the crestfallen Moses to stick to the plan, assuring him that Pharaoh will eventually relent and be forced to let the Israelites go.

With their spirits crushed, the Israelites refuse to listen to Moses as he reveals God's message. Moses, in turn, questions how he could convince Pharaoh if he couldn't convince his own people. God again assures him that Aaron will be his spokesman.

Take Ten—Plagues, That Is

Moses and Aaron again face off with Pharaoh. Anticipating that Pharaoh will be impressed by such wonders, Aaron casts down his rod. Sure enough, it transforms into a serpent. But the Egyptian magicians easily duplicate the feat. Although Aaron's serpent turns back to a rod and proceeds to swallow all the magicians' rods, Pharaoh is unmoved and unfazed.

However, Pharaoh won't remain recalcitrant very long. He's in for a very unpleasant surprise in the form of ten nasty plagues, each of which lasts seven days:

- ◆ **The Plague of Blood.** After warning Pharaoh, Aaron followed Moses' instructions and waved his staff over the Nile. The result was blood in place of all the water. It killed the fish and caused an unbearable stench throughout the land.

The Egyptians begged the Israelites (whose water supply was unaffected) for water. When the Egyptian sorcerers duplicated it, Pharaoh wasn't impressed and remained obstinate.

- **The Plague of Frogs.** For this plague, Aaron stretched out his hand over the Nile and frogs swarmed the land. Pharaoh begged Moses to stop the plague and promised to let the Jews leave. As soon as Moses accommodated, Pharaoh reneged on his promise.

- **The Plague of Lice.** Aaron drove his trusty staff into the dust and kicked up lice that swarmed all over the Egyptians and their cattle. The Egyptian magicians couldn't duplicate the feat and were forced to admit that the God of Israel possessed superior powers. Pharaoh, however, still didn't budge.

- **The Plague of Wild Animals.** Moses warned Pharaoh that the Egyptians' homes would be invaded by wild animals if he didn't relent. After the ensuing devastation of the land, Pharaoh agreed to let the Jews bring sacrifices to God within the borders of Egypt. Moses, however, insisted they be allowed to remove themselves from the defilement and decadence of Egypt by traveling into the wilderness for three days to bring such sacrifices. Pharaoh initially agreed but recanted when the plague stopped.

- **The Plague of Cattle.** After Pharaoh again failed to heed Moses' warning, the Egyptian cattle were stricken with disease. Again, Pharaoh didn't budge.

- **The Plague of Boils.** In Pharaoh's presence, Moses sprinkled ashes toward the skies. The ashes turned into dust and then into boils on the Egyptian people and their animals. Pharaoh still didn't relent.

- **The Plague of Hail.** Following a familiar pattern of warning and deliverance of the promised plague, a torrent of hail hit the Egyptian people, crops, and cattle. These weren't ordinary hailstones; God combined ice and fire in a miraculous harmony of opposites. Pharaoh at first acknowledged his folly; but when the hail ceased he became that same old stubborn mule of a man.

- **The Plague of Locusts.** Moses warned that a plague of locusts would descend upon the Egyptian crops; Pharaoh's advisors urged him to let the Jewish males leave. Moses and Aaron weren't looking for compromise and insisted that all the Jewish people (and their flocks) be allowed to leave. Pharaoh drove Moses and Aaron from his presence. The next day, Moses extended his rod and a swarm of locusts descended and devoured the Egyptian vegetation. After Moses stopped the plague, Pharaoh remained obstinate.

♦ **The Plague of Darkness.** The next plague enveloped the Egyptians in darkness for six days. During the last three, they couldn't move about at all while the Israelites were given light in all their inhabitations. Pharaoh again drove Moses and Aaron from his presence.

♦ **The Plague of Death of First Born.** Moses warned there would be one last plague that would kill all Egyptian firstborn—including Pharaoh's own son—and departed for the last time. At midnight, God smote the Egyptian firstborn people and animals. Pharaoh and his fellow Egyptians arose in the middle of the night, lamented their loss, and finally begged the Israelites to leave Egypt.

When God informed Moses that redemption was at hand, He commanded that on the tenth of the Jewish month of Nissan (spring) the head of each household should set aside an unblemished young male lamb. On the evening of the fourteenth of Nissan, the lamb would be sacrificed and some of its blood would be spread on the doorposts of the home symbolizing that its inhabitants were Jewish. That night, the meat of the sacrifice would be roasted and eaten with unleavened bread and bitter herbs. Any remains would be burnt in the morning. This meal was to be consumed in haste and the Jews were to be ready to begin their journey, for that night God would smite the Egyptian firstborn but spare those homes whose doorposts were sprinkled with blood. God further commanded that Pesach (Passover) be observed annually as a permanent reminder of the liberation from Egypt. Only unleavened bread would be eaten for seven days, and the first and seventh days of Pesach were to be days of celebration on which all work was forbidden.

The Israelites Leave Egypt

Approximately 2.5 million men, women, and children left Egypt saddled with donkeys and camels. They were laden with a tremendous wealth of gold and silver that the Egyptians had given them in fulfillment of a promise God made to their forefather, Abraham, 400 years earlier. (Genesis 15:14)

They left in such haste that their leavened bread didn't have time to rise. This is the main reason Jews eat Matzot (unleavened bread) on Passover.

When the Jews left Egypt, God had to lead them toward the Land of Israel via a circuitous route. He wished to avoid taking them through the land of the hostile Philistines, lest the nascent Israelite nation encounter war-hardened armies there and desire to return to Egypt.

The Israelites were led by a miraculous pillar of cloud by day and a pillar of fire by night. (Exodus 13:21) Moses performed a kindness for his ancestor Joseph and brought his remains to the Land of Israel for burial. The Israelites arrived at Etham on the wilderness's edge and were commanded to turn back and camp by the Red Sea. God maneuvered them around in such a fashion as a ploy to entice Pharaoh to pursue them—with the thought that they were confounded or lost in the wilderness. God reassured the Israelites that He would protect and deliver them.

The Splitting of the Red Sea

Pharaoh regretted letting the Jews leave and assembled his entire army to pursue them. When they were breathing down the Israelites' backs, the Jews panicked and complained bitterly to Moses, saying, "It would have been better for us to serve in Egypt than we die in the wilderness." (Exodus 14:12) However, Moses assured them that God would again save them. The Pillar of Cloud moved to the rear, creating a buffer of darkness that stalled the Egyptian advance. Moses then stretched his hand over the Red Sea and divided the waters, allowing the Jews to cross on dry land.

The maniacal Pharaoh and his hoards attempted to follow them, but were thrown into confusion by God, who caused their chariot wheels to become stuck in the wet sand. Moses then stretched out his hand again over the sea and the waters returned to their original place, drowning the Egyptians in the process. Upon witnessing this miracle, the Jews sang a song praising God for His infinite power and guidance in destroying their enemy and leading His people to their destiny.

The remaining part of chapter 15 and all of chapter 16 relate the following events:

♦ **The Waters of Marah.** The Jews continued their journey, reaching Marah ("bitterness"), so named because of its bitter waters. The people became thirsty and murmured against Moses, who was shown a branch from a species of tree which when thrown into the waters made them sweet.

Tower of Babel

Manna or Mann (in Hebrew) was the "Bread from Heaven," that God miraculously sent to sustain the Israelites during their 40-year sojourn in the wilderness.

♦ *Manna* from Heaven. One month after leaving Egypt, the Jews entered the wilderness of Sinai. Soon their lack of food made them wish they had died amidst the "luxuries" in Egypt. God made it known that He would cause bread to rain from heaven and would test whether the Jews obeyed His law. In the evening, quails came to the camp, providing the Jews with meat; in the morning, the ground was covered with manna. The Jews were commanded to each gather no more than an *omer* (approximately four pints) of manna per day; however, on the sixth day, they were told to gather a double portion so that they would have manna on Sabbath, when work, including gathering, was prohibited.

♦ The Second Complaint About Lack of Water. At a place called Rephidim, the people again complained to Moses about the lack of water. At God's command, Moses struck a rock on nearby Mount Sinai with his staff. Rivulets of water gushed forth and the people drank to their hearts' content.

♦ Attack by the Tribe of Amalek. The tribe of Amalek, descendants of Esau, attacked the Israelites at Rephidim. The Jews, led by Joshua, fought back. Although the war escalated, Moses went to the top of the hill holding his staff. When he raised his hands in prayer to God, the Jews prevailed. The battle lasted until sunset when Amalek was decisively defeated.

Moses and the Mountain

On the first day of the month of Sivan (late May into June), just 45 days after leaving Egypt, the Israelites arrived in the Sinai wilderness and made their camp in front of a mountain. Moses made an initial ascent on the mountain. As he did, he heard God's voice instructing him to remind the Jews how He delivered them from Egypt and that, if they obeyed Him, they would be transformed into a "kingdom of priests and a holy nation."

Moses descended from Mount Sinai and repeated God's exhortation to the elders and people, to which the people responded in unison "All that the Lord has spoken we will do!" (Exodus 19:8)

Moses then reported these words back to God (not that He didn't already hear them). God told Moses that He would "appear" in a thick cloud and speak to him before the entire assembly of Jews so that His divine mission would never be second-guessed.

Lord Knows
God's speaking to Moses before the entire assembly of Jews distinguishes Judaism from the two other major religions, Christianity and Islam. The latter are based on the testimony of an individual or small group of people who proclaim a revelation or divine instruction. The entire nation of Israel, by contrast, was told to prepare for three days to receive the Torah and personally experienced the revelation.

The Ten Commandments

On the sixth day of Sivan, thunder and lightning erupted and a cloud descended over Mount Sinai. The sound of the trumpet permeated the rarified air and Moses brought the Jews to the foot of Mount Sinai. God then called Moses up to its summit. Instructed by God, Moses told the Jews not to gaze upon His Manifestation.

Then God began the 10 Devarim or Utterances. The people heard the first two and their souls fled them. After restored, they bid Moses to ascend alone and received the remaining commandments:

> I am the Lord your God who delivered you from Egypt …
>
> You shall have no other gods before Me …
>
> You shall not take the name of the Lord your God in vain …
>
> Remember the Sabbath day to keep it holy …
>
> Honor your father and mother …
>
> You shall not murder
>
> You shall not commit adultery
>
> You shall not steal (or kidnap)
>
> You shall not bear false witness against your neighbor
>
> You shall not covet your neighbor's house, wife, servant, ox, donkey, or any of his possessions

The Sages Say

The Ten Commandments are divided into two categories. The first category is comprised of five laws between man and God and the second category has five related to laws between man and man. Why is honoring one's parents in the first five? The sages had three plausible explanations. First, the Talmud teaches that whoever honors his parents honors God because it indicates a willingness to accept authority and to carry on the tradition. Second, respect for them is part of one's obligation to God. Finally, respect for one's parents is a cornerstone of faith in the entire Torah, for Jewish tradition is based on the chain from Abraham to Sinai and beyond. This is a chain in which the links are successive generations of parents and children.

The people were so struck with fear by what they had witnessed that they withdrew after the second commandment and pleaded with Moses to speak to God in their place lest they die. Moses then drew near to the thick darkness and received a series of laws—613 of them, to be exact—over the following 40 days and nights.

Chapters 21–24 contain dozens of civil laws that include torts (personal injury) and property damage. The juxtaposition of the portion dealing primarily with civil and tort law with the Ten Commandments provides an astounding insight into Judaism. The Torah doesn't recognize a distinction between church and state; to the contrary, all areas of life are interwoven. Holiness is a state of being that emanates from correct business dealings as well as piety in ritual matters. In Judaism, the concept of the "temple" is in the courtroom, or any room for that matter, be it in the home, in the office, or in the synagogue.

The following is just a sample of some of the laws that God imparted on Moses during his time on the mountain:

- If one injures another during a fight, he's liable for his loss of earning, medical expenses and pain, embarrassment, and physical injury.

- If during a fight one accidentally strikes a pregnant woman and causes her to miscarry, one is liable for damages: "an eye for an eye, a tooth for a tooth …" (which, although commonly misinterpreted, always means the monetary value of an eye, and so on).

- If the owner of a dangerous animal fails to take proper precautions and the animal kills a person, the animal is killed and the owner is punished.

- If an animal kills a non-Jewish slave, the slave's owner is given 30 shekels of silver.

The civil laws covered in the Book of Exodus are so many and so detailed that it is not within the scope of this guide to discuss them all or to go into any great detail. Here are a few of them, just to give you an idea:

- A stranger (or a convert) isn't to be wronged or insulted in any way. Similar consideration must be shown to widows and orphans.

- Loans between Jews must be interest-free; if one takes a garment that is used as a blanket at night for a pledge, he must return the garment to its owner before sunset.

◆ One must extend a helping hand to a fellow Jew, even if there is a rivalry between them. If one comes upon a rival's lost animal, he must return it to its original owner. Similarly, if one finds an animal lying helplessly under its burden, one should assist it.

◆ The first fruits and produce of land and vineyards must be offered to God; similarly, the firstborn of men and animals are to be dedicated to God.

Miscellaneous laws also included in this section include the following:

◆ The prohibition against eating *treifah* (the meat of an animal torn by beasts in the field).

◆ The Shemitta (seventh Sabbatical) year, during which the land is to lie fallow. This allows rejuvenation of the soil and provides an additional benefit—the owner, freed from working the field, can direct his energies to spiritual pursuits.

◆ The complete abstention from work on Shabbos.

◆ The pilgrimage to Israel on the three Festivals (Passover, Pentecost, and Feasts of Booths or Sukkot).

◆ The prohibition against cooking a kid goat in its mother's milk. This actually applies to any species of kosher mammal in kosher milk.

God's concluding message here is this: He promises the Jews that if they obey the divine law, He will support them in their gradual conquest of Canaan, and their victory will be assured.

How to Build a Tabernacle

With the exception of the story of the Golden Calf (explained in the section that follows), the balance of Exodus is devoted to the preparations for and the construction of the Tabernacle.

God commanded Moses to build a sanctuary symbolizing His presence among the Jewish people and constructed per His divine pattern. The Jews were asked to voluntarily give offerings of precious metals, fabrics, skins, wool, oil, spices, incense, and precious stones.

The sanctuary consisted of the following:

◆ The outer court, which contained the altar for burnt offerings and the laver used by the priests.

◆ The Tabernacle, which was divided into two chambers (a) the outer chamber (the holy) to which only priests who performed sacred duties had access and which contained the table of showbread, menorah (candelabra), and altar of incense; and (b) the inner chamber (holy of holies), which only the high priest entered on *Yom Kippur* and which contained the sacred ark holding the Ten Commandments.

The instructions respecting the construction of the utensils and the actual building needed in the Tabernacle are detailed in great length throughout the remainder of the Five Books of Moses.

Tower of Babel

Yom Kippur is also called the Day of Atonement, as it is a time when Jews confess their sins, resolve to improve, and look forward to divine pardon. It is the holiest day on the Jewish calendar.

The Sin of the Golden Calf

After the greatest national revelation experience in human history, Moses goes up the mountain and comes down 40 days later to find a large idol-worshipping group session.

Chances are, if you were just elevated to the level of prophet and had a personal encounter with the Almighty and He told you "Hello, I am your God, don't worship any thing/one else," you'd get the message. So what possessed the Israelites?

First off, not all the Israelites participated in the debauchery. Scripture explicitly teaches in Exodus 32:28 that there were only about 3,000 people—pretty much a motley hoard of people—who Moses took mercy on and allowed to leave with the Jews because they were so impressed by that awesome demonstration of might God revealed to the world during the Ten Plagues.

If we do the math, that makes a little more than .1 percent—meaning that the vast majority of them did not participate. So why does the Book of Exodus make it seem as if they were all to blame and that God was prepared to wipe them all out and start over with just Moses?

Here is the answer, and it explains many such events in Jewish history—accountability. The Jewish people had been given the responsibility to uphold a high level of morality for the entire world at Mount Sinai. The guiding principle is that the greater the potential, the greater are the ramifications of one's actions. That is why God holds certain people to a higher standard.

The relay baton was being exclusively passed to the Israelites at Mount Sinai. The Jewish people were collectively being given the privilege to win the gold, and they dropped it.

Being a "chosen person" carries with it certain liabilities. Three people can run perfect legs of a relay race but if the last handoff is flawed, the entire race is lost. All members of the team must be accountable.

Moses pleads for mercy for the remainder of his flock. God acquiesces, but the damage is done. They will be vulnerable for other glitches in their development as a nation, as we will see later.

The Least You Need to Know

- The Book of Exodus details Moses' birth and development as a leader amidst the persecution of the Jewish people at the hand of Pharaoh.

- Exodus describes the liberation of the Jewish people from Egypt and the Ten Plagues that were unleashed on Pharaoh and his nation.

- Moses' brother Aaron helped him deliver the Jewish people from slavery. They left Egypt with a great amount of wealth in fulfillment of a promise to Abraham.

- The Book of Exodus relates the travels of the Jewish people out of Egypt, including the miraculous crossing of the Red Sea.

- Exodus contains an account of the revelation at Mount Sinai and the giving of the Torah through Moses. It also relates the subsequent sin of the Golden Calf committed by a very small minority while Moses was up on the mountain.

God's Guidebook: The Book of Leviticus

In This Chapter

- ◆ Guiding your way to priestly worship
- ◆ Learning God's diet plan
- ◆ Keeping things clean
- ◆ Reciting the blessings and curses

The Israelites have been freed from slavery and are camped beneath Mount Sinai. They have followed God's plans for the Tabernacle, their portable place of worship, and they have their first priests.

Sacrifices, purity regulations, and other technical religious details of priestly worship are all grist for the mill for Leviticus, the third book of the Five Books of Moses.

Leviticus offers a window into a religious system that had, at its core, the idea of coming close to God through ritual action. We take a look at how that worked in this chapter.

A Guide to Priestly Worship

Leviticus, the Greek title for this book, is fitting as it is primarily concerned with Levitical or priestly worship. It's somewhat like a manual or a how-to guide as it details how the priests and the people are supposed to worship.

Leviticus, which means "belonging to or relating to the Levites," is the Greek title of this book. Jews also know it as *Vayikra*, which means "He called." This book is also known as *Torat Kohanim*, or "Instruction of the Priests."

Lord Knows

In the Torah scroll, the first word of the book Vayikra is written with a small aleph at the end. Why shrink the letter? Moses was a man of extreme humility. He didn't want to boast of his special relationship with God or that God singled him out from others. Of course, he couldn't change God's words, but he could lessen the impact by reducing one letter.

As is the case with the other books of the Pentateuch, Moses is credited as the author of Leviticus.

The guidance in Leviticus falls into four main areas: sacrificial rituals and offerings, ordination ceremonies, laws on legal purity, and the code of holiness.

Offer It Up

Leviticus opens with God giving Moses rules for bringing various types of offerings:

◆ *Olah*, or burnt offerings. These were animal offerings. They provided a pleasing odor to God and served as a metaphor for appeasement.

◆ *Minchah*, or meal offering. This was an offering of grain without leavening. Olive oil was added to most minchah offerings.

◆ *Zevach shelamim*, or peace offering. These offerings could be of cattle, sheep, or goats and were primarily eaten by the donor. However, as with all other sacrifices, fat and blood could not be consumed.

◆ *Chatat*, or sin offering. This was an offering submitted with the unintentional commission of 207 prohibited acts. There are some sins that the Torah delineates specifically as requiring a sin offering. Incidentally, these offerings were only proscribed for unintentional sins. A person who sinned willfully needed a higher-level atonement that included serious moral rehab. In cases of inadvertent sins, there was a sliding scale of choices depending on financial ability. One could choose between smaller animals, birds, or a meal offering, if they could not afford a larger domesticated animal.

♦ *Asham*, or guilt offering. This offering was made for robbery, fraud, misappropriation of temple property, and unintentional violations of ordinances.

How each offering was to be made is explained in some detail in Leviticus. Most details, however, are provided through Oral Law in the Talmud.

Lord Knows

As mentioned in Chapter 3, Fundamentalist Christianity bases a major tenet of its belief system—there is no forgiveness without the shedding of blood—on the concept of the animal offerings found in the Book of Leviticus. The difficulty with this line of reasoning is that it is refuted by the text. Although these verses do indeed illustrate an aspect of importance in blood sacrifice, nowhere does it say that blood is the exclusive means of expiation of sin. Furthermore, careful analysis of these verses demonstrates that these offerings were only brought for unintentional sins. Finally, atonement for a poor person could be achieved by merely bringing a meal offering—where no blood was included.

To the modern man, ritual sacrifices of animals sounds barbaric. It's hard to argue otherwise. However, if we transcend conventional thinking, we can get a glimpse at the role they played in ancient Israel.

First, many of the sacrifices provided food for the priests of the Temple. These priests did not own land or real property. Instead, they were sustained by the tithes and gifts of their co-religionists. Second, the bringing of something of value was a sign of commitment and loyalty to God. Though one might not understand the deeper significance behind animal offerings, faith is strengthened by obedience to the law.

Furthermore, a person who erred and committed a sin would be required to travel to Jerusalem to meet with the priests who conducted the Temple service. This would bring the transgressor into close proximity with these holy, spiritual, and educated people and help them rectify their deeds. Moreover, the sacrifices were a form of repentance in which a person would imagine his own limbs and fats being burnt on the altar, thus motivating him to change.

Lord Knows

After the Romans destroyed the Second Temple in Jerusalem in 70 C.E., the sacrificial system of worship ceased to exist. As such, the Kohanim (the priests whom God had appointed as the religious functionaries of the community) no longer had an official role. Now each Israelite had the opportunity to draw closer to his or her Creator through studying the laws of the offerings, meditating on their deeper meaning, and praying.

Ordaining the First Priests

Leviticus 9 and 10 give an account of the dedication of the sanctuary and inauguration of the priestly service with the ordination of Aaron and his sons. Moses instructed Aaron and his sons on the rules for bringing offerings to the sanctuary as atonement for unintentional sins that they or the people had committed. Aaron followed Moses' instructions and placed offerings on the sanctuary altar. The celebration suddenly went sour: "The sons of Aaron, Nadab and Abihu, each took his fire pan, they put fire in them and placed incense upon it; they brought before the Lord an alien fire that he had not commanded them." (Leviticus 10:1)

Immediately after Aaron placed the offering on the sanctuary altar, his two sons, Nadab and Abihu, decided to bring a fire and incense offering of their own. They brought offerings not commanded by God and their souls were consumed by fire. The Sages offer a unique insight into Aaron's sons' indiscretion. On the eighth day of the inauguration of the Tent of Meeting, the Heavenly fire descended and consumed the sacrifices. Nadab and Abihu decided that they should place their own fire on the altar based on a verse from the Torah that they interpreted, despite the presence of God's own Heavenly fire. It was alien in the sense that God's glory was already present, what they offered was superfluous and insulting. In a way it was like bringing a gift of ice to Eskimos, except much worse.

The message, once again, is that God must be obeyed. Nor should his word be taken lightly.

Clean and Unclean

Cleanliness, it's often said, is close to Godliness. The basis for this saying can be found in Leviticus.

Those who wish to approach God and worship Him must be ritually clean. Leviticus presents the guidelines for being so. In Chapter 11, for instance, we find "contamination" from contact with the carcass of certain animals, and a remedy if that happens: "Only these are contaminated *(Tamei)* to you among all the teeming animals; anyone who touches them when they are dead shall be contaminated until the evening. And when they are dead, anything upon which they fall shall become defiled, whether it is a sackcloth, any utensil made for work, shall be brought into water and remain defiled until evening—then it becomes cleansed." (Leviticus 11:31–32)

The word *Tamei* connotes a spiritual contamination or defilement. Although these passages speak of garments or utensils, even humans can become *tamei*, or defiled from contact with these types of dead creatures. (An even stricter course of purification was required if one came in contact with a human corpse.) The gist of these directives was to avoid physical proximity to death—the antithesis of vitality and holiness. A rectification allowed the contaminated person or item to be restored to its ideal state of purity. This notion is implied in the next step: "… shall be brought into water."

One of the major institutions that preserved the sanctity of the Jewish people was the *Mikvah*, or ritual pool. The waters of the *Mikvah* need to be connected to an artesian well, or natural water source. In addition to serving as part of the purification process for defiled garments and utensils, the *Mikvah* was generally used for the following purposes:

- Immersion was necessary for a man who had a seminal emission, before he could resume service or bring an offering into the tabernacle.

- Entering the waters of the *Mikvah* was one of three prerequisites for conversion to Judaism. The others were circumcision and sacrifice.

- Ritual purification by immersion was required of a woman after her monthly period. (Leviticus 15:28)

The last one in this list is still practiced today.

God's Diet Plan

Eating properly plays a big role in the Jewish faith. Judaism, in fact, finds the entire enterprise of eating to be filled with both complications and growth opportunities. It takes discipline and commitment.

To the uninitiated, the various dietary restrictions, called *Kashrut*, are as foreign to most as an iPod would be to an Aborigine. Yet to an observant Jew, the mundane act of eating is an opportunity to elevate oneself through the medium of thought, speech, and action.

Tower of Babel

Kashrut comes from the Hebrew kasher, meaning fit, proper, or approved. The more commonly known word "kosher," which describes food that meets these standards, comes from the same root. The word kosher is also used to describe ritual objects that are made in accordance with Jewish law and are fit for ritual practice.

In the realm of thought, eating is perceived as an act of fulfilling the Almighty's will. As for speech, Jews are accustomed to reciting a blessing over the food they eat. Finally, in the sphere of action, the food is selectively eaten with care and gratitude for God's kindness.

One expression of that care and gratitude is to select food that is not only nourishing for the body, but also "clean" for the soul. In chapters 9–11 of Leviticus, Scripture delineates between those species that are kosher or fit for consumption, and those that are not.

What does keeping kosher have to do with holiness? The answer is simply this: holiness begins with self-sanctification, self-discipline and development, and personal growth. Personal growth begins with self-control and self-restraint. The Creator in His infinite wisdom deemed it desirable to reach up by pulling in. That is, by controlling our most basic appetite, that for food, and utilizing it for the service of God, we are sanctifying ourselves and becoming holy. This path will eventually lead toward achieving an intimate relationship with God.

Many Jewish scholars have held that these dietary laws should simply be categorized within a group of laws that are considered irrational in that there is no particular explanation for their existence. The reason for this is that there are some of God's regulations for mankind that the human mind is not necessarily capable of understanding. Related to this is the idea that the dietary laws were given as a demonstration of God's authority and that man should obey without asking for a reason—though one is certainly invited to delve into their possible rationale.

Four-Legged Animals

Any four-legged animal must possess two characteristics to be kosher, or spiritually clean for food consumption. They must have split hooves and they must chew their cud. As such, cattle, buffalo, goats, sheep, deer, antelopes, and even giraffe are included in the species of four-legged mammalian creatures that are biblically kosher.

The most likely rationale for certain domesticated mammals being designated kosher touches the realm of the symbolic and spiritual. Many cultures believe in the concept of "you are what you eat." A placid noncarnivorous animal does not exhibit the characteristics that would render its flesh a product of aggression and violence. The fact that it is docile and slowly regurgitates partly digested food to chew it again demonstrates an existence that is radically different from that of a lion, wolf, or any other animal of prey. Jewish philosophers suggest that only such nonhunters are suitable to serve the dietary needs of a *homo sapien* who aspires to also become a *homo spiritus*.

Fish and Seafood

Scripture also makes distinctions between kosher and nonkosher fish and seafood: "And all that have not fins and scales in the seas, and in the rivers, and all that move in the waters, and of any living thing which is in the waters, shall be an abomination to you." (Leviticus 11:10)

To be kosher, a fish has to possess both fins and easily removable scales. Mystical writings explain that these components can be likened to crowns atop the fish, alluding symbolically to the kosher fish's elevated spiritual status. Another distinction is that such fish tend to swim in the upper echelons of the ocean where the water is less contaminated and purer. This would exclude lobster, crabs, oysters, shrimp, and many other bottom-dwelling scavengers.

As mentioned earlier, there is another component of the dietary (and other ritual) laws and that is the concept of prohibition of mixing diverse species. What immediately comes to mind for most is the forbidden mixture of meat and milk. Although this restriction is not mentioned in the Book of Leviticus, it fits in with the general dietary laws.

One rationale offered by the sages is that certain substances that are independently "kosher" form spiritually unhealthy by-products when combined. A cheeseburger, for instance, consists of opposite forces: milk, which is the consummate life-giving and -promoting substance, and meat, representing the termination of life. The Almighty requests that never the twain shall meet, in traditional Jewish practice.

Birds

"And these are they which shall be an abomination among the fowl. They shall not be eaten …. The eagle, the ossifrage, and the osprey. And the vulture, and the kite after his kind; Every raven after his kind; And the owl, the nighthawk, the cuckow, and the hawk after his kind; And the little owl, the cormorant, and the great owl. And the swan, and the pelican, and the gier eagle; And the stork, the heron after her kind, and the lapwing, and the bat." (Leviticus 11:13–19)

The exact identification of these species is not 100 percent known. Those listed here are based on some historical and cultural factors. Birds are categorically different from domesticated mammals and fish. The Bible offers no identifying features to distinguish kosher from nonkosher species. It simply provides a listing of the 24 species or categories of birds that are not kosher. By inference, the vast number of other bird species are, de facto, kosher. Today, when the 24 nonkosher species can no longer be accurately identified, things are a bit more complex.

Although the Torah did not provide physical indicators by which to identify kosher fowl, the rabbis provided identifying features to help categorize birds that were considered kosher:

- ♦ An extra toe

- ♦ A crop

- ♦ A gizzard whose inner lining can be peeled

Predators such as vultures are not considered kosher.

Lord Knows

There are people in the world today who question the divine origin of the Five Books of Moses. The Talmud invokes the two signs of domesticated animals to prove the Bible could not have been fabricated by mortal man. There are three animals mentioned that chew their cud but don't have split hooves: the camel, the hyrax, and the hare. Also, there is one animal which the Torah names as having split hooves, but doesn't chew its cud—the pig. (Leviticus 11:4–7) Playing the devil's advocate for a moment, if a human actually "invented" the Bible—is there anyone who would be so bold as to list these four "exceptional" animals, without being afraid that maybe, by some far-out chance, there might be another type of animal in the world that also has one kosher sign but not the other? Was Moses a zoologist who traveled around the world? Only the omniscient Creator could write that these are the only exceptions; no more, no less!

Insects and Swarming Things

The last verses in the section dealing with dietary laws include a prohibition of insects and other swarming creatures. The people are reminded that the Egyptians and Canaanites amongst whom they dwelled before they were liberated consumed these creatures, which included mice, scorpions, lizards, and the like. They are bidden to wean themselves away from these practices and commanded: "Do not become defiled with these because I am The Lord, your God, sanctify yourselves because I am holy …." (Leviticus 11:43–44)

Keeping Things Clean

Another key area of Leviticus relates to the ritual purification that women followed after they gave birth. Interestingly, after a woman completed her ritual purification, she was commanded to make a sin offering.

"Upon the completion of the days of her purity for a son or a daughter, she shall bring a sheep within its first year for an Olah (elevation offering), and a young dove or a sin offering to the entrance of the Tent of Meeting, to the Priest." (Leviticus 12:8)

But having a child is not a sinful act. What is the Torah prescribing here?

In the days before anesthesiology, childbirth was the most painful experience a woman might endure. (Even with pain-numbing chemicals, childbirth is, frankly, no piece of cake.) The sages related that while a woman is writhing in pain during the birthing process, she might swear under her breath (or with a scream) that she refuses to cohabit with her husband ever again.

After she survives the ordeal, amnesia sets in and she regrets having made such an oath. Therefore, she must bring atonement for her ill-spoken words. She is then reunited with her husband and they live happily ever after.

Spiritual Leprosy

Not only does the Bible contain directives concerning what goes into our mouth, but also that which emanates from it. Chapters 12–15 also contain passages that detail the methods for diagnosing and remedying *Tzaras* or spiritual leprosy—an affliction that would come upon a person when they spoke evil or slander against others—in Hebrew, *loshon harah*.

This affliction was not physical in nature, and as such it did not have a physical remedy, only a spiritual one. Because these actions of slander and libel are antithetical to the teachings of God, He demands that a priest should examine a person with a suspicion of this disease.

If the priest deems the sufferer to indeed be infected with spiritual leprosy, he might be quarantined and isolated from the rest of the people. This isolation would allow the victim to reflect on how he or she can attain greater honesty, integrity, and respect for his or her fellow people and initiate the healing process.

Cleanliness and Holidays

The concept of cleanliness spills over into the major holiday on the Jewish calendar—Yom Kippur, The Day of Atonement. In fact, the verses from chapters 16–18 contain instruction concerning observance of all the celebratory days on the Jewish calendar—Shabbat, Pesach, Shavouot, Rosh Hashana, and Sukkot.

Forbidden Relationships

Chapter 18 of Leviticus deals exclusively with commandments delineating forbidden relationships. This section culminates in another area of cleanliness, but it is far from the conventional understanding of the word. The Almighty reveals here a form of cleanliness in sexual behavior that upholds the integrity and purity of the lineage of the Jewish people.

Most forbidden relationships deal with adultery and incest. These restricted unions might result in a child. Such a child, by no fault of its own, is stigmatized with the title *mamzer*, or bastard, and ostracized from the community. Incidentally, in contra-distinction to certain forms of Christianity, a child born out of wedlock (for example, two unwed parents), does not yield the title mamzer.

The Holiness Code

Leviticus is indeed the book of the Levites, the consummate spiritual leaders of the people. As such, it stands to reason that it contains numerous rules central to proper religious living.

Chapters 19 and 20 contain a set of laws called The Holiness Code, for they begin with the ringing statement, "You shall be holy, for I, the Lord your God, am holy." (Leviticus 19:1)

The laws within this Holiness Code concern many things:

◆ The way we live our lives ("You shall not sow your field with two kinds of seed. You shall not wear garments made of two kinds of cloth.")

- The way we relate to and care for each other ("You shall not place a stumbling block before the blind." "You shall not measure falsely either length, weight, or volume," forbidden unions.)

- The way we relate to God ("Do not turn to idols or make molten gods for yourselves.")

- The way we relate to the Land (The laws regarding the sabbatical and the jubilee year. For six years the people are to sow their fields and prune their vineyards, but in the seventh year, the land must be allowed to lay fallow. In other words, it must be given a rest—a Sabbath for the land.)

> **The Sages Say**
>
> Chapters 19 and 20 sit at the center of Leviticus, which, in turn, is at the center of the Torah. From their central position in the Torah we learn that these laws should similarly be at the center of our lives.

Every fiftieth year is a jubilee year. The Torah states that the jubilee year is to have all the rules of a sabbatical year and in addition proclaims that liberty will be granted to all Israelites enslaved during the previous 49 years. Property (especially land) is also to be returned to the original owner-families. Thus the original distribution of land among the tribes of Israel is to be preserved forever.

Blessings and Curses

The Book of Leviticus ends on a somber note with a rather long recitation of blessings and curses, mostly the latter. In this portion God tells the people about the benefits of loyalty and of keeping the laws, and also the consequences of not following them:

"But if you will not listen to me and carry out all these commands, and if you reject my decrees and abhor my laws and fail to carry out all my commands and so violate my covenant, then I will do this to you: I will bring upon you sudden terror, wasting diseases and fever that will destroy your sight and drain away your life. You will plant seed in vain, because your enemies will eat it ...." (Leviticus 26:14–16)

The curses end with the most profound promise of ultimate consolation:

> **Lord Knows**
>
> When these verses are recited in the synagogue in the course of the yearly cycle, it is very difficult to find people willing to be called up to the Torah as they don't like to read the curses. Thus, the custom in most houses of worship is to have the rabbi read them.

"Yet in spite of this, when they are in the land of their enemies, I will not reject them or abhor them so as to destroy them completely, breaking my covenant with them. I am the LORD their God. For their sake I will remember the covenant with their ancestors whom I brought out of Egypt in the sight of the nations to be their God. I am the LORD." (Leviticus 26:44)

The opening message of Leviticus contains the concept of sacrificial offerings as a tool to bring people closer to their Creator after having distanced themselves through misdemeanors. The concluding message of Leviticus is essentially the same. The Jewish people are eternal. They might suffer, but they will never be entirely despised by their God. They will undergo exile but eventually they will return. That process has already begun.

The Least You Need to Know

- Leviticus is the Greek name for the third book of the Bible. It means "pertaining to the service of the Levites," or priests in the temple or sanctuary. In Hebrew the word is *Vayikra*, which is an affectionate summons or call (for example, God to Moses).

- Leviticus also deals with details of the dietary laws, identifying the species that are kosher to consume and which are not. Cleanliness is a theme that also relates to childbirth and proper speech, among other topics.

- The middle section of the book relates a Holiness Code that warns against forbidden sexual relations, slanderous speech, and business ethics.

- The book closes with both encouragement for keeping the law and admonishment for violating it. God promises that the Jewish people are eternal.

Chapter 8

Counting Up: The Book of Numbers

In This Chapter

- ◆ Counting heads
- ◆ Living in a holy camp
- ◆ Learning that Israel has failed
- ◆ Counting again

Leaving behind the old for the new and trusting God while you do it are just two of the main themes in the Book of Numbers.

Having been freed from slavery, the Children of Israel now have much to look forward to in the land God promised them long ago. But first they have to get there, and the journey is full of tests and challenges.

Israel Organizes

Numbers, which covers events that span 39 years from 1445 to 1406 B.C.E., begins with yet another census. There's a practical reason for another head count—the Israelites need to know how many adult men they have for their militia—but there's more to it than that. It also unites the people as one body, and shows that there's actually a nation of Israel.

This census was also important for the following reasons:

◆ It classified the people of Israel according to specific family divisions within the tribes, under flags and following their tribal leaders.

◆ It clearly established the ancestry of the Children of Israel that caused the Divine Presence to reside in their midst.

◆ The eventual apportionment of the Land of Israel would be according to these tribal divisions.

The Levites, however, were not counted with the rest of the tribes. Their members were given special attention: "God spoke to Moses saying 'But you shall not count the Tribe of Levi, and you shall not take a census of them among the Children of Israel … The Levites shall encamp around the Tabernacle so that there be no wrath upon the assembly of the Children of Israel.'" (Numbers 1:48–52)

> **Lord Knows**
>
> Numbers, a term borrowed from the Greek translation of the Bible, reflects the Rabbinic name of Chumash HaPikudim (The Book of the Two Censuses). Bamidbar, which means "In the Wilderness," is the Hebrew title of this book.

This distinction and the role the Levites played was partially attributed to their loyalty to God and Moses in the wake of the Golden Calf debacle. In honor of their role, God claimed the Levites as His own, in place of the Israelite firstborn whose lives He spared in Egypt.

God gives the Levites the elevated responsibility for bearing the Holy Ark and all the vessels of the Tabernacle. They were also charged with dismantling and erecting the structure itself. They had exclusive privilege to perform these tasks and were the only tribe to directly encircle the portable sanctuary. The rest of the tribes camped around them.

Bearing Standards

The people were instructed to pitch their tents in a boxlike square. The Tabernacle stood in the center, with the tents of three tribes each set to the north, south, east, and west.

Each tribe had a flag to represent it. The colors, shades, and content were different on each flag.

Each standard or flag expressed a particular ambition or objective unique to each specific tribe. Moreover, each banner represented the special personality of that tribe.

This organization, with the Tabernacle at the center, symbolized the particular strength and unique role of each tribe—the 12 flags symbolized this most vividly—and that all Israelites possessed a unifying force that would bind them as one. The sanctuary, with the Divine Presence hovering over it, stood in the center, constantly reminding the Israelites that they were united as a people.

> **The Sages Say**
>
> Rashi explains that the color of each standard or flag corresponded to that tribe's precious stone that was affixed to the breastplate worn by the High Priest. (Exodus 28:15–21)

Purification of the Camp

The camp of Israel did not simply refer to the place where the different tribes lived and expressed their unique talents.

Because it was also a repository for the Divine Presence, a certain level of sanctity had to be maintained. This meant quarantining and/or separating anyone who became ritually impure for any reason while they were in the camp.

Separating for Sin

The people of Israel could also be separated from the camp if they committed an offense against God. As an example, Numbers 5:5–8 relates a case of someone committing an offense against God by illegally withholding the money of a fellow Jew. It might be in the form of a loan, theft, withheld wages, and so on, where the offender compounds the iniquity by swearing falsely that he owes nothing.

Any man or woman who committed such a transgression against God in this fashion had to make restitution to the aggrieved for the amount owed, plus an additional fifth of the sum owed as a fine. If there was no one to whom restitution could be paid, the amount was to be brought to the priest. In addition, the atonement process was not complete until the offender brought a sacrifice and voluntarily confessed his sin.

Hidden Sins of the Adulterer

The ritual procedure of *sotah* was another way in which the sanctity of the camp was maintained.

Sotah is one of the most unusual rituals mentioned in Scripture. It didn't happen often, but when it did, it must have been downright scary. Sotah involved a woman whose husband suspected her of committing adultery by secluding herself with a man who the husband had expressly warned her not to be alone with.

> **Tower of Babel**
>
> **Sotah** means "to turn away," as in turning away from the proper path. The seemingly bizarre ritual of sotah was intended to remove the suspicion of marital infidelity from the midst of Israel. It also protected an innocent wife from unreasonable suspicions by her husband.

If there were not two witnesses of her guilt, she was to drink a sacred potion consisting of the dust of the sanctuary floor, a dissolved parchment with the ineffable name of God, and water. She also must accept an oath from the High Priest stating that the potion would cause her grim and visible injury if she was in fact guilty. Confirmation of her guilt would be that her reproductive organs would distend, or possibly explode, leading to her demise. But if she was innocent, she would immediately become pregnant.

If her husband was equally guilty, he also would meet a gruesome death.

> **Tower of Babel**
>
> **Nazirite** comes from the Hebrew *nazir*, which means "delineation" or "designation."

The Vows of the Nazirite

In what seems to be a bit of a segue, Numbers also presents the guidelines for becoming a *Nazirite*. Nazirites were individuals who vowed to dedicate themselves to special sacred service. The dedication could last for a limited period or a lifetime.

Nazirites held holy status tantamount to that of the High Priest. Contact with a corpse was forbidden. So was cutting hair, drinking wine, or deriving any benefit from grapes or grape products.

The most famous Nazirite was Samson (you'll learn more about him in Chapter 10), whose unshorn hair held the secret to his extraordinary strength.

First Rebellion

After leaving Mount Sinai, things started falling apart for the people of Israel. They were venturing into vast, desolate, and uncharted wilderness—truly a frightening prospect for just about anyone. Instead of trusting God, however, they panicked and doubted their ability to endure.

"The people began seeking complaints; it was evil in the ears of the Lord, and God listened and His wrath flared, and a fire of God burned against them and consumed at the border of the camp." (Numbers 11:1)

What were they complaining about? They were tired of the heavenly manna that rained down 24/6 (not on the Sabbath) and they started craving the "fleshpots" of Egypt.

What is particularly galling about the Israelites' attitude is not only that they were grumbling ingrates concerning this divine nourishment of the manna, but that they insisted it would have been better for them to remain slaves in Egypt than to bask in God's Divine Presence.

"… And the Children of Israel also wept once more and said, 'Who will feed us meat? We remember the fish we ate in Egypt free of charge; and the cucumbers, melons, leeks, onions, and garlic. But now, our life is parched, there is nothing (to eat), we have nothing to anticipate but the manna.'" (Numbers 11:4–6)

Nevermind that manna had a miraculous quality that made it taste like whatever food a person fantasized about (the default flavor was delicate wafers fried in honey—not too shabby). The people wanted meat, and they wanted it now.

The answer was not long in coming. God granted their request in the form of a massive flock of quail. He sent them enough meat for an entire month and told the people that they should eat "not one day, nor two days, nor five days, nor ten days, nor twenty days but for a whole month, until it comes out of your nostrils and becomes loathsome to you …." (Numbers 11:19–29)

The instigators of the rebellion died immediately, and the rest of the nation ate quail for a month.

The basic lesson here: No task is beyond God's ability, but irrational complainers will not be rewarded.

The Family Rebels

It's not enough that Moses has his hands full with the Israelites. Even his own brother and sister voiced a complaint against him. They spoke against Moses because he married an Ethiopian woman, Zipporah, and then chose to abstain from marital relations with her, which, in effect, made her a living widow.

Although Moses claimed that such a separation was necessary because he had to stand ready to communicate with God at any time, Aaron and Miriam argued that they too were prophets, but were not commanded to do as Moses did.

God calls the three of them to the Tabernacle. There he reproves them and reminds them of His special relationship with Moses: "When a prophet of the Lord is among you, I reveal Myself to him in visions, I speak to him in dreams. But this is not true of my servant Moses …. With him I speak face to face, clearly and not in riddles; he sees the form of the Lord." (Numbers 12:6–8)

For her transgressions, God punishes Miriam with leprosy. Recoiling in horror at the horrific sight, Aaron cries out to Moses and asks for this sin to pass him by.

Moses petitions God with the shortest prayer recorded in Scripture, "O, God please heal her now," and Miriam is healed. God tells Moses to keep Miriam out of the camp for seven days, after which she can return. During this time, the camp has to remain in place.

The Trouble with Spies

God led the Israelites to the southern border of Canaan. Now that they're there, God commands Moses to dispatch spies to explore and report on the Promised Land. He selects one leader from each tribe. Their 40-day trip turned out to be a pivotal event that affected the people for the next 40 years, and, by extension, for their entire history.

The spies returned from their scouting mission with samples of produce, affirming it was indeed a land flowing with milk and honey. Almost immediately thereafter, however, they launched into a fear-laced diatribe describing Canaan as a land that devours its inhabitants. Wherever they went, they said they saw burials, so they assumed it would be extremely dangerous to live there.

The spies could have asked Moses, or perhaps even God, why so many people died in the Land of Canaan. Instead, based on their misinterpretation of the facts, they criticized both Moses and the land. This error in judgment caused the people to become frightened at the prospect of facing off with the Canaanites.

By this point, God was so incensed with His people that He was ready to exterminate them and start over with Moses: "God spoke to Moses 'How long will this people provoke Me, and how long will they not have faith in Me, despite the signs that I performed in their midst? I will afflict them with the plague and annihilate them and I shall make you a greater and mightier nation than they.'" (Numbers 14:11–12)

Moses, the consummate advocate for his people, once again argues with God to spare them, and is successful with his plea. However, God decrees that the Israelites will now wander the desert for 40 years—one year for every day the spies were away. It's enough time for all those over 20 years of age (the ones most culpable for causing the panic over the Promised Land) to die.

> **It Is Written**
>
> Joshua and Caleb, 2 of the 12 spies, were the only Jewish males between 20 and 60 years of age to survive and enter the Promised Land. The 10 spies whose pessimistic reports caused the rebellion were immediately struck down. (Numbers 37:14)

The Second Rebellion

Not long after the incident with the spies, the Israelites were on the brink of another rebellion. In contrast with the other misdeeds, which were basically complaints about God's "accommodations" in the wilderness, this one threatened to overthrow the divinely ordained leadership of Moses and Aaron.

This rebellion was caused by Korach, who challenged Moses' and Aaron's special status, saying that he and his followers—some 250 people of the congregation—should also be given the honor of service. However, Korach's logic was flawed. It wasn't Moses or Aaron who designated themselves leaders—it was God who did so.

Moses fell to the ground in despair and dismay, for he felt powerless to appeal to God to pardon the people over this one. Instead, he pleaded with the upstarts to refrain from this coup. He tried to reason with them and proclaimed, "I have not taken even a single donkey of theirs, nor have I wronged even one of them." (Numbers 16:15)

Moses then challenged Korach and his people to a "duel." He bade them to take censers with incense to the altar (censers are used to burn the incense). Aaron, his brother, would do the same thing. There, they would see whose offering was accepted. He also tried to negotiate with Korach's allies Dathan and Aviram, but they refused to meet him. This so angered him that he prayed to God not to accept their offerings.

Predictably, God rejected the rebels' offering, and they were swallowed up by the earth. A flame then came down from above and consumed the other 250 men from the Tribe of Reuven who sided with Korach.

The net effect of this rebellion should have been "Wow, when you mess with Moses you are messing with God." Remember, however, the Israelites were a stiff-necked people. The effect wore off the next day as the people complained, "You have killed the people of God!" (Numbers 17:6)

At this precise moment a cloud appeared over the Tent of Meeting where the assembly had gathered against Moses and Aaron. The glory of God appeared and He spoke "Remove yourselves from among this assembly and they shall be destroyed in an instant." (Numbers 17:10)

Moses was helpless to avert what came next. From the plague, 14,700 died; Aaron, at his brother's instruction, took his censer from the altar, along with fire and incense, and ran among the people atoning for their sins. Some were saved by his action. The damage was done, however, and the Torah teaches us a most severe lesson in distancing oneself from disputes and quarrels.

Striking the Rock

The only glitch in an otherwise stellar career of leadership by the dynamic brother duo of Moses and Aaron happened at a placed called Marah.

After Miriam died, the special well that miraculously supplied water to the Israelites ran dry. God told Moses to bring his rod and speak to the rock. Instead, Moses spoke angrily to the people and struck the rock.

God wasn't pleased, and issued what appears to be a harsh sentence: "God spoke to Moses and to Aaron, 'Because you did not believe in Me to sanctify Me in the eyes of the Children of Israel, therefore you will not bring this congregation into the Land that I have given them.'" (Numbers 20:12)

> **Lord Knows**
>
> Many commentators have grappled with what the brothers' transgression actually was. Nachmanides simply writes, "This matter is a great secret concealed within the mysteries of the Torah."

Why is God so angry? We don't know the exact reasons, but it could be because Moses' actions indicated a lack of trust in God. He diminished what would have been a most miraculous feat of bringing forth water from a rock by merely speaking to it. When Moses didn't obey God, God saw his response as similar to the people's earlier refusal to enter Canaan. So the punishment would be the same: Moses, like the rest of the adults among the Jews, would die before the Israelites would enter the Promised Land.

Travels and Travails

Scripture not only relates the various detours and travels of the Israelites as they were poised to enter the Promised Land, but also their battles against hostile Canaanite nations restricting their passage.

In Numbers 21:21–35, we learn of their encounters with Sihon and Og, two kings of Amorite nations (Amorites were descended from Canaanites) located just to the east of the Jordan River. As a peace-loving leader, Moses extended a courtesy to the monarchs by sending emissaries to ask for the right to cross through their land. The kings, however, refused right of passage. This was a fatal mistake.

God Almighty, who already deemed these lands sacred to the Jewish people, did not look favorably on such lack of social grace. His chosen people were earmarked to take these lands eventually, but for now God merely wanted them to pass by and gather at the Jordan River. What's more, he wasn't against his people waging a little war to get to where they needed to go: "… Israel smote him (the Sihon the Amorite) with the edge of the sword and took possession of his land, from Arnon to Jabbok to children of Ammon—for the border of the children of powerful. Israel took all these cities, and Israel settled in all Amorite cities …." (Numbers 21:24–25)

The Israelites, now settled in the land of the Amorites, set their eyes on Og, their other nemesis. Things didn't go well for Og, either. As Scripture puts it, "They smote him, his sons and all his people, until there was no survivor left to him, and they conquered his land."

The Nefarious Prophet Balaam

Balak, the king of neighboring Moab, saw what happened to the two Amorite kings and became frightened of the Israelites. He mobilized into action, not in the conventional sense of preparing to wage war, but to solicit the help of an old sorcerer who could "curse this people for me, for it is too powerful for me … For I know that whomsoever you bless is blessed and whomsoever you curse is cursed!" (Numbers 22:5–6)

Balaam, an infamous soothsayer (predictor of the future), is Balak's choice for doing his dirty work. Balak promises Balaam great wealth and honor if he can pull off the crime. God, however, tells Balaam the Jewish people are already blessed and that he is to do no such thing.

In almost comical form, Balaam and Balak go through a dance of trying to find the perfect spot to curse the Israelites. However, every time Balaam opens his mouth to curse, only blessings come out. Balak gets angrier by the minute.

Balak is frustrated and returns home, thwarted in his efforts to harm the Jewish people. Balaam returns to his place, riding his donkey. But the donkey sees the Angel of the Lord along the way and shies away from it. Balaam, irritated, strikes the donkey. She shies again and is struck again. After a third refusal, and a third striking, God opens the donkey's mouth, and she asks, "What have I done to you, that you have struck me these three times?"

> **Lord Knows**
>
> "Ma Tovu" (how goodly are your tents, Jacob), the very first prayer a Jew recites upon entering the synagogue, is taken from Balaam's feeble attempt to curse the Jewish people.

After a brief discourse, God opens Balaam's eyes, and he too sees the Angel of the Lord.

Balaam's attempts to curse the Jewish people were not entirely unsuccessful. Near the end of his efforts, he tells Balak that if he wishes to undermine the strength of the Israelites, he should cause them to engage in the vices of idolatry and sexual immorality. As it turns out, the Israelites end up doing exactly that.

The people of Israel had settled in an oasis called Shee'tim. There, Moabite women (Scripture refers to them as "the daughters of Moab") invited the Israelite men to feast with them, and subsequently seduced them to worship Baal Peor, a generic idol.

Their act incited God's wrath once again, and Moses called upon the judges of Israel to exact vengeance against the perpetrators of the orgy. By the time the dust settled, 24,000 Israelites were dead.

Another Head Count

In the aftermath of this disaster, God commanded Moses and Elazar to take yet another census. It was similar to the counting that Moses conducted 39 years earlier. This census was done to determine how the Land of Canaan would be divided among the twelve tribes.

The census taken of the Israelites when they were on the brink of entering the Promised Land revealed that there were 601,730 men available for army duty (between the ages of 20 and 60). Interestingly, the Jewish population in May 1948, when the State of Israel was declared, was about 625,000. In June 1967, approximately 600,000 Israeli soldiers, including reservists, were poised to defend the land against a coalition of four Arab armies.

Moses' Successor

Shortly after the census, Moses, mindful of the fact that he would not be allowed to lead the people into the Promised Land, asked for a successor. God selected Joshua to be ordained by Moses, who thereby indicated him as his successor. (Numbers 27: 22–23)

Joshua was ordained via *Smicha*, or "laying of the hands." The custom of Smicha is a very ancient one and is only mentioned in Numbers. It went something like this: Moses placed Joshua before the priest Elazar and the congregation and laid his hands upon him while giving him instructions. A portion of Moses' spirit was transferred to Joshua through Moses' hands.

Tower of Babel

Smicha is derived from the Hebrew word lismoch, which means to rest or to support.

Laying on of hands was the only way the transference of spirit could take place. Moses also used it to ordain the 70 elders who helped him govern the people during their journey to the Promised Land. According to tradition, the elders who Moses ordained, then ordained their successors, who in turn ordained others. In this way, an unbroken series of ordainers and ordainees existed until the time of the Second Temple.

Claiming the Promised Land

The closing chapters of Numbers include a travelogue of the route taken by the people of Israel from the Exodus until they were poised to cross the Jordan River into the Holy Land. There were 42 encampments in all. They suggest that despite the decree to wander 40 years in the wilderness, God gave the Israelites ample time to rest and regroup. Also there were details about several laws regarding conquest and destruction of pagan worship sites after the Israelites entered the Promised Land.

Also significant here is "God's road map" (Numbers 34:1–15), which describes in great detail the divinely ordained borders of Israel.

These biblical boundaries may have reflected the actual extent of Jewish sovereignty at some point in the past, or they might be an as-yet-unfulfilled vision that will be realized in the Messianic future. Regardless, the Land of Israel, within its biblical borders, has a lofty eternal quality.

Every bit of its territory, every clump of earth, is holy as Scripture declares. God delineates these boundaries primarily because of the numerous commandments that are mandatory only within the borders of the Holy Land. Moreover, this holiness is derived from the nature of redemption that the Israelites were commanded to accomplish in fulfillment of God's promise to Abraham 400 years earlier. It is the fervent aspiration of millions of Jews and Christians the world over that this redemption will take on practical applications in the very near future.

The Least You Need to Know

- The Book of Numbers is primarily a narrative describing the journey of the Israelites from Mount Sinai toward the Land of Canaan.

- Numbers derives its name from the two censuses that were conducted; one at the beginning and one near the end.

- There are several intrigues involving complaints against Moses for bringing them into a wilderness and denying them their fleshpots of Egypt, the negative report of the spies, and the rebellion of Korach against Moses' and Aaron's leadership.

- The Book of Numbers gives a careful account of the Israelites' journey of 40 years in the Sinai wilderness and delineates the ancient borders of the Promised Land.

Chapter 9

Saying It Twice: The Book of Deuteronomy

In This Chapter

- ◆ Moses' rebuke
- ◆ The covenant renewed
- ◆ The Ten Commandments restored
- ◆ Moses' last acts

Having led his people to the edge of the Promised Land, Moses now has to let them enter it alone. But he won't allow the people he has led and loved to enter without some final words of wisdom.

The Book of Deuteronomy is primarily an account of one very long speech that Moses gave 37 days before he was "gathered unto his people." It also contains several shorter speeches and one that culminates in an esoteric poem, the "Song of Moses," saturated with both chastisements and prophetic messages concerning the end of days.

A Book of Words and Speeches

Deuteronomy, the English name for the last book of the Torah, stems from the name which the book bears in the Septuagint, the Greek translation of the Five Books of Moses made in the second century B.C.E. Although the name is a bit misleading, it is not entirely without merit, for the book includes a repetition of a significant part of the laws found in sections of Exodus, including the Ten Commandments.

Deuteronomy was transmitted directly by Moses to the Israelites in the last weeks of his life. In that spirit, they serve as a quasi "last will and testament" to the flock he shepherded and cherished for so long.

The first five verses contain a rebuke of the people and remind them of a long sequence of errors in judgment and rebellions committed during the 40-year sojourn in the Sinai wilderness that was coming to an end. However, like a doting uncle, Moses was mindful of the somewhat fragile psyche of his beloved people. As such, he didn't come right out and remind them of their shortcomings. Instead, he alluded to their infractions by referencing where they took place or with some other identifying factor.

Regardless, Moses didn't mince words when taking the Israelites to task. The fact that he didn't is reflected in the Hebrew title of Deuteronomy—Devarim—which means "words." In context, this connotes a more forceful way of communication. In other words, Moses wasn't speaking just any old way. Instead, he was speaking words of reprimand and chastisement.

Moses' words are organized in a group or series of three speeches or sermons:

◆ Chapters 1–4: First or introductory speech, discussing what God has done for Israel.

◆ Chapters 5–26: Second speech, discussing life under God's covenant and what God expects of Israel.

◆ Chapters 27–30: Third speech. This is a prophetic speech on what God will do for Israel.

Some of what Moses says throughout Deuteronomy recaps certain commandments that he previously conveyed to his people. He withheld the remaining commandments—more than 100—until the people were poised to enter and inhabit the Promised Land.

What God Has Done for Israel

Moses began his final teachings by reminding his people of two things: the value of being obedient and what it brings, and what happens when one is disobedient. He does so by recounting two stories. The first tells of Israel's initial military march to conquer the Promised Land, which ended in the nation's downfall and resulted in its retreat. (Deuteronomy 1:6–46) The second tells of the Israelites' successful military campaign and the victories already achieved, which would bolster the successful outcome of the nation's conquest by Joshua, who had been appointed leader in Moses' stead.

In both stories, Moses clearly illustrates for the people the blessing and the curse associated with their actions. He demonstrates how rebellion against God led to catastrophe, undermined the people's will, and caused their 40-year desert wanderings. Conversely, repentance and following in God's ways leads to success and victory, a formula for future prosperity.

> **It Is Written**
>
> Moses wrote 13 letter-perfect Torah scrolls during the last 37 days of his life. One was given to leaders of each of the twelve tribes, and one was placed in the Holy Ark next to the Ten Commandments tablets to serve as the standard for all Torah scrolls to be transcribed from. Although it's believed they've all been lost, some Jews believe that one of them remains in hiding with the Ark of the Covenant and the tablets.

A Firm Rebuke

Near the end of his first speech, Moses issues a firm rebuke and admonishes the people to remain loyal to God and His commandments and not to stray after false gods: "Now, O Israel, listen to the statutes and the judgments which I teach you to observe that you may live, and go in and possess the land which the Lord God of your fathers is giving you." (Deuteronomy 4:1)

Here, Moses is counseling the people to stay obedient to God. If they do, they will live in tranquility and not be driven from the land. He also tells them to be careful in their observances of God's laws: "You shall not add to the word which I command you, nor take anything from it, that you may keep the commandments of the Lord your God which I commanded you." (Deuteronomy 4:2)

Bold Words

Moses also utters several statements whose sheer boldness only makes sense if divinely inspired, as no leader would make such claims if he were acting on his own: "For inquire now regarding the early days that preceded you, from the day when the Lord created man on the earth, and of those which are from one end of the heavens to the other end of heaven, has there ever been anything like this great thing or has anything like it been heard?

Or have a people ever heard the voice of God speaking from the midst of the fire as you have heard, and survived?

Or has any god ever performed miracles to come to take for himself a nation from amidst a nation, with challenges, with signs, and with wonders, and with war, and with a strong hand, and with an outstretched arm, and with great awesome deeds, such as everything that the Lord, your God, did for you in Egypt before your eyes?

You have been shown tangible proof to give you direct knowledge that the Lord, He is your God; there is none beside Him." (Deuteronomy 4:32–35)

Here, Moses is referencing the exodus from Egypt and the revelations on Mount Sinai. These two events are considered the most significant world events of recorded history. They were one-time deals.

No other nation in history makes the claim, as the Jewish nation does, that an entire nation, including its ordinary folk, witnessed a revelation of God. Nor in the annals of history has a "force" ever extracted any nation or entity from amidst another nation—as Moses testifies about God and the Israelites. It is indeed a bold assertion, and Moses was taking a big risk in saying it—unless of course, God was speaking through him!

These events were intended to be a lasting, convincing force for all Jews and for all mankind, for all times. The Jewish people, recipients of this legacy, have been entrusted with a mandate to stress the uniqueness of the Sinai revelation, making the claims of the truth of the Torah very logical and plausible. The effect of this objective is in order that even the nations of the world will say: "… The Lord, He is your God; there is none beside Him." (Deuteronomy 4:35)

Life Under the Covenant

Moses' main monologue, which spans a whopping 22 chapters, is prefaced with a simple introduction of what he wishes to accomplish with the revelation of additional divine laws.

"Hear O Israel, the ordinances and laws that I speak in your ears today; learn them, and be careful to perform them." (Deuteronomy 5:1)

Moses then references the experience at Mount Sinai in communicating the new legislation, for he wanted them to know that these laws were also given during his initial 40-day sojourn on the mountain. They are only new inasmuch as Moses hasn't yet revealed them to the nation. They all come from the same source and hold the same authority.

> **Lord Knows**
>
> Moses' main speech in Deuteronomy is often referred to as Ne'um HaMitzvoth or The Speech of the Commandments.

Before Moses launched into a presentation of a long set of rules and regulations, he let the people know that they are all bound by these new laws in the same way they were at Mount Sinai. All of them must be observed vigilantly.

Why did Moses wait so long to share the rest of the law? The simple answer is that many of these laws would only take on practical application as the people entered the Promised Land. For instance, one set of laws pertains to the sanctity of the land, private altars, sacred foods consumed only in Jerusalem, permission to eat unconsecrated meat, and not following the rites of the Canaanites.

Thou Shall Love the Lord

It is clear now why Moses waited all those years to relate many of the mitzvoth he received at Mount Sinai. What isn't so obvious is why the very first mitzvah mentioned here wasn't mentioned back in the Book of Exodus, yet it formed such a fundamental part of the Jewish belief system. What is that mitzvah?

"Hear O Israel, the Lord is our God, the Lord is One!" (Deuteronomy 6:4)

Jewish children are taught this verse almost as soon as they're able to speak. It quite literally carries a Jew from the womb to the tomb, for it is recited at a circumcision service as well as by a person who is at the throes of death.

In between those stages, Jewish people are commanded to repeat this verse, and several that follow, twice daily in a ritual observance called Kriat Shema. The main objective of this observance is to accept upon oneself the "yoke of heaven," acknowledging the Oneness of the Almighty and acceptance of all the commandments.

The very next verse is also a tenet of Jewish faith: "You shall love God with all your heart, with all your soul, and all your resources." (Deuteronomy 6:5)

Why are these passages and the observances they convey relegated to first mention in the last book of the Torah? Jewish tradition holds that the commandment to recite the Kriat Shema and to profess a love for God were given to the people at Mount Sinai and practiced 40 years earlier. These concepts form the essence of Judaism.

Tower of Babel

Tefillin (frontlets or phylacteries) is derived from the word *tefilah*, meaning "prayer." **Mezuzot** means "doorposts."

Their initial mention in Deuteronomy, however, is to also set the tone for the people's entry into the Promised Land.

In addition, these passages instruct male Jews to place *tefillin* (frontlets) on the heads and arms and *mezuzot* on their doorposts so that the meditations contained in the Kriat Shema should serve as a constant reminder of their origins and their commitment to God.

In recognition of these commandments, a small ornamental case made of plastic, metal, wood, or clay is placed on the right-side doorposts of observant (and even not-so-observant) Jewish homes. A mezuzah is not a talisman or good-luck charm. It simply serves as a constant reminder of God's presence and His covenant.

Like the mezuzah, tefillin are meant to remind Jewish people of God's mitzvoth. At weekday morning services, one case containing special scrolls is tied to the arm, with the case at the biceps and leather straps extending down the arm to the hand. The second case housing identical scrolls is tied to the head, with the case on the forehead and the straps hanging down over the shoulders. The tefillin are removed at the conclusion of the morning services, although some very pious individuals wear them the entire day.

The dictionary definition for phylacteries—amulets—is misleading as it implies that tefillin are some kind of protective charm. Although some trendy new-age groups might represent them as such, they certainly are not.

Trust in the Lord Your God

In addition to emphasizing these "constant reminder" mitzvoth, Moses admonishes the people not to succumb to the temptations associated with material prosperity. (Deuteronomy 6:10–15) He also includes in his pep talk a reminder to fortify their absolute trust in the Almighty, and concludes the introduction to the Featured Speech with one of the most important themes:

"If your child asks you tomorrow, says 'what are these testimonies, decrees and precepts that the Lord, God has commanded you?' You shall say to him, 'We were slaves to

Pharaoh in Egypt, and God took us out with an outstretched arm … And He took us out to bring us to the land … God commanded us to perform all these decrees, to fear God … for our good, all the days to give us life … and it will be a merit for us ….'" (Deuteronomy 6:20–25)

A sampling of these decrees, which are interspersed throughout the 22 chapters of Moses' magnum opus, include the following:

- The material gifts that were given to the Kohanim, or priestly caste. These included certain parts of animals and their sheerings, gifts of grain, wine, and oil. (Deuteronomy 18:1–8)

- The laws governing prophets and prophecy. (Deuteronomy 18:9–22)

- The laws dealing with Cities of Refuge, preserving boundaries, and conspiring witnesses. (Deuteronomy 19)

- Circumstances dictating going to war, those unqualified to fight, overtures of peace, and preserving fruit-bearing trees during a siege. (Deuteronomy 20)

- The case of the unsolved murder, the woman of beautiful form taken in captivity during war, the wayward and rebellious son. (Deuteronomy 21)

- Private property rights, wearing cross-gender apparel, sending mother bird away before taking eggs or chicks, protective fences placed on rooftop, defamation of a married woman and violation of a maiden. (Deuteronomy 22)

Mostly basic civil laws comprise the rest of this section of Moses' main speech.

What God Will Do for Israel

Moses' third speech is contained in chapters 27 through 30 of Deuteronomy. It opens with God spelling out, through Moses, the blessings that will accrue for fulfilling the commandments and walking in His ways: "And all these blessings shall come upon you and overtake you, because you obey the voice of the Lord your God." (Deuteronomy 28:2)

However, the proverbial "but" follows where Moses lays out in gruesomely graphic detail what will befall the people should they mess with their Maker! Here are a few of the more horrific curses:

- God will strike you with lesions, with fever, with burning heat, with thirst and with sword …

- Your carcass will be food for every bird of the sky and animal of the earth and nothing will frighten them …

- God will smite you with madness and with blindness, and with confusion of the heart …

- You will betroth a maiden, but another man will lie with her …

- You will take abundant seed into the field, but you will harvest little, for the locust shall consume it …

- A nation unknown to you will devour the fruit of the ground and all your labor …

As mentioned, this is just a sampling. Between chapters 27 and 28, there are no less than 98 curses!

More Blessings and Curses

Chapter 28 is very much a "yes, but" chapter, as it details various blessings for obedience and curses for disobedience. One of the key verses and overriding themes of this section is found in Deuteronomy 28:47: "They will be a sign and a wonder for you and your offspring forever, because you did not serve the Lord, your God amid joy and goodness of heart, when all was abundant."

Scripture constantly beckons one to heed God's Will so that Israel will experience happy times, exuberance, and material prosperity. But when those good times roll in, and a person doesn't serve his/her Creator with a good heart, gladness, and appreciation, God's wrath is kindled. Instead of closeness to God, the result of ingratitude is subservience and humiliation to one's enemies, coupled with starvation, depravation, and disease.

Writing It Down (Again)

Chapter 27 also contains one of the very last assignments God asked Moses to give to the people. He instructed the elders that, on the day they cross the Jordan River to enter the Land of Israel, the people must set up 12 great stones and cover them with plaster: "And you shall write upon them all the words of this law when you pass into the land. And when you reach the land, you shall set these stones on Mount Abel, build an altar there, and offer up sacrifices." (Deuteronomy 27:3)

Furthermore, Moses commands "And you shall write upon the stones all the words of this law, clarify them very well." (Deuteronomy 27:8)

The Sages Say

The Talmudic commentators teach that "very well" means to write them in 70 languages. The purpose? Testimony. They would affirm their allegiance to God and His Torah and proclaim it to the entire world. Furthermore, the ability to transcribe the Torah into 70 languages, most of which they had never heard, could only be accomplished in a miraculous fashion—a subtle reminder of the same miraculous God-orchestrated feat of crossing the Red Sea.

Everyone's Law

In this speech, Moses also recounts the giving of the Torah and its accessibility: "For this law that I command you today is not hidden from you and it is not distant; it is not in the heaven for you to say, 'Who will ascent there and take it for us, so that we can listen to it and perform it.'" (Deuteronomy 30:11–12)

In other words, Moses was telling the people that the Torah was not intended for flawless angelical beings. Instead, it should be accessible to mortals with all their imperfections and foibles.

Foretelling the Future

Near the end of this speech, Moses also seems to prognosticate about the future, and envisions some of these curses and exiles befalling the people sometime down the road. However, he consoles them by promising there will be redemption and sincere repentance that will again have them finding favor in the eyes of the Lord. (Deuteronomy 30:1–10)

The Time Is Drawing Near

Following Moses' third speech is a chapter that sets the stage for the great leader's last days. In it he tells the people of Israel that he has grown old and "can no longer go out and come in." (Deuteronomy 31:2) He also tells them that the Lord has prohibited him from crossing into the Promised Land. However, he again reminds the people that they won't be alone: "The Lord your God Himself crosses over before you; He will destroy these nations from before you, and you shall dispossess them." He also reminds the people that Joshua is their new leader and will cross over before them, "just as the Lord has said." (Deuteronomy 31:3)

The Song of Moses

Moses then tells the people that he wants the elders of all the tribes and their officers gathered together so that he may "speak these words into their ears." (Deuteronomy 31:28)

The words he speaks is called The Song of Moses. It is a most esoteric and troubling poem, full of recaps of what happened when the people forgot God in the past and what will happen if they forget Him in the future:

"And Jeshurun became fat and rebelled; you grew fat, thick and rotund; [Israel] forsook the God Who made them, and spurned the [Mighty] Rock of their salvation … I will hide my face from them. I will see what their end will be, for they are a generation of changes; they are not [recognizable] as My children whom I have reared." (Deuteronomy 32:15–18)

Moses ends with a prophecy of a war of retribution against God's enemies, who are also enemies of the Jewish people and state: "'When I sharpen the blade of My sword, and My hand grasps judgment, I will bring vengeance upon My adversaries and repay those who hate Me. I will intoxicate My arrows with blood, and My sword will consume flesh, from the blood of the slain and the captives, from the first breach of the enemy.' Sing out praise, O you nations, for His people! For He will avenge the blood of His servants, inflict revenge upon His adversaries, and appease His land [and] His people." (Deuteronomy 32:41–43)

When Moses is done speaking, God speaks to him "the very same day" and tells him to go to Mount Nebo, "which is in the Land of Moab, across from Jericho." (Deuteronomy 32:49) From there, Moses will be allowed to see the Promised Land and behold with his eyes and heart that which the people will experience with their entire being. After this, God tells him, he'll die.

Final Blessings

Before Moses carries out God's last commandment to him, he blesses the tribes of Israel in a string of inspiring and uplifting prose. He personalizes the blessings for each tribe, imparting praise, predictions, commands, and prayers on each. For example:

♦ "May Reuven live and not die and may his men be counted among the tribes." (Deuteronomy 33:6) The tribe of Reuven, the first born, is the first to settle in Israel, as the land they choose to live on is east of the Jordan in the Land of Moab. Because they are outside the main borders of the Promised Land, however, they need a special blessing to defend them against the enemies that surround them.

♦ "And this to Judah, and he (Moses) said; Harken, O God, to the voice of Judah and return him to his people; may his hands fight his grievance, and may You be an aid against his enemies." (Deuteronomy 33:7) This is a reference to Judah maintaining rulership and vanquishing enemies in war.

♦ "Of Levi he said Your oracles befit Your devout one (reference to Aaron the High Priest) whom You tested at Massah and Merivah … for they (the Levites) have observed Your word and Your covenant they persevered." (Deuteronomy 33:8) Here, Moses praises the steadfast loyalty and courage of the Tribe of Levi in the wilderness.

♦ "Of Dan he said; Dan is a lion cub, leaping forth from the Bashan." (Deuteronomy 33:22) Samson hailed from this tribe. Moses might be forecasting a personality who would emerge from this tribe and "leap forth" and defeat the Philistine enemy who dwelt along the Mediterranean coast, the area in proximity to Dan's portion.

The blessings Moses bestowed upon the Tribes of Israel go on for 29 verses. They end with these inspiring words for the entire nation: "Fortunate are you, O Israel: Who is like you! O people delivered by God, the Shield of your help, Who is the Sword of your majesty; your enemies will try to betray you, but you will trample their haughty ones." (Deuteronomy 33:29)

The Death of a Great Leader

The Torah ends with Moses' ascent of Mount Nebo, where he finally views the land that his people will inhabit. Here, God delivers a final *coup de grace:* "This is the land of which I swore to give Abraham, Isaac and Jacob, saying 'I will give it to your descendants. I have caused you to see it with your eyes, but you shall not cross over there.'" (Deuteronomy 34:4)

After Moses dies, he is buried in a valley in the Land of Moab, opposite Beth Peor. However, as noted in this chapter, no one knows exactly where his grave is. To prevent the Jewish people from behaving like other cultures who deify their exalted leaders, God concealed Moses' burial place. There is no shrine, no monument, no temple to venerate or worship his remains. The only "shrine" to Moses is the legacy of the Torah he left humanity.

Moses' level of prophesy was unique among all prophets because God spoke with him directly and not through dreams or visions, which was the case for all other prophets. History has borne out the veracity of this passage. Moreover, Moses did not expire from natural causes or in the conventional sense as the Torah proclaims "… his eyes had not dimmed and his vigor had not diminished." (Deuteronomy 34:7)

Moses' role shepherding his flock is over. He departs and is gathered to his people, his task completed. The era of Torah is now finished, and the story of the judges and prophets is about to begin.

The Least You Need to Know

- The Book of Deuteronomy is a series of four speeches given by Moses to the Jewish people over the last 37 days of his life.

- Parts of these speeches contain admonitions to the people for previous misbehaviors and warnings to adhere to the mitzvoth of the Torah and to remain loyal to God.

- Although Moses conveyed more than 100 new mitzvoth in this book, the English name of this book implies a review or repetition of the laws. Many of these laws were being taught to the Jewish people as they were poised to enter the Promised Land, as they could only be fulfilled there.

- In addition to reprimands, Moses also conferred upon each tribe a blessing most suited to its temperament, situation, and goals.

Part 3

The Major Prophets

The Major Prophets (a.k.a. the Early Prophets) get their name because their prophecies came earlier than the others, not necessarily because they're more significant than the others. These books contain chronological accounts of ancient Israelite history, but this isn't their main concern. Instead, they're replete with profound prophetic messages that address past and future generations.

Chapter 10

Triumph and Victory: The Book of Joshua

In This Chapter

- ◆ Moses' chief disciple
- ◆ Canaan's defeat
- ◆ Land distribution
- ◆ Joshua's farewell

Written in the narrative style of Deuteronomy, the Book of Joshua seems to pick up the story of the Jewish people where Moses ends it. In fact, many Bible commentators have pointed out that Joshua is almost a clone of the Five Books of Moses. This stands to reason to a certain extent, as Joshua was Moses' chief disciple and handpicked by God to be Moses' successor.

With all the miraculous events related in the Torah over the course of Moses' 40-year reign, one might think crossing the Jordan River into the Promised Land would be a piece of cake. Not so fast. There were a number of hostile nations living in Israel at the time. As you might imagine, they were not terribly excited about the new kid on the block suddenly staking claim to their turf.

The task of dispossessing nations one at a time would take nearly 500 years. A great deal of the Book of Joshua is devoted to the efforts of the people to conquer the land and then divide it among the twelve tribes.

Preparing for Conquest

As the sages taught "all good beginnings are difficult," Joshua's first mission was exactly that. Moses, the greatest prophet in history, was dead. It was Joshua's charge to help the Jews regroup after their devastating loss and lead them across the river Jordan into the Land of Israel.

Joshua had big shoes to fill—the ones imprinted with the footsteps of Moses. Moses had led the people of Israel through the greatest exodus of an enslaved people of all time. Now it was Joshua's turn to fulfill God's promise to His people.

> **Lord Knows**
>
> Moses' leadership would be a tough act for anyone to follow. Through trials, tribulations, and challenges to his authority, Moses never faltered. But his actions also provided a formula for success.

Before he did, he received a divine pep talk: "But be very strong and determined to guard to do all the Torah which My servant Moses commanded you, don't stray from it left or right." (Joshua 1:7)

God gave Joshua a truly significant bit of advice—uphold the Law of Moses and all will be good.

Joshua didn't wait long to emulate his mentor. Like any good military commander, he first gathered intelligence. Just as Moses sent out spies to scope the lay of the land, Joshua dispatched two spies to "reconnoiter the Land and Jericho." (Joshua 2:1)

When the men reached Jericho, they entered the house of a harlot named Rahab, where they lodged. But the king of Jericho somehow learned that Rahab was harboring spies, and he ordered her to "Put out the visitors who have entered your house, for they have come to spy out the entire land." (Joshua 2:3) Rahab, however, told the king's representatives that the two men had already left.

"True, the men you speak of came to me, but I did not know where they came from. At dark, when it was time for the gate to be shut, they left, and I do not know where they went. You will have to pursue them immediately to overtake them." (Joshua 2:4–6)

What's interesting here is the tremendous risk that Rahab took to harbor Joshua's spies. She literally lied to the officers to protect the interlopers. Why? She knew that

God had given the land to the Israelites, and she believed their actions were divinely ordained.

"… I know that the LORD has given you the land, that a dread of you has come upon us, and that all the inhabitants of the land are overcome with fear of you. For we have heard how the LORD dried up the waters of the Red Sea before you when you came out of Egypt, and how you dealt with Sihon and Og, the two kings of the Amorites beyond the Jordan, whom you doomed to destruction. At these reports, we are disheartened; everyone is discouraged because of you, since the Lord, your God, is God in heaven above and on earth below." (Joshua 2:8–12)

In exchange for harboring the spies, Rahab asked them to "show kindness to my family; and give me an unmistakable token that you are to spare my father and mother, brothers and sisters, and all their kin, and save us from death." (Joshua 2:13)

Rahab's exemplary behavior was not lost on the spies. They guaranteed her safety when the Jewish army eventually invaded Jericho.

"We pledge our lives for yours," the men answered her. "If you do not betray this errand of ours, we will be faithful in showing kindness to you when the Lord gives us the land." (Joshua 2:14)

The Sages Say

The Bible notes that Rahab let the spies down through a window with a rope. Rashi explained that Rahab used the rope to raise and lower adulterers and other customers in and out of her house. When she used it to aid Joshua's spies, she was, in essence, petitioning the Almighty to forgive her as she was now using the rope for a good deed. The symbolic message is that the very item used in sin could also be used for beneficence and even to bring salvation.

Conquering the Land

Thanks to Rahab's kindness, Joshua's spies were able to leave the land unscathed. They returned to where the Jews were camped and told Joshua all that had happened to them.

The next morning, the people got up early and traveled to the banks of the Jordan River. Once there, the marshals of the camp told them that they couldn't cross the river until they saw the Ark of the Covenant, which the Levites would carry before them to show them the way.

The Fall of Jericho

Jericho was the first city to fall to Joshua and his soldiers. How it fell is a well-known story. Joshua's army walked around the walled city of Jericho once a day for six days. Each time they walked, priests blew trumpets. On the seventh day they circled seven times. As they did, Joshua told the people to "Cry out, for the Lord has given you the city!" (Joshua 6:16) They did so, and the walls fell down before them.

It Is Written

Jericho was the most heavily fortified city in the Land of Canaan. No other nation or force had ever conquered the city. Excavations of the ancient city of Jericho revealed that it was surrounded by two walls, both 12 feet thick with a space of at least 12 feet between the walls.

Joshua and his army conquered the city, setting the city and everything in it ablaze. Only the vessels of gold, silver, copper, and iron were declared sacred and consecrated for the treasury of the Lord. Only Rahab and her family were spared, in keeping with the promise made to her. Joshua goes one step further, Rahab commits herself to the tenets of Judaism, and the Talmud relates that Joshua eventually took her as his wife!

Joshua then pronounced a solemn curse on any man who should rebuild Jericho. (Joshua 6:26)

Defeat at the City of Ai

Joshua and his people then continued to destroy other towns and cities, and they succeeded in conquering Canaan. However, not only does the process take 14 years to accomplish, the Israelites stub their toes with a form of defeat at the city of Ai.

It turned out that not all the soldiers heeded Joshua's call to refrain from taking of the spoils of Jericho. One of them went against his wishes and took the consecrated items. Predictably, God wasn't pleased.

"But the children of Israel committed a trespass concerning the consecrated items; for Achan, the son of Carmi, the son of Zabdi, the son of Zerah, of the tribe of Judah, took of the consecrated items; and the anger of God was kindled against the children of Israel." (Joshua 7:1)

What happened next is considered the greatest defeat and casualty toll in the many battles Joshua fought to conquer the land. First, Joshua followed standard operating procedure and dispatched spies to Ai. The spies told him that it wasn't necessary to send the entire army.

"The entire people need not go up; about two thousand men or three thousand men should go up and smite Ai. Do not weary the entire nation there, because they are few." (Joshua 7:3)

Joshua accepted the spies' report and sent about 3,000 men to the city. There, the men of Ai ambushed the men and killed about 36 of them—sending the rest of the army into retreat.

The setback perplexed and greatly troubled Joshua, and he openly questioned God's guidance: "Joshua tore his garments and fell on his face before the ark of God until evening ... and Joshua said 'Alas, O Lord God, why did you bring this people across the Jordan to deliver us into the hand of the Amorites, to make us perish? If only we had been content to dwell on the other side of the Jordan!'" (Joshua 7:7)

God told Joshua that the stunning defeat was the result of Achan's plundering of the gold and silver vessels of the city of Jericho. Joshua confronted Achan, who readily confessed his crime.

Joshua had Achan put to death. Shortly thereafter, the Israelites waged a second attack against Ai and were successful.

> **Lord Knows**
>
> As difficult as it is to believe, Ai is the only battle in which the Israelite army suffered any casualties during the entire military campaign to conquer the Land of Canaan. This speaks of a supernatural relationship between the Jewish nation and God in waging war, as if God Himself was vanquishing the enemy.

The Treaty with Gibeon

The breathtaking initial success of the upstart Israelites was not lost on the people of Gibeon, who were the next city in the crosshairs of Joshua's deadly bow. But the Gibeonites came up with a crafty ploy to avoid becoming the Israelites' next victims: "They also did work subtly, and went and made as if they were ambassadors, and took old sacks on their asses and wine containers, old and torn and bound up." (Joshua 9:4)

It was clearly well known that Israel was set to destroy all Canaanites. Their probable alliance with Shechem, who you met in Genesis, was also well known. These two factors explain the Gibeonite approach. If they could pretend to be non-Canaanite Israelite admirers, such as Shechem, they might be able to unite with these tenacious and uncompromising warriors.

With their "old sacks," the Gibeonites wanted to give the impression of having come on a long journey: "And they went to Joshua, to the camp at Gilgal, and said to him, and to the men of Israel, 'We have come from a far country. Now therefore make yourselves a covenant-treaty with us.'" (Joshua 9:6)

The Israelites believed the Gibeonites and struck an agreement with them.

> ### It Is Written
>
> A covenant such as the one that the Gibeonites wanted to strike with the Israelites would involve mutual protection and responsibility and would be looked on as secure and sacred. Even when it was discovered that it had been obtained by false pretences, it could not be changed or cancelled. And it was binding through the centuries. When King Saul slew some Gibeonites without good reason, he violated this pact, and he was punished for it. (2 Samuel 21:1)

However, after a few days, the Israelites learned that the Gibeonites were, in fact, their neighbors: "And so it was that at the end of three days, after they had made a treaty-covenant with them that they heard that they were their neighbors and that they dwelt among them." (Joshua 9:16)

Lord Knows

"Hewers of wood and drawers of water" were the lowest of the low. (Deuteronomy 29.11) Their slavery would involve the most menial service in the sanctuary and also consisted of meeting the general and continual need for wood and water throughout the tribes of Israel.

It wasn't the kind of secret that could be kept for long. Soon everyone would know about it. People would begin gloating and laughing at the way the Israelites had been duped.

The Children of Israel were naturally incensed and wanted to slay every last one of the Gibeonites. However, their leaders thought differently, and counseled the Israelites to honor the pact and let the Gibeonites live so they could become "woodchoppers and water drawers for the entire assembly ...." (Joshua 9:20)

The wisdom of the leaders is borne out by their restraint. They reasoned that slaughtering the Gibeonites outright would only embolden other Canaanites and leave the impression (as false as it might be) that Israelites did not honor their oaths.

Defeat of the Canaanite Confederacy—The Invasion of the South

Next up was the Canaanite Confederacy, which was an alliance of five Canaanite kings against the Gibeonites. In accordance with their treaty with the Israelites, the Gibeonites asked Joshua for assistance, which he granted.

There followed the slaughter of the Canaanite armies by the forces of Israel. Here, the battles took on a decidedly supernatural bent, as the armies were vanquished by such things as hailstones from heaven and of the standing still of the sun and of the moon.

The battle against the Canaan Confederacy was followed by the taking of Makkedah, Libnah, Lachish, Eglon, Hebron, and Debir, which completed the conquest of the southern part of the hill country.

The first verse in chapter 10, which chronicles the conquests in the hill country, also contains the first mention of Jerusalem in Scripture. The holiest of cities to the Jewish people is mentioned no less than 800 times throughout the Bible.

Dividing and Settling the Land

No fewer than eight chapters in the Book of Joshua detail how the land was divided amongst the Israelites. At the end, God's promises were fulfilled.

"Thus God gave to Israel the entire land that He swore to their forefathers to give; they inherited it and dwelled in it." (Joshua 21:41)

Joshua and his armies had accomplished great things in Canaan, and had conquered much of the land. However, it was not entirely under his control. In ancient times, when relatively minor kings moved into a land and conquered it, they didn't necessarily remain there or station troops there. Instead, they followed up their conquests by demanding tribute.

The question then was whether the conquest would hold. Would the people accept the position as subject people? That depended on both the strength of the king's forces and the strength or weakness of the conquered people. It was a position that would have to be continually maintained by force.

That was also true in this case. Joshua had conquered the land. But settlement was a different matter. The conquered people might object, especially as they were to be driven out. And he hadn't left occupying forces. Returning refugees and those who had avoided his forces would soon fill the vacuum left by his invasion. Thus the conquest would need to be enforced, or otherwise. That was to be the task of the Israelite tribes.

The Memorial Altar

With the initial war with the Canaanites being over, Joshua summoned to him warriors from the two tribes of Reuben and Gad, and the half tribe of Manasseh, who had come over the Jordan River with him to assist in the warfare. He commended them for their obedience to Moses, to himself, and to God, telling them they had fulfilled their solemn oath. (Numbers 32:20–31) Then he blessed them, told them to return home, and gave them careful instructions about maintaining rightful worship of God.

The warriors departed. When they came to the border, they erected a memorial altar by the Jordan River. This concerned the rest of the Children of Israel who feared that the warriors were going to turn from the pure worship of God.

They sent a delegation of princes to the warriors, along with Phinehas, the son of Elazar (the High Priest), to both ask what was going on and to rebuke them. But the warriors told the Israelites that God knew what they were doing. What's more, they told the Israelites to let God be the rebuker.

"Almighty God … He knows and Israel shall know. If it is in rebellion or in treachery against God, save us not this day. [If we meant] to build an altar for ourselves to turn away from following God, or to offer an elevation-offering or meal-offering upon it, or to offer peace-offerings upon it, let God Himself exact [retribution] …." (Joshua 22:22–23)

The Israelites did the wise thing and backed off.

Joshua Says Goodbye

"And so it was after many days, when God had given rest to Israel from all their enemies round about, and Joshua was old and well stricken with years, that Joshua called for all Israel, for their elders, and for their heads, and for their judges, and for their officers, and said to them, 'I am old and well stricken with years.'" (Joshua 23:1–2)

Near the end of his life, Joshua again emulated the actions of Moses, his mentor. Just as Moses gathered the people for a final address before his death, so did Joshua. It is not clear exactly where the venerable leader gathered the people. It might have been at the sanctuary in Gilgal or in Shechem, which is where Moses stationed the people for his final address.

Lord Knows

Moses and Joshua both ruled their people for 40 years.

In his address, Joshua reminded the Israelites of what God had done and of what He would do, and exhorted them to keep God's commandments. He warned them not to mix with the Canaanites nor join them in their idolatrous practices. Should they depart from God and do so, it wouldn't be pretty.

"For if you should turn away and cling to the rest of these nations … by intermarrying with them and coming into them and they into you, you should know with certainty that God, your God, will not continue to drive these nations out from before you; they will be a snare and an obstacle to you, a lash in your sides and thorns in your eyes, until you are banished from this goodly land that God, your God, has given to you." (Joshua 23:12–13)

The Great Covenant Ceremony

The Book of Joshua closes with an account of a covenant ceremony in the Samarian city of Shechem. Previously, Joshua had written the words of the covenant on stones there and had built an altar and sanctuary as God had commanded. It was also the place where Moses had declared that such a covenant ceremony should take place upon entering the land. (Deuteronomy 27:2–8)

At Shechem, Joshua again gathered and addressed the people. He reminded them once more of the many great and good things that God had done for them and again implored them to fear and serve God and to reject idols.

Then he laid before them the stark choice as to whether they would serve the true God, or the gods of the Canaanites. He did so not just once but three times. Each time, the people told Joshua they would serve only God.

Joshua accepted their pledge and finalized a covenant with them. He then wrote down decrees and laws for them, and sealed their covenant with a visual reminder of their promise.

"Joshua wrote these words [and placed them] with the Book of God's Torah. He took a large stone and stood it there beneath the doorpost that was in the Sanctuary of Hashem, and Joshua declared to all the people, 'Behold, this stone will be a witness for us, for it has heard all the words of God that He has spoken to us; it will be a witness against you if you ever deny your God.'" (Joshua 24:26–27)

> **Lord Knows**
>
> According to tradition, Joseph's bones were submerged with his coffin in the Nile until the Israelites of the Exodus retrieved them and buried him in the Holy Land.

After the stone was placed, Joshua sent the people away.

The chapter concludes with an account of the death and burial of Joshua and Eleazar, and of the interment of the bones of Joseph, which the Children of Israel had carried with them from Egypt in accordance with Joseph's request that he not be buried there.

After much effort, all the tribes of Israel had found somewhere to settle. Some tribes were well established; others, such as Dan, which had to settle in hill country because the enemy would not allow them on lower ground, were finding things more difficult. But at least they were at rest. They were established in the land without fear of being driven out.

The next phase—the gradual subjection and driving out of the Canaanites—lay ahead. It would take place over the next 400 years. The new leadership were "the elders that outlived Joshua" (Joshua 24:31) who would guide the people. They were the precursors to a new form of quasi-monarchy—the Judges—who would lead the people for more than 350 years before an official king would be anointed in Israel.

The Least You Need to Know

- The Book of Joshua picks up where the Five Books of Moses ends.

- Joshua's military campaigns in conquering the Land of Canaan are a major theme of the Book of Joshua.

- The first verse in chapter 10, which chronicles the conquests in the hill country, also contains the first mention of Jerusalem in Scripture.

- Although the tribes had not completely dispossessed the Canaanites by the end of the Book of Joshua, they had found places to settle throughout the land, just as Moses had planned many years earlier.

Chapter 11

Sitting in Judgment: The Book of Judges

In This Chapter

- ◆ Israel's new leadership
- ◆ Canaan is purified
- ◆ Deborah the warrior prophet
- ◆ Gideon, Abimelech, and Jepthah
- ◆ Samson and the Philistines

Joshua is gone and the Israelites have settled into their tribal cities. There is relative peace and tranquility in the land. Complacency sets in. But foreign influences begin to erode the moral fabric of the people. The enemy begins to rattle its saber.

The nascent Israelite nation is clamoring for a new champion. Enter the period of the judges.

A Time of Transition

The Book of Judges (in Hebrew, Shoftim) traces nearly 350 years of history of the Jews in Israel, from the death of Joshua in 1227 B.C.E. to 890 C.E. when a united monarchy was established under Saul, the first king of Israel. Tradition holds that Judges was written by Samuel, the last judge and the first major prophet after Joshua.

The book unfolds along two themes. The first details what happened to the nation as a whole. The second describes each generation's leader—its judge.

As discussed in Chapter 9, although Joshua and his armies had conquered much of the land, it was not entirely under their control. The question then was whether the conquest would hold. That would depend on the strength of the new leader's forces. It would also depend on the resolve and confidence of the people in their new champion.

Commentators have characterized this transitional period in contradictory ways. Some suggest that these nearly four centuries of Jewish history were an era of disorder and lawlessness. There are two key verses to support this contention: "In those days there was no king in Israel; each person did that which was right in his eyes." (Judges 17:6, 21:25)

These words speak of a period when no ruler exercised control over the Jewish people. It might have been a time when lesser men who were unable to ascend to higher positions on their own merit usurped power, and thus everyone acted independently.

"And it came to pass in the days when the Judges judged, that there was a famine in the land." (Ruth 1:1) This verse is most intriguing. Certain commentators interpret it to mean that it was a generation that "judged its judges" during a period of anarchy and rebellion against authority. In other words, it's an indictment against the people themselves. In the words of the Talmud, "If a judge ordered a litigant, 'take that toothpick from between your teeth'" (for example, beware of a minor infraction), the man would counter, "Take the beam out from between your eyes!" If a judge said to a defendant, "Your silver is dross!" the defendant would retort, "Your wine is diluted with water!"

On the flip side is the school of thought that praises the young nation for its success in self-government. The Lord, as it were, was testing the people to see if they would remain loyal to the Law of Moses, reinforced by Joshua, without coercion. As such, the words "each person did what was right in his own eyes" indicate that the people intuited the correct path without a king, minister, or policeman to compel them.

Likewise, when "the Judges judged"—the people listened! They honored their acknowledged leaders. A system like this boded well for them centuries later when they would be led into exile far away from their central halls of justice and Holy Temple. Alien people and cultures with their opposing values could not hold sway over a people tenaciously dedicated to Torah observance.

Who were the judges? Were they rulers, prophets, neither, or both? Let's see.

The Judges of Israel

Judges were not legal decision makers in the conventional sense. They did more than sit on a bench and hold court. Instead, the judges of early Israel were the quasi-political and religious moral leaders of their generation.

Judges were faced with many leadership challenges, most typically military in nature. One of Israel's mortal enemies would oppress a particular tribe and all of Israel suffered, for they realized they could be next. Suddenly, an inspired judge would arise and lead a collection of fighters recruited from among the tribes. He would liberate that tribal region, and the people would breathe a collective sigh of relief. With the acute problem under control, the judge would return home and tend to less serious, noncrisis affairs.

Certain judges, such as Ibzan and Eli, were also important links in the chain of the oral tradition and preferred educational tasks to military ones.

The following chart details the 14 judges who led Israel over a span of close to 350 years.

Judges of Israel	Major Accomplishment
Othniel 1227 B.C.E.	First judge after Joshua's death, defeated the Arameans. Judged 40 years.
Ehud 1187 B.C.E.	Fought the Moabites; slew its king, Eglon.
Shagmar	Led Israelites against the Philistines.
Deborah 1106 B.C.E.	Prophetess, guided Barak to victory over the Canaanites. Only female judge.
Gideon 1066 B.C.E.	Defeated Midianites with 300 men.
Abimelech 1026 B.C.E.	Only judge to win leadership through treachery.
Tola	Judged Israel for 23 years.

continues

continued

Judges of Israel	Major Accomplishment
Yair	Judged Israel for 22 years.
Jepthah 981 B.C.E.	Defeated Ammonites, made fateful careless vow that some say caused death to his daughter.
Ibzan	Judged people for seven years.
Elon	Judge for 10 years.
Abdon	Ruled for eight years.
Samson 950 B.C.E.	Fought Philistines single-handedly for 20 years. Was a Nazirite from his birth.
Eli 930 B.C.E.	Priest who ruled people from the sanctuary at Gilo for 40 years.

The battles of most of the judges are recorded in the Hebrew Bible. However, details of the battles of the minor judges—Abimelech, Tola, Yair, Ibzan, Elon, and Abdon—are not.

Let's take a closer look at what they did.

Trouble from the Neighbors

A pattern that recurs throughout Judges (and several books that follow) is a weakening of pure worship of the God of Israel that led to intermarriage, idolatrous paganism, and trouble from the neighbors: "And the children of Israel dwelt among the Canaanites, the Hittites, and the Amorites, and the Perizzites, and the Hivites, and the Jebusites; and they took their daughters to be their wives, and gave their own daughters to their sons, and served their gods. And the children of Israel did that which was evil in the sight of the Lord, and forgot their God, and served the Baalim and the Asheroth." (Judges 3:5–7)

The people were in hot water again and in need of a new champion to rid themselves of this menace. When they cried for mercy, God responded with a deliverer.

The mantle of leadership was first passed on to the Tribe of Judah: "And it came to pass after the death of Joshua, that the children of Israel asked God, saying: 'Who shall go up for us first against the Canaanites, to fight against them?' And God said: 'Judah shall go up; behold, I have delivered the land into his hand.'" (Judges 1:1–2)

What is interesting here is that Scripture first mentions: "Judah shall go up," without specifically mentioning an individual. The implication is that whoever followed after Joshua would not be considered his successor, as there simply wasn't anyone great enough to follow him.

Nonetheless, the people would rally behind Othniel ben Kenaz, the first of the judges. A distinguished scholar and war hero, he was the brother of Caleb (ben Yefuneh) who was a disciple of Moses and one of the 12 spies Moses sent as the people were about to enter the land.

As it is written: "And the spirit of God came upon him, and he judged Israel; and he went out to war, and God delivered Cushan-rishathaim king of Aram into his hand; and his hand prevailed against Cushan-rishathaim. And the land had rest forty years. And Othniel the son of Kenaz died." (Judges 3:9–11)

Othniel, with the "Spirit of God" pulsing through his veins, delivered the Israelites from foreign oppression. It was by this Spirit of God that came upon him that he routed the king from Mesopotamia and saved Israel. But this respite of "And the land had rest forty years," would not have been possible unless the people, led by Othniel, changed their wayward behavior.

Othniel served the Israelites well. His gravesite in the holy city of Hebron, in the Land of Judea, is a memorial prayer-site frequented by many people even today.

Enter Ehud

It didn't take long after Othniel's death for the Israelites to revert to their old ways: "And the children of Israel again did that which was evil in the sight of God; and God strengthened Eglon the king of Moab against Israel, because they had done that which was evil in the eyes of God. And he gathered unto him the children of Ammon and Amalek; and he went and smote Israel, and they possessed the city of palm-trees. And the children of Israel served Eglon the king of Moab eighteen years." (Judges 3:10–12)

The Israelites again cried out to God for a new leader. As it is written: "But when the children of Israel cried unto the Lord, God, He raised them up a savior, Ehud the son of Gera, the Benjaminite …." (Judges 3:15)

Ehud made a dagger and paid a visit to Eglon, the king of Moab. He offered a tribute to Eglon. After he did, he sent away the people who bore the present. But Ehud stayed on and told Eglon he had a secret message for him. As Eglon got out of his seat, Ehud stabbed him through the stomach.

Ehud fled the scene but not before cleverly locking the doors behind him enabling him to escape undetected while Eglon's servants lingered. He sounded a loud horn-blast from the hill country of Ephraim (north) and the Children of Israel amassed to wage war on the newly crippled and leaderless Moabites.

After they slaughtered the Moabites, the Israelites enjoyed 80 years of peace, the longest continuous period of quiet during the era of the judges. This testifies to the righteousness of this generation who, notwithstanding a few glitches, faithfully adhered to the teachings of their forefathers. Consequently, Moab never again even attempted to wage war against Israel.

Shamgar the Son of Anath

Shamgar, of whom only one verse is written, follows Ehud: "And after him was Shamgar the son of Anath, who smote of the Philistines six hundred men with an ox-goad; and he also saved Israel." (Judges 3:31)

Shamgar's was the initial encounter with the Philistines. They won't reappear until much later, which again attests to the relative calm and peaceful prosperity the Israelites enjoyed during this pre-monarch epoch of self-government. But there were a few more pitfalls and dark moments, as we will see. Here is one of them: "And the children of Israel again did that which was evil in the sight of God, when Ehud was dead. And God gave them over into the hand of Jabin king of Canaan, who reigned in Hazor; the captain of whose host was Sisera, who dwelt in Harosheth-goiim. And the children of Israel cried unto God; for he had nine hundred chariots of iron; and twenty years he mightily oppressed the children of Israel." (Judges 4:1–3)

As in the past, the Israelites petitioned the Almighty to deliver them from this threat. The answer, however, was anything but business as usual. This time the response came in the form of a woman.

Israel's First Lady

"Now Deborah, a prophetess, the wife of Lappidot, judged Israel at that time. And she sat under the palm-tree of Deborah between Ramah and Beth-el in the hill-country of Ephraim; and the children of Israel came up to her for judgment." (Judges 4:4–5)

The Israelites' oppression at the hands of Jabin, the Canaanite king, had been so grievous that they stopped using the main highways for travel. They also cramped themselves into overcrowded cities, abandoning the more vulnerable villages and hamlets.

Deborah, the sole female judge, successfully led Israel to victory over the Canaanites with Barak, her general, whom she appointed through the spirit of prophecy. The account of the victory against Sisera, the captain of Jabin's army, introduces us to another female heroine, Yael, who fearlessly decapitates Sisera and helps rout the enemy: "And Sisera gathered together all his chariots, even nine hundred chariots of iron, and all the people that were with him, from Harosheth-goiim, unto the brook Kishon. And Deborah said unto Barak: 'Up; for this is the day in which HaShem hath delivered Sisera into thy hand; is not HaShem gone out before thee?' So Barak went down from Mount Tabor, and ten thousand men after him. And HaShem discomfited Sisera, and all his chariots, and his entire host, with the edge of the sword before Barak; and Sisera alighted from his chariot, and fled away on his feet.

But Barak pursued after the chariots, and after the host, unto Harosheth-goiim; and all the host of Sisera fell by the edge of the sword; there was not a man left. However Sisera fled away on his feet to the tent of Yael the wife of Heber the Kenite; for there was peace between Jabin the king of Hazor and the house of Heber the Kenite. And Yael went out to meet Sisera, and said unto him: 'Turn in, my lord, turn in to me; fear not.' And he turned in unto her into the tent, and she covered him with a rug.

And he said unto her: 'Give me, I pray thee, a little water to drink; for I am thirsty.' And she opened a bottle of milk, and gave him drink, and covered him. And he said unto her: 'Stand in the door of the tent, and it shall be, when any man doth come and inquire of thee, and say: Is there any man here? thou shall say: No.' Then Jael Heber's wife took a tent peg, and took a hammer in her hand, and went softly unto him, and smote the peg into his temples, and it pierced through into the ground; for he was in a deep sleep; so he swooned and died.

And, behold, as Barak pursued Sisera, Yael came out to meet him, and said unto him: 'Come, and I will show thee the man whom thou seeks.' And he came unto her; and, behold, Sisera lay dead, and the tent peg was in his temples. So God subdued on that day Jabin the king of Canaan before the children of Israel." (Judges 4:13–23)

> **Lord Knows**
>
> The fifth chapter of Judges is commonly referred to as Shirat Devorah (The Song of Deborah). It is publicly read in synagogue one Sabbath during the year.

The entire fifth chapter of Judges is devoted to hefty praise of God, these heroes, and the individual tribes.

The victory against Jabin was total and never again did the Israelites hear from the northern Canaanites. They had another 40 years of tranquility to grow and prosper as a Torah nation. But in an already familiar pattern, they stumbled yet again: "And the children of Israel did that which was evil in the sight of God; and God delivered them into the hand of Midian seven years. And the hand of Midian prevailed against Israel; and because of Midian the children of Israel made them the dens that are in the mountains, and the caves, and the strongholds." (Judges 6:1–2)

The Midianites forced the Jews to cower in caves along the mountainous regions. That national pastime of crying out to God during crises was not forgotten. God responded with their fifth major judge and champion—Gideon.

Gideon and His Trumpet

The story of Gideon illustrates the sometimes paranormal or miraculous nature of military campaigns of this era. It goes like this …

God sends an angel to a man named Gideon. The angel tells Gideon that God has chosen him to deliver the Israelites. Gideon isn't sure about this and asks God for signs or wonders to prove that God was really with him.

Gideon starts out with an army of 32,000 men. God commands him to tell all who are afraid to go home, and 22,000 of his troops depart. The next test is to have these men get a drink of water. Some of them get down on their knees and put their faces in the water. These are rejected. Some take water in their hands and lap it up as a dog laps water. Only these were chosen.

Gideon's army now numbers 300 men. They surround the Midianite army that is camped in a valley. Each man has a trumpet in his right hand and a pitcher with a lighted torch in his left hand. When Gideon gives the signal, each man blows on the trumpet, breaks the pitcher to let the torch shine, and shouts, "The sword of the Lord and of Gideon!" The Midianites think they are surrounded by a much larger army and become so confounded that they kill one another.

Gideon, with God's help, won a battle with just 300 men. He fought many other battles with great success as well.

The Sages Say _____

"Then the men of Israel said unto Gideon: 'Rule thou over us, both thou, and thy son, and thy son's son also; for thou hast saved us out of the hand of Midian.' And Gideon said unto them: 'I will not rule over you, neither shall my son rule over you; only God shall rule over you.'" (Judges 8:22–23)

The sages note that these verses recognize the free spirit of the leaders who eschewed honor, glory, and kingship, and rather attempted to instill their charges with the attitude that they did not need a mortal king to rule over them. Only God would be their king.

Abimelech, the Jealous Judge

The only blot on this period in terms of leadership was Abimelech. The son of Gideon, with a concubine for a mother, he used extreme violence to gain office and didn't really serve in the capacity of a recognized judge. Instead, he coerced the men of Shechem to coronate him as their king. To do so, Abimelech followed the pagan practice of killing off 70 brothers.

Abimelech's end came after three years of civil war and strife and occurred in a most embarrassing fashion: "Then went Abimelech to Thebez, and encamped against Thebez, and took it. But there was a strong tower within the city, and thither fled all the men and women, even all they of the city, and shut themselves in, and got them up to the roof of the tower. And Abimelech came unto the tower, and fought against it, and went close unto the door of the tower to burn it with fire. And a certain woman cast an upper millstone upon Abimelech's head, and broke his skull. Then he called hastily unto the young man his armour-bearer, and said unto him: 'Draw thy sword, and kill me, that men say not of me: A woman slew him.' And his young man thrust him through, and he died. And when the men of Israel saw that Abimelech was dead, they departed every man unto his place. Thus God requited the wickedness of Abimelech, which he did unto his father, in slaying his seventy brethren." (Judges 9:50–56)

Jepthah, the Hero of the Common Folk

Jepthah, who hailed from the Land of Gilead, was the next judge. He was an outcast, born of an unwed mother. Questioned about his paternity, his half brothers (who were born to a better-bred mother) banished him from their father's estate, and he relocated to a place called Tov on the boundary with Aram (Syria) where he attracted landless, unemployed vagabonds to his army.

Known for his fearless fighting prowess, the elders of the Sanhedrin called on him to save Israel. Jepthah agreed on the condition that if he prevailed he would head the land. His terms were accepted, and Jepthah, as the first order of action, tried to negotiate peace.

Although not the greatest scholar, Jepthah held his own against the king of Ammon when the latter insisted on restoring their old territory of Ammon on the East Bank of the Jordan River, now settled by the tribes of Reuben and Gad: "So said Jepthah; Israel did not take the land of Moab and the land of the children of Ammon." (Judges 11:15)

Jepthah then went into an epic monologue in which he reviewed the entire account exactly as it is found in the Torah. (Numbers 21, Deuteronomy 2) There were no compromises. God gave the land to the Israelites—no land for peace!

Lord Knows

The face-off between Judge Jepthah and the king of Ammon reminds one of the present-day Middle East peace efforts and the notion of "Land for Peace." The king of Ammon brazenly demands that Israel return to him the territories that were conquered, and if Israel refuses, there will be war. Compared to the demands of today's Arabs, this demand is quite "moderate." The king of Ammon, unlike the Palestine Liberation Organization (PLO), does not call for the total destruction of the Jewish State. He only wants that which he believes was taken from his people. In words that echo in the UN and in Washington, D.C., the king concludes his demand in the following manner: "Now, therefore, restore those lands *peacefully.*" The response of Jepthah to the king of Ammon is far different than Jewish leaders told Arafat and the PLO. Jepthah recounts all the past history, and then concludes: "So now the Lord of Israel has driven out the Amorites from before his people—Israel—and you should possess the land?! Will you not possess what your god, Kemosh, gives you to possess? And all whom the Lord, our God, shall drive from before us that we shall possess." (Judges 11:23–24) Many religious-minded people believe this is the proper reaction of a true Israelite leader. The land belongs to the Jewish people not just because of a historical claim or because of the defeat of the former inhabitants in battle. Rather, the land is theirs because God gave it to them and they have no right to give it up ... not even for promises of peace.

When Jepthah's efforts failed, he took on the Ammonites and won. However, before he waged war he swore to God that he would submit as sacrifice the one that would be the first to welcome him on his return. He reckoned it would be one of his farm animals. Sadly, his only child instead ran out to meet her victorious father.

Jepthah, horror-stricken, broke down on the spot. But his valiant daughter strengthened him to do what he must. She asked for two months to mourn her lost youth, and then submitted herself to be sacrificed by her father.

Samson and the Philistines

Samson is without a doubt the most famous and colorful of all the judges. Much has been written about his extraordinary physical strength and weakness for women. His unique and original escapades in the service of God led to incredible feats that were motivated by a single-minded focus to exploit both his proclivities for the sake of the Jewish people. No less than four chapters of Judges are dedicated to this remarkable hero.

God designated Samson as a judge even before his conception. Remember the judge Shamgar? He gave Israel respite from the Philistines for a few years. But Israel returned to its sinful ways and God placed them under the rule of the Philistines for 40 years. Time again for a new hero.

God designated a man named Manoach and his wife to sire the new savior. A messenger from God told the hitherto infertile wife that she would give birth to a son who would be solely dedicated to God. So much so that she should avoid alcohol and sinful food. Once born, the young boy should leave his hair uncut and become a Nazir (see Chapter 7), dedicated to saving Israel from the Philistines. The infertile woman did indeed have a son. She called him Samson, and he was blessed that God's spirit pulsed through him.

Samson and His Women

Samson's penchant for Philistine women was a ruse to infiltrate their ranks and begin his campaign as a one-man wrecking crew against their army and leadership.

Young Samson found a Philistine woman and invited his parents to purchase her for him. On their way, they encountered a lion. Samson, buoyed by God's spirit, wrestled the attacking beast and killed it with his bare hands.

Some days later, Samson came to the same spot and saw the corpse of the lion housing bees and honey, which he spooned and ate. When he married the Philistine woman, he threw a seven-day party for her family and friends and challenged them with a riddle: "Which is that was the eater, and became the eaten, the fearsome that became a sweet thing?" (Judges 14 :14)

Samson and his wife's family bet on whether they'd be able to solve the riddle. After three days of partying, the family was not even close, and they blackmailed Samson's bride into getting him to tell her the solution. The wife was scared and pleaded with Samson to tell her the answer. He did, and she immediately passed it on to her family, who announced it with bravado: "What is sweeter than honey, and who is more fearsome than a lion?" Samson answers: "If you had not ploughed with my she calf, you would not have solved my riddle." (Judges 14:18)

Angry Samson went to Ashkelon, robbed 30 Philistines, and gave the loot to his wife's family as their reward for solving the riddle. He then abandoned his wife and her father gave her to one of Samson's friends.

Making Amends

A considerable time after the wedding fiasco, Samson returned to his wife to make amends. Her father revealed that his daughter was now married to a Philistine. He then tried to pacify Samson by offering his younger daughter who is "much better."

Samson had been looking for a pretext to wreak havoc on the Philistines and responded by devising a clever scheme to burn the Philistines' grain crop. He caught 300 foxes and tied each two of them by their tails, placing a torch in the knot. Samson then lit the torches and released the foxes. The wild beasts ran amok through the Philistine's crops and set a large area on fire.

The Philistines realized who had done it, and for what, and in revenge they burned to death the father and his daughter—Samson's former wife—in their house. Samson learned of their treachery and slaughtered the Philistines mercilessly. He then went into hiding. The Philistines were incensed and gathered over Israel demanding Samson be delivered to them. The Israelites complained to Samson that he angered the Philistines who had a dominion over Israel. He agreed to be arrested by his countrymen, provided they didn't hurt him.

Delivery to the Philistines

Tied up, Samson was delivered to the cheering Philistines. Then divine power began to flow through his veins and the ropes on his arms melted. He found a fresh donkey's jawbone, rendered it into a weapon, and killed 1,000 Philistines on the spot.

Samson became very thirsty, prayed to God, and God created a fountain to save him from death by thirst. Samson went on to judge Israel for 20 years.

The Power of a Woman

Samson couldn't kick his womanizing tendencies and fancied a Gazan whore who allowed the Philistines an opportunity to ambush him. When he realized this, he unhinged the big gate of the city, and carried it on his back all the way to Mount Hebron—a considerable distance. Finally, he set his eyes on one other Philistine woman, the seductive Delilah. Philistine officers seeking to extract the secret of his immense power approached Delilah for help.

Delilah accommodated and started driving Samson crazy with her inquiries. She teased, begged, seduced and implored him to tell. Each time, Samson put her off with a deception.

Ironically, every time Delilah asked, she intimated to him that she used this knowledge to hurt him, but Samson didn't pick up the hint.

Delilah's nagging was so extreme that Samson eventually relented and told her that his power emanated from his uncut hair. She cut his hair while he slept, and the Philistines captured the now weakened warrior. They bore his eyes out and brought him to their main temple called Beit Dagon to make sport of the Israelite hero. But the last laugh would be on them: "Now the house was full of men and women; and all the lords of the Philistines were there; and there were upon the roof about three thousand men and women that beheld while Samson made sport. And Samson called unto the Lord, and said: 'O Lord God, remember me, I pray Thee, and strengthen me, I pray Thee, only this once, O God, that I may be this once avenged of the Philistines for my two eyes.' And Samson took fast hold of the two middle pillars upon which the house rested, and leaned upon them, the one with his right hand, and the other with his left. And Samson said: 'Let me die with the Philistines.' And he bent with all his might; and the house fell upon the lords, and upon all the people that were therein. So the dead that he slew at his death were more than they that he slew in his life." (Judges 16:27–30)

Israel Falls to Idolatry

The age of the charismatic judges comes to an end shortly after Samson. The Israelites would soon be asking for a king, and the last chapters of Judges painfully demonstrate why they need one. Chapters 17 and 18 tell the story of the people of Dan, who settled themselves into Israel and contended with a man named Micah who established a shrine to idolatry in their midst. Chapter 19 describes a brutal, senseless gang rape of a man's concubine by certain lowlife characters from the tribe of Benjamin.

The last two chapters of Judges convey the story of the war that ensued when the mistress who was brutally raped eventually died from the abuse. The enraged Benjaminite sliced up her body and sent pieces in a gruesome package to the other tribes of Israel, demanding justice.

The tribes of Israel, outraged at the absence of justice in Benjamin, amassed an army and defeated their brethren in a civil war. Killed in the ranks of Israel were 40,000 men, and 25,000 soldiers were lost to Benjamin—the smallest of tribes—who were left with 600 men. It was the most horrendous episode in Israel's history. But that wasn't all. The victors imposed a suicidal ordinance restricting anyone marrying the women of Benjamin to repopulate the tribe. Eventually reconciliation prevailed, and Israel arranged for keeping the oath, while allowing the Benjaminites to find wives from among women of the other tribes.

The Least You Need to Know

- The Book of Judges covers nearly 350 years of Jewish history and introduces us to several amazing leaders who tried to consolidate Joshua's victories in Israel.

- Judges were quasi-kings, political and military leaders during a period of Israeli self-government.

- The military victories against hostile enemies allowed Israel to prosper in their land and experience extended periods of quiet and tranquility.

- Samson, who had a weakness for women, was a Nazir from the womb and used his extraordinary God-given strength to deliver Israel from 40 years of Philistine subjugation.

From Judges to Kings: The Book of Samuel

In This Chapter

- ◆ Eli, Samuel, and Saul
- ◆ Saul and David
- ◆ David's rise to power
- ◆ David's reign

As could be expected of a young nation, Israel underwent many transformations. The Book of Samuel documents one such transformation by describing the events that took place as Israelites switched from judges to kings for their leaders.

Although the Book of Samuel focuses on three great Jewish leaders—Samuel, Saul, and David—it is essentially a book about one of the greatest biblical personalities of all—King David.

Samuel's Book

Tradition holds that the Book of Samuel was written by none other than Samuel himself. However, I Chronicles 29:29 notes that Samuel had two co-authors—Gad the Seer and Nathan the Prophet. It is believed that their contributions account for the inclusion of Samuel's death in this self-titled book.

The Book of Samuel covers the period from Samuel's birth in approximately 928 B.C.E. to shortly before David's death in 836 B.C.E.

The Birth of a New Leader

The Book of Samuel begins with the transition of leadership from Eli to Samuel. Interestingly, however, Eli makes only a brief appearance, doing so in a long story about Samuel's birth. As such, the main reason for Eli's appearance in this book is to introduce us to Samuel.

> ### Lord Knows
>
> The Christian canon splits the Book of Samuel into two—I Samuel and II Samuel. There was no such split originally in the Jewish canon; however, many modern translations do split the book into two.

We are first introduced to a man named Elkanah, a prophet who was a member of the Levitical tribe. Elkanah had two wives—Hannah and Peninah.

Although Hannah was barren, Scripture notes that Elkanah loved her very much. However, after 10 years of marriage, Hannah encouraged her husband to take another wife in the tradition of Sarah, who gave her handmaiden, Hagar, to Abraham to build a home.

Peninah had 10 children. But she didn't have them quietly: "Her rival (Peninah) provoked her again and again in order to irritate her, for God had closed her womb." (I Samuel 1:6)

The Talmud suggests that Peninah's actions were meant to provoke Hannah to pray for a child more fervently. However, her good intentions didn't justify her cruel taunts, and we are taught that she lost eight of her ten children.

As she did every year, Hannah went to Shiloh, where the Tabernacle had rested for 369 years, with her husband and her co-wife. There, she prayed tear-laden, heartfelt prayers before Eli, the High Priest and judge. At first, Eli thought she was drunk because Hannah prayed silently. He confronted her and told her to sober up.

Hannah assured Eli that she was far from drunk—only heavy of heart—and confided the reason for her sadness.

Asked of God

Eli blessed Hannah and told her she would bear a son. She vowed to God that she would dedicate her baby to the service of the sanctuary.

Hannah's desire for a child was answered. She named the baby Samuel, which is variously translated as "Asked of God," "The name of God," "Heard of God," and "His name is God."

After Hannah weaned her small son, she fulfilled her vow by bringing him to Eli, telling the judge: "For this child I prayed, and the Lord has granted me my request which I asked of him. Therefore I also have given him to the Lord; as long as he lives he shall be devoted to the Lord." (I Samuel 1:27–28)

Hannah's Prayer

The next chapter opens with Hannah's Prayer (or Poem). In it, she thanks God, rejoices in His salvation, and states that nothing is outside of the realm of God's power. She also predicts that God will crush the Philistines—Samuel's enemies.

In recognition of Hannah's faithfulness, God also blesses her with more children—three sons and two daughters.

The Little Minister

The Bible tells us quite a bit about Samuel's childhood. Under Eli's tutelage, Samuel "ministered before the Lord, even as a child, wearing a linen ephod." (I Samuel 2:18) Hannah even made him "little robes," which she brought to him when she visited the Tabernacle with Elkanah to make their annual sacrifice. Samuel continued to grow in favor with both God and his people.

A Godly Warning

Sadly for Eli, he had two sons of his own—Chofni and Pinchas—who, although scholars and priests, were noted as being "corrupt; they did not know the Lord." (I Samuel 2:12) Eli was a doting father, but he eventually had enough and chastised his sons for their indiscretions, telling his sons that God would judge them if they continued their evil ways.

Soon after, Eli was visited by a "man of God" who chastised him for favoring his sons over the Lord: "Did I not choose him out of all the tribes of Israel to be my priest, to offer upon My altar, to burn incense, and to wear an ephod before me? … Why do you kick at My sacrifice and My offering which I have commanded in My habitation, and honor your sons more than Me …?" (I Samuel 3:28–29)

Eli's visitor ends by telling him that his sons will die, after which the Lord will "raise up for Myself a faithful priest who shall do according to what is in My heart and in My mind." (I Samuel 2:35)

Samuel's First Vision

Eli and his sons soon die as a result of Philistine aggression. Samuel's first prophecy was a vision of their downfall.

Samuel heard what he thought was Eli calling to him. As it turns out, the voice he was hearing was God's. The Lord called to him three times. Each time, Samuel went to Eli. Each time, Eli told Samuel he hadn't summoned him.

The third time, Eli figured out that God was calling the boy. He told Samuel to tell God that he was listening. Samuel did so.

The Lord told Samuel: "Behold, I will do something in Israel at which both ears of everyone who hears it will tingle. In that day I will perform against Eli all that I have spoken concerning his house, from beginning to end." (I Samuel 3:12)

Samuel was afraid to tell Eli about his vision, but Eli wormed it out of him. Samuel spilt the beans and held nothing back. Eli told Samuel "It is the Lord. Let Him do what seems good to Him." (I Samuel 3:18)

After his revelation to Eli, Samuel was then recognized as a prophet of the Lord.

Israel Loses the Ark

Israel had enjoyed a 20-year reprieve from war following Samson's death. It came to an end soon after Samuel made his prophecy to Eli when the Israelites took the Philistines. Some 4,000 Israelites lost their lives in an epic battle at Ebenezer, near Shiloh.

The people rallied and sounded the ram's horn as a call to battle. The Philistines were initially bewildered by the sound, but they regrouped and fought again. This time, they killed 30,000 Israelites. Among them were Eli's two sons. Even worse, the Philistines captured the Ark of the Covenant.

A messenger brought news of the battle to Eli. When he heard it, he fell backward in his chair, broke his neck, and died.

The Philistine celebration over this victory was short-lived. With great bravado, they brought the Ark to their idol, Dagon. Their intention was to mock the God of Israel, but God mocked them right back and toppled their idol onto its face. Twice more they found their idol prostrated on its face in front of the Holy Ark.

The Philistines ended up transferring the Ark to each of their cities. The people of Beth Shemesh, who first received the Ark, didn't treat it properly and many died as a result. They then transferred the Ark to Kiriath Yearim, where its inhabitants welcomed and afforded it due respect. This ushered in a national movement of repentance and rejection of foreign gods under Samuel, who reigned as judge for the next 20 years.

Samuel was a dedicated and indefatigable servant to his people. As long as he led, the Philistines remained subdued and the Israelites were able to resettle the border towns that had been seized by their nemesis. Peace and prosperity abounded.

> **The Sages Say**
>
> The most active of all the judges, Samuel traveled throughout the land to teach, elevate, guide, and judge. The sages teach that he accepted no compensation for his teaching and established a level of integrity that was legendary and a standard for Torah scholars for generations.

Passage of Power

Samuel might have been a great leader, but his prowess didn't transfer to his sons. He had two, Joel and Abijah, and he made them judges, but they were corrupt and definitely didn't walk in their father's footsteps.

The elders of Israel came to Samuel and told him they wouldn't accept his sons as their leaders. They asked Samuel to name a king in their stead.

Their request didn't rest well with Samuel. He felt they were asking for a king for the wrong reasons. Their motivation should have been their desire for such a leader to help them reach a higher level of service to God. Instead, they seemed more captivated by the image of a king who would bring them honor through conquests, spoils of war, and great riches.

Although Samuel was affronted by their request, he told them he would seek God's assistance. God told him the following: "Listen to the voice of the people in all that they say to you, for it is not you whom they have rejected but it is Me whom they have rejected from reigning over them, like all the deeds that they have done from the day I brought them up from Egypt until this day—they forsook Me and worshipped other gods. So are they doing to you, as well, and now, heed their voice but be sure to warn them, and tell them about the protocol of the king who will reign over them." (I Samuel 8:7–9)

Samuel told the people what God said, and warned them of the price they were going to pay for their request. He told them their king would take their sons to be his horsemen, and their daughters to be his perfumers, cooks, and bakers. He would also take the best of their fields and a tenth of their flocks for his own, and that the people would be his servants. But the people didn't care. They wanted their king to allow them to be like everyone else.

The Lord told Samuel to heed the people's voice.

Enter Saul, the first king of Israel.

A Reluctant King

God told Samuel that Saul, a humble man from the tribe of Benjamin, was His choice for king. It was an interesting choice as Saul hailed from the smallest tribe, and his family was "the least of all the families of the tribe of Benjamin." (I Samuel 9:21) As such, he questioned Samuel's choice, but Samuel assured him he was indeed God's appointed and anointed him as such.

Saul Stumbles

Saul reigned for only two and a half years. Although foremost a Torah scholar, he waged successful battles against both the Ammonites and the Philistines. However, he made significant mistakes along the way that hinted at his being a less-than-effective ruler, including the following:

- Not able to keep his troops gathered together during battles with the Philistines.

- ◆ Not trusting that Samuel would come and join him as he said he would.

- ◆ Being vainglorious in battle by not taking any strong or valiant man for himself (in other words, going it alone).

Samuel repeatedly warned Saul about going against God's wishes and told him he was not keeping God's commandments. But Saul continued his disobedience. As is always the case, doing so would eventually catch up with him.

> **Lord Knows**
>
> Remnants of the special blend of oil that Moses used to anoint and dedicate the Tabernacle, all its vessels, and its priests, were also used to anoint all the kings and High Priests. Tradition has it that both the oil and the Ark would remain concealed until the final Messianic king was anointed.

Saul's Comeuppance

Samuel commanded Saul, in the name of God, to battle the evil Amalekite people. Saul achieved a complete victory over Amalek, but he failed to totally annihilate the Amalekites. Instead, he disobeyed God by sparing the life of Agag, the Amalekite king, along with the best of the Amalekite herds.

God came to Samuel and told him how much He regretted appointing Saul as king. Samuel, dismayed, went to Saul and gave him one last chance to plead his case. Saul did so and asked Samuel to pardon his sins. Samuel, however, told Saul that he had "rejected the word of the Lord." (I Samuel 15:26) In return, the Lord had rejected Saul as king.

In a dramatic encounter, Samuel sliced Agag in half. He told Saul that his kingdom would be "cut asunder" and given to a man greater than he.

The Good King David

Samuel would not see Saul again until Saul died, and he mourned for him. God, however, would have none of it and commanded Samuel to anoint the next king. He was to travel to Bethlehem, where, God said, the next king awaited.

Samuel, however, feared for his life and asked God "How can I go? If Saul hears it, he will kill me." (I Samuel 16:2) God told Samuel to engage in a bit of subterfuge. He was to travel with a heifer, ostensibly as a sacrifice. When he reached Bethlehem, he was to meet up with a man named Jesse, who was the father of the next king. After this, God said, "I will show you what you shall do; you shall anoint for Me the one I name to you." (I Samuel 16:3)

Samuel, ever the obedient servant, did what God asked and traveled to Bethlehem. There, he invited Jesse and his sons to the sacrifice. They came, and Samuel tried to identify the next king from them. He looked at seven of Jesse's sons and figured that one of them must be the new king. However, God told him to look past their outward appearance because "the Lord looks at the heart." (I Samuel 16:7)

The new king wasn't among Jesse's seven sons. Samuel asked him if there might be another young man lurking about. As it turned out, there was. Jesse's youngest son, David, didn't come with the others as he needed to keep their flock of sheep. Samuel asked for David to be brought before him. The young man, who was "ruddy, with bright eyes, and good-looking," was God's anointed one.

Saul's Melancholy

After Samuel anointed David in the spirit of the Lord, God's spirit departed from Saul and was replaced with "a distressing spirit." Saul's servants suggested that his bad humor might be relieved with some good music, and encouraged their leader to summon a "skillful player on the harp." (I Samuel 16:16) Saul agreed that a little music might lift his spirits, and he asked his servants to bring him a "man who can play well."

One of Saul's servants spoke highly of David, telling the king that he had "seen a son of Jesse the Bethlehemite, who is skillful in playing, a mighty man of valor, a man of war, prudent in speech and a handsome person, and the Lord is with him." (I Samuel 16:18) Saul asked that the young man be brought to him. When he saw David, he was instantly impressed with the young man. He asked Jesse to allow David to minister to him with music. Whenever the spirit of melancholy descended on Saul, David played and the distressing spirit departed from Saul.

David and Goliath

Just prior to meeting David, Saul and his son Jonathan (who would become David's closest friend) had handed the Philistines a rousing defeat. Ironically, the Philistines were ready to go at it again with another offensive only a few months later.

Jesse, David's father, sent him to visit three of his older brothers who were fighting the Philistines with King Saul. When he arrived, he found both sides ready for battle.

David's brothers told him of a man named Goliath who was challenging the Israelites to put up a champion to fight him.

The stakes were simple: If Goliath prevailed, the Jews would be slaves to the Philistines. If the Jewish champion prevailed, the Philistines would be slaves to the Jews. Because of Goliath's mammoth size and terrifying appearance, none of Saul's warriors wanted to accept the challenge.

Goliath had been issuing his challenge for 40 days, and the morale of the Jewish forces was shrinking exponentially. David said he'd fight the Philistine giant, but Saul argued against it. "David's only a lad," he said, while Goliath was a seasoned killing machine from his early childhood.

But David convinced Saul by telling him that the Almighty had given him the strength to fight against powerful enemies, such as the mighty lion and the ferocious bear, when they had stolen sheep from his flock, and he had pursued them, rescuing the sheep from their grasp, and killing them. (I Samuel 17:34–36) It was a compelling enough argument for Saul.

David approached the Philistine brute and said, "You come against me with a sword and with a spear and with a javelin; but I come against you in the Name of the Lord of Hosts, the God of the armies of Israel, Whom you have taunted ...." (I Samuel 17:45) He killed Goliath with a single, precisely aimed stone from his slingshot, then took his sword and decapitated the beast on the spot.

In honor of his courage, despite his youth and lack of military experience, Saul appointed David as the head of his armies. David became more successful as a military leader than his boss, so much so that the women of Israel lifted their voices in song and praise, "... Saul has slain his thousands, and David his tens of thousands." (I Samuel 18:7)

Understandably, their adulation made Saul a bit paranoid. It wasn't long before he turned on David.

Saul Versus David

The rivalry heated up between old King Saul, who hadn't quite figured out that he'd been deposed, and a new king, David, designated in his stead. Saul commanded his servants to kill David. When they failed, Saul told Jonathan to bring David to him. But David successfully eluded both father and son. In fact, during the course of his struggles with the old king, he actually ended up saving his life more than once.

During this period of warfare, Saul sought God's advice, but the Lord didn't answer him. Thus thwarted, he turned to seers and mediums, specifically, the witch of Endor, and asked her to conjure up the spirit of Samuel, who had recently died. She did so and Samuel's spirit told him that he and his sons, including Jonathan, would fall in battle the next day.

Despite Samuel's dire prediction of death, Saul put on his armor, took his position in his chariot, and rode off into battle with a sense of purpose and duty to defend his people. In the ensuing battle, Saul's only fear was that he would be wounded and captured alive and paraded around the enemy camp to make a mockery of him. Indeed the Philistine archers got to him and he was mortally wounded. But Saul chose to die by his own hand rather than be captured alive, abused, and be made into a living source of desecration of God's name: "Saul said to his armor-bearer 'Draw your sword and stab me with it, lest these uncircumcised people come stab me and make sport of me.' But his sword bearer did not consent, for he was very afraid, so Saul took the sword himself and fell on it." (I Samuel 31:4–5)

The Sages Say

One of the commentators takes the position that Saul did not actually kill himself. In the beginning of II Samuel, an Amaleki tells David that he had killed Saul (which was a foolish mistake, as David puts him to death).

Saul clearly committed suicide, or at least tried to. In the code of Jewish law, suicide is clearly proscribed, and is viewed as the worst form of homicide, but Jewish law also teaches that a king who realizes his capture is imminent and wishes to avoid torture or desecration of his person at the hands of his captors may take his own life.

David's Reign

The second Book of Samuel records the highlights of King David's reign. It begins with David's elegy for Saul and Jonathan, which is a stirring collection of verses filled with love and respect for these fallen heroes.

However, David's rule is not *fait accompli* (irreversible). He faces opposition from a number of sides, including Ish-bosheth, one of Saul's surviving sons.

When David declared his kingship in Hebron, Ish-bosheth did the same. A showdown was inevitable and a bloody duel ensued that left David and his servants the victors, but that nearly led to a civil war.

With David clearly established as supreme ruler over Judah, he was able to supervise the material and spiritual welfare of God's people. It was in this time that the tribes of Israel solidified into a nation, and the nation transitioned from a people who constantly had to pay tribute to their Philistine occupiers to one of wealth and prosperity.

David accomplished this transition in part by subduing many foreign entities, which were then forced to pay him a tribute. He also increased Israel's geographic size tenfold.

David was a beloved and successful king, but his reign was never easy. The Talmud says that during his 40 years as ruler he never dreamt a pleasant dream. He continued to have problems with the Philistines. He incurred the wrath of Michal, Saul's daughter, when she saw him rejoicing (supposedly, dancing wildly) when the Ark of God was returned. His family is best described as dysfunctional. And David himself suffered one of the greatest dysfunctions of them all—infidelity.

A Woman Named Bathsheba

David had one fatal flaw: he had an eye for women—or at least "a woman." It resulted in the only blemish on the record of one of the greatest personalities in Jewish history.

One day, while standing on the roof of his palace, King David spotted Bathsheba, the wife of one of his soldiers, Uriah. He was immediately love-struck.

David had a prophetic vision that he was destined to marry this woman. He summoned her to his palace and slept with her.

Bathsheba conceived from this tryst. The quick-thinking monarch then ordered her husband Uriah back from war so that he would have marital relations with Bathsheba and conceal David's paternity. But Uriah, smelling a rat, refused to return to his house. David insured Uriah's death by sending him back to war and ordering the general to place him in the front lines. He reasoned that this would be a more honorable death for the soldier, and it covered up his own deed. The plan seemed to work. After Bathsheba's period of mourning ended, King David married her.

Lord Knows
Technically, David and Bathsheba's coupling did not constitute adultery. Since the time of King Saul, soldiers who went out to battle granted their wives a bill of divorcement (a Get) so that in the event they are captured or killed in battle and their bodies are not discovered, their wives would be able to remarry. If they indeed returned they would simply take their wives back with a new ceremony.

Scripture then introduces us to the wisdom of the prophet Nathan, who was Samuel's successor. He came to David with a dilemma. He told the king of two men, one rich and one poor. The rich man had very large flocks and herds, but the poor man had only one little lamb, which he cared for with great tenderness.

One day, the rich man received a traveler, but was loathe to take any of his own livestock to prepare a meal for the guest. So he took the poor man's only lamb and prepared it for the traveler.

Upon hearing this, David flew into a rage. "As God lives," he told Nathan, "the man who did this deserves to die!" Nathan responded, "You are the man!" Nathan then explained how David was the rich man, whom God had blessed in numerous ways. His soldier Uriah, however, was blessed with just one "lamb," his wife, Bathsheba. David answered Nathan with just two words, "Hatati LeHashem—I have sinned before God."

The proud king immediately rended his garment, put on sackcloth, and sat on the floor as if in mourning. David took full responsibility for his transgression, and his repentance was accepted. He showed remorse over this deed for the rest of his life. Eventually, Bathsheba bore for him a son, Solomon, who would continue the Davidic dynasty for his offspring, and the Messiah himself will sprout from his line.

Building a Permanent Temple

A final note about David's reign as king over Israel is that he prayed to be given the privilege to build a permanent Temple to house the Ark of the Covenant and provide a central location for the revelation of the Shechina, or divine presence, on earth.

God responded to David's offer through the prophet: "And it came to pass the same night, that the word of the Lord came unto Natan, saying: Go and tell my servant David, 'Thus says the Lord: shall you build a house for Me to dwell in? For I have not dwelt in a house since the day that I brought up the Children of Israel out of Egypt, even to this day, but have walked in a tent and a tabernacle. In all the places that I walked among the Children of Israel, did I speak a word with any of the tribes of Israel whom I commanded to pasture My People Israel, saying: "Why have you not built Me a house of cedar?" When your days are fulfilled, and you will sleep with your fathers, I will set up your seed after you, who will proceed from your body, and I will establish his kingdom. He shall build a House for My Name, and I will establish the throne of his kingdom forever.'" (II Samuel 7:4–7)

God told David that because he offered to build a "House for the Divine Presence," that house would indeed be built, but by a son of his (Solomon), whose very name connotes peace. David himself would not be allowed to build the physical house of God, for his hands had shed much blood. But God promised to build a "House" for David, an eternal dynasty of kings, which would serve the Jewish people. That dynasty would be eclipsed during the Exile of the Jewish People, but it would come back and be reinstated to its former glory, at the time of the Messiah.

The Least You Need to Know

- The Book of Samuel begins with an account of Samuel's birth. It also teaches us of Eli, the High Priest and second-to-last judge.

- Following the period of judges, the people were harassed by the Philistines and implored the prophet Samuel to anoint for them a king "like the other nations."

- Samuel accommodated and God pointed out a great and humble scholar from the Tribe of Benjamin, Saul, who reluctantly became the nation's first official king.

- Saul stumbled in the campaign to wipe out the archenemy of the Jewish people—Amalek—and Samuel prophesied the disintegration of his kingdom and ascendancy of David.

- The major theme of the Book of Samuel is the life of David, his great military accomplishments, and the many intrigues he endured to consolidate his kingdom.

- King David's only glitch as a leader involved his affair with Bathsheba. He had remorse for this deed the rest of his life. The act, however, was providential as Bathsheba became David's wife and bore him a son, Solomon, who would succeed him and continue the Messianic lineage.

Glory and Disaster:
The Book of Kings

In This Chapter

- ◆ From David to Solomon
- ◆ A splendid temple
- ◆ The wise Solomon
- ◆ A split kingdom
- ◆ Good kings and bad kings

King David's 40-year rule was coming to an end. His reign brought tremendous growth and prosperity to the nation. His kingdom was secure, powerful, and united; the royal coffers overflowed with wealth, and the first commonwealth of Israel was sitting pretty.

It looked like the Israelites were finally in a position to fulfill the destiny promised to them in God's covenant with Abraham. It was almost too good to be true. And, it was.

The Book of Kings tells the sad story of the factors and forces that once again prevented the fulfillment of God's ancient promises.

Royal Intrigues

The Book of Kings opens with royal intrigues, similar to how the Book of Samuel closes. With King David so close to death, there is fear of another coup.

> ### It Is Written
>
> In the Hebrew Bible, the Book of Kings is technically a single book instead of two; however, even the Jewish world identifies it as two. The prophet Jeremiah wrote most of the Book of Kings shortly after the last of the kings, Jehoiachin, was released from Babylonian captivity around 561 B.C.E., and 538 B.C.E., the date of the decree of deliverance by Cyrus the Great. Evidence of his authorship is found in the fact that some portions of the Book of Kings are identical to the Book of Jeremiah. An alternative supposition is that the leader Ezra, after the Babylonian captivity of Judah, compiled them from official court chronicles of David, Solomon, and the prophets; Nathan, Gad, and Iddo, and that he arranged them in the order in which they now exist.

David had designated Solomon, his son by Bathsheba, to succeed him. However, Adonijah, the son of Haggith (David's first wife), gathered a following and poised to proclaim himself king—even while David was still alive. The fifth verse of the Book of Kings announces the coup: "Adonijah son of Haggith, exalted himself, saying, 'I shall reign!' He provided himself with a chariot and riders, and fifty men running before him. All his life his father (David) had never rebuked him saying, 'Why do you do this or that?' Additionally, he was handsome and born after Absalom (making him the next eldest son)." (I Kings 1:5)

King David definitely had his flaws, and they included his parenting skills. Commentators did not refrain from pointing them out. The disastrous consequences of never having disciplined his son led to this serious rebellion.

Adonijah was no slouch. Intelligent and strikingly handsome, his magnetic power of persuasion naturally endeared him to his countrymen. His father was also seduced by his charm. Aided by Joab, a seasoned general from King Saul's reign, his other brothers, and the king's servants, Adonijah continued his plan to usurp the throne. Among those not on the invited list: Nathan the prophet and Adonijah's brother Solomon.

Nathan, the trustworthy prophet, went to Bathsheba and told her about Adonijah's plans. Together, they went to tell the infirm king.

When David learned of the plot, he didn't leave his legacy up to providence alone. He girded his loins for one last encounter with his internal foes. He publicly re-affirmed his pledge and wasted no time in having Solomon anointed.

Adonijah and his cronies heard the horns and celebration from the ceremony cele-brating Solomon's anointing from afar. When word came to them that David had anointed Solomon, they all dispersed to the four winds fearful of the repercussions.

Adonijah sought refuge in the sanctuary, grabbing hold of the corners of the altar as a tacit petition for amnesty. Solomon, the new king, ostensibly honored his request and wisely chose to wait until David expired before taking action against the upstart.

Shortly after David's death, Adonijah came knocking on Bathsheba's door and re-quested one of David's widows as a wife. The wise Solomon knew very well what that meant (in those days, taking a dead monarch's wife was a way of staking a claim to the throne) and immediately had Adonijah exe-cuted. Likewise, Solomon meted out appropri-ate punishments to all those miscreants and at the ripe "old" age of 12 became the monarch of the most impressive kingdom in the world!

> **Lord Knows**
>
> David and Solomon both reigned for 40 years. David lived until the age of 70 and Solomon was 52 when he died.

A Boy King Talks to God

What would a typical 12-year-old who just gained such extraordinary power want to do with it? Throw opulent feasts? Charge his fawning courtiers to lavish him with praise? Be entertained by all the national treasures amassed by his father?

No on all counts. Solomon instead communicated with the Almighty. God appeared to Solomon for the first time on the day that Solomon was anointed and told him: "'Request what you desire that I should give you.' And Solomon requested, 'Give to your servant a heart which hears (discernment), to judge your people to understand between good and evil.'" (I Kings 3:5,9)

God did as Solomon requested—in spades. He imbued Solomon with uncanny wis-dom, greater than that of all humankind. Scripture teaches that the idealistic monarch became a beacon to all who sought the fountain of wisdom that burst from his sub-lime intellect: "And God gave Solomon wisdom and understanding exceedingly much, and expansiveness of heart, even as the sand that is on the seashore. And Solomon's wisdom excelled the wisdom of all the members of the east, and all the wisdom of Egypt. For he was wiser than all men: than Ethan the Ezrahite, and Heman, and Calcol, and Darda, the sons of Mahol; and his fame was in all the nations round about. And he spoke three thousand proverbs; and his songs were a thousand and five. He spoke of trees, from the cedar that is in Lebanon even unto the hyssop that springs out of the wall; he spoke also of beasts, and of fowl, and of creeping things, and of fishes. And there came of all peoples to hear the Wisdom of Solomon, from all kings of the earth, who had heard of his wisdom." (I Kings 4:29–34)

Never before or since had there been a person who understood the conversation of the birds, trees, and other creatures, communicated with angels and demons alike, wielded those communications for useful purposes like a skilled swordsman, and adjudicated legal cases by simply gazing upon the litigants.

A Splendid Temple

One of Solomon's allies was Hiram, the king of Tyre, who was also close to King David. Solomon enlisted the king's help in bringing to fruition David's unrealized plans for building a "house for the name of the Lord …." (I Kings 5:3) He asked Hiram to help his workers supply the cedar and cypress logs for the temple, and Hiram agreed to it.

In the fourth year of his reign—480 years after the exodus from Egypt—Solomon began construction of the Holy Temple in Jerusalem. He sent 30,000 men to Lebanon to bring wood; 40,000 more hewed stones from the Judean hills.

It took seven years to complete the Temple. Chapters 7 and 8 of Kings goes into great detail on the structure, which by all accounts was simply magnificent. Here are just some of the details:

- The edifice and virtually all its vessels were overlaid with pure gold—another common commodity in Solomon's royal coffers.

- The inside of the Temple was cedar, carved with "ornamental buds and open flowers." (I Kings 6:18)

- Carved cherubim graced many areas, including the inner sanctuary.

Pillars of bronze, cast by none other than Hiram himself (the king was a skilled bronze worker), detailed the vestibule of the Temple.

Chapter 7 relates the dimensions of the house, and chapter 8—with 66 verses—is one of the longest in Tanakh, and demonstrates just what Solomon had in mind in constructing a "house" for the divine presence. It is spelled out in his enthusiastic dedication prayer he delivered to God in the presence of his people.

Scripture notes that God was pleased with this most impressive building. It would stand for 410 years until it was sacked by the Babylonian conqueror Nebuchadnezzar in 587 to 586 B.C.E.

It Is Written

Based on the measurements and description of the Temple given in the Book of Kings and in Second Chronicles, both Jewish and secular reference works depict the holy house as a rectangular building with a triple-tiered row of cells wrapping around three of its sides: north, south, and west, and with an entrance toward the east.

Solomon's Wisdom

Solomon captivated dignitaries who traveled long distances to pay tribute to the wisest king of them all. No one, however, was more impressed with Solomon's keen mind than the fabled Queen of Sheba, who we meet in chapter 10 of Kings.

The queen posed many riddles to the young prodigy. As Scripture notes: "… she spoke with him of all that was in her heart. And Solomon answered all her questions; there was not any thing hid from the king that he told her not. And when the Queen of Sheba had seen all the wisdom of Solomon, and the house that he had built, and the food of his table, and the sitting of his servants, and the attendance of his ministers, and their apparel, and his cupbearers, and his burnt-offering which he offered in the house of God, there was no more spirit in her. And she said to the king: 'It was a true report that I heard in my own land of your acts, and of your wisdom. Howbeit I believed not the words, until I came, and my eyes had seen it; and, behold, the half was not told me; thou hast wisdom and prosperity exceeding the fame that I heard. Happy are your men, happy are these servants, that stand continually before thee, and that hear thy wisdom. Blessed be the Lord thy God, who delighted in thee, to set thee on the throne of Israel; because God loved Israel forever, therefore made He thee king, to do justice and righteousness.'" (I Kings 10:2–9)

God's gift of wisdom to Solomon proved to be a double-edged sword. And paradoxically, it was Solomon's wisdom—the very same wisdom that had enabled him to orchestrate the construction of the Temple—that sowed the seeds of its eventual destruction.

Girls, Girls, Girls!

Despite the fact that Solomon, like his father, reigned 40 years and brought virtually unlimited wealth, prestige, power, and influence to the nation, he doomed his own kingdom by succumbing to his greatest weakness.

Solomon had a penchant for women. The wisest king of Israel, who contributed thousands of brilliant proverbs, parables, and prose—miscalculated his ability to control his harem and took 1,000 wives and concubines.

According to traditional sources, Solomon's intentions were mostly noble—he married only princesses from neighboring kingdoms. His goal was to influence those kingdoms through proxy by making his wives ambassadors for his plan to spread ethical monotheism. However, his plan backfired.

Samuel (remember him?) told the people their request for a king would have consequences. He also reiterated the Torah's admonishment that a king should not have more than 18 wives, should refrain from accumulating too much gold and silver, and should not maintain more than the number of horses needed to wage war or defend a kingdom. (Deuteronomy 17:14–20) Solomon violated all three by thinking he was above the purpose of these restrictions and could abrogate them.

> **Lord Knows**
>
> King Solomon's unprecedented wisdom contributed three significant books to the 24 books of Jewish Scriptures: the deeply symbolic Song of Songs, which he wrote in his youth; Proverbs, which he wrote in midlife; and the often-cynical Ecclesiastes, which he penned in his declining years.

Such hubris would not go unnoticed. As Scripture notes: "For it came to pass, when Solomon was old, that his wives turned away his heart after other gods; and his heart was not whole with the Lord his God, as was the heart of David his father." (I Kings 11:1–4)

Although Scripture here, read literally, implies that Solomon himself worshipped foreign gods, the Talmud makes it abundantly clear that this is not the case. Rather, because his wives proliferated idolatry under his very nose, and he did not sufficiently rebuke them, Scripture reckons as if he was guilty himself of the same transgressions as his wives.

God's Rebuke

"So the Lord became angry with Solomon because his heart had turned from the Lord God of Israel … Therefore the Lord said to Solomon, 'Because you have done this, and have not kept My covenant and My statutes, which I have commanded you, I will surely tear the kingdom away from you and give it to your servant." (I Kings 11:9–11)

God clearly wasn't going to let Solomon's actions go unpunished. However, in honor of Solomon's father, His actions would not manifest during Solomon's life. Instead, God told Solomon that He will "tear it out of the hand of your son." (I Kings 11:12)

And indeed He did. He raised several adversaries, and unrest settled over the people and the land. Although Scripture is vague here, the state of unrest seemed to hasten Solomon's death. He died at age 52 after ruling Israel for 40 years.

Rehavam, Solomon's son, is the next king.

A Kingdom Divided

The Kingdom of Israel was divided after King Solomon's death, in great part due to Rehavam's lack of insight. Solomon had imposed some heavy taxes during his reign. With Solomon dead, the people of Israel decided to petition his son for relief. Rehavam listened to their pleas, and then sent them away for three days so he could consult with his advisors.

The elders, men who had counseled his father, advised the young king to listen to his people and be a servant to them. Doing so, they told him, would ensure that they'd "be your servants forever." (I Kings 12:7) But Rehavam opted instead to listen to the counsel of his young friends, who told him to increase the people's burden.

What happened next is in fulfillment of God's vow to Solomon. Remember when He said He would tear Israel out of the hand of Solomon's son? That's exactly what happened.

The seeds were now sown for a confrontation, and Rehavam assembled his warriors to fight against the people of Israel. However, God intervened and told the people not to fight against each other. In this way civil war was averted, but the Kingdom of David would never be entirely united. That unity, according to tradition, would only come about with the advent of the Messiah.

Jeroboam, one of Solomon's generals and a leader in the civil uprising, took 10 tribes in the northern half of the country and kept the name Israel. Rehavam took two tribes—Judah and Benjamin—in the southern half of the country and called it Judah. Each claimed to be God's chosen king.

For his part, God promised Jeroboam that if he were to abandon his idolatrous practices, the line of kingship would pass through him and he would unite the nation. But Jeroboam couldn't quite give it up for the Lord: "… Jeroboam returned not from his evil way, but made again from among all the people priests of the high places; whosoever would, he consecrated him, that he might be one of the priests of the high places." (I Kings 13:33)

The Northern Kingdom of Israel lasted just over 200 years and was conquered by Assyria around 722 B.C.E. The Southern Kingdom of Judah lasted just over 300 years and was conquered by Babylon around 586 B.C.E.

Good Kings and Bad Kings

The two kingdoms would now decline and slip even further away from worshipping God, thanks to a host of evil kings who followed Solomon and Jeroboam. And despite the attempts of Elijah and Elisha—two main prophets of the time—who would try to halt Israel's wrongdoing.

Although the Kingdom of Judah remained relatively loyal to God and the Torah—though with frequent lapses—the Kingdom of the 10 Tribes fell into a downward spiritual spiral.

Trouble in Israel

In Israel, wicked King Ahab of Israel was lead astray, mostly by his vicious wife Jezebel who impelled him to pursue the righteous prophets, including Elijah. They both met untimely deaths—Jezebel was attacked and killed by dogs. Only her hands and feet remained from their feast—while Ahab fell in battle.

> **Tower of Babel**
>
> **Baal** worship, a generic name for the main idolatry of the time, was taken from the religion of the Canaanites, the god who controlled rain and thunder.

One story that stands out here is that of Ahab and Jezebel instituting the greater worship of *Baal* in the land, including having built a temple for Baal. And having built Asherim, God sent Elijah to Ahab with a message of judgment: "And Elijah the Tishbite, of the inhabitants of Gilead, said to Ahab, 'As the Lord, God of Israel lives, before whom I stand, there shall not be dew nor rain three years, except at my word.'" (I Kings 17:1)

Elijah made a dire prediction of drought and fled into a cave to hide with other prophets who were being pursued by Ahab. Ravens miraculously brought them food. The significance of this story is that the ravens, by sustaining Elijah, aroused him to have mercy and removed his curse.

> **It Is Written**
>
> Elijah and his disciple Elisha are among the main prophets of the time. Their fervent dedication to God allowed them to reprove their people and perform miracles.
>
> Elisha, the student successor to Elijah, is also earmarked for greatness and miraculous deeds. In his first act, he encountered a noble woman of Shunem who would regularly host the prophet but was childless. He predicted her fate, "At this season, when the time comes round, you shall embrace a son." (II Kings 4:16)
>
> The woman conceived and bore a son at that season when the time came round, as Elisha had said to her. He also resuscitated her son when he later died.
>
> Elisha also healed the leprosy of the Aramian general Naaman by having him immersed in the Jordan River seven times, thus creating a tremendous sanctification of God and cessation of hostilities between Israel and Aram. (II Kings 5:1–18)

During the imposed drought, God then sent Elijah to the home of a poverty-stricken widow in Zarephath, where God again performed miraculous provisions for both Elijah and for the widow and her son. When the widow's son fell sick and died, God resuscitated the boy through Elijah, confirming both His power and the calling He had placed upon Elijah.

That calling would be manifested into one of the greatest episodes of the book, where Elijah faces off with 450 worshippers of the Baal at Mount Carmel.

Before this confrontation, Elijah entered into a heated debate with Ahab over who was responsible for the terrible situation that the drought had brought. Ahab accused Elijah, saying that he had brought upon the demise of Israel. Elijah countered that Ahab himself was responsible because of his alliance with Jezebel and the Baal worship which she had instituted.

Elijah then commanded Ahab to gather his people at Mount Carmel so that he might speak to them. He asked them the following: "And Elijah came near unto all the people, and said: 'How long shall you waver between two opinions? If the Lord be

God, follow Him; but if Baal, follow him.' And the people answered him not a word." (I Kings 18:21)

Frustrated, Elijah calls a challenge. He's just one man against 450 of Baal's, but God's on his side and he knows he'll be the victor: "Let them therefore give us two bulls; and let them choose one bull for themselves, and cut it in pieces, and lay it on the wood, and put no fire under; and I will dress the other bull, and lay it on the wood, and put no fire under. And call ye on the name of your god, and I will call on the name of the Lord; and the God that answers by fire, let him be God." (I Kings 18:23–24)

The prophets of Baal do as they're commanded. As detailed in Scripture: "And they took the bull that was given them, and they dressed it, and called on the name of Baal from morning even until noon, saying: 'O Baal, answer us.'" (I Kings 18:26)

But Baal doesn't answer. They then take to dancing around the altar they had fashioned. Still no Baal.

Returning to Scripture: "And it came to pass at noon, that Elijah mocked them, and said: 'Cry aloud; for he is a god; either he is musing, or he is gone (to the bathroom), or he is in a journey, or peradventure he sleeps, and must be awakened.'" (I Kings 18:27)

The prophets of Baal gave it one last go. They cried out loud and cut themselves with their swords until their blood gushed. Still no Baal. The prophets of Baal kept it up until evening, but as Scripture notes, "there was neither voice, nor any to answer, nor any that regarded."

Elijah then called the people to him. He repaired the altar of God that had been dismantled. Then: "… Elijah took twelve stones, according to the number of the tribes of the sons of Jacob, unto whom the word of God came, saying: 'Israel shall be thy name.' And with the stones he built an altar in the name of God; and he made a trench about the altar, as great as would contain two measures of seed. And he put the wood in order, and cut the bullock in pieces, and laid it on the wood. And he said: 'Fill four jars with water, and pour it on the burnt-offering, and on the wood.' And he said: 'Do it the second time'; and they did it the second time. And he said: 'Do it the third time'; and they did it the third time. And the water ran round about the altar; and he filled the trench also with water.

And it came to pass at the time of the offering of the evening offering, that Elijah the prophet came near, and said: 'O Lord, the God of Abraham, of Isaac, and of Israel, let it be known this day that Thou art God in Israel, and that I am Thy servant, and that I have done all these things at Thy word. Hear me, O Lord, hear me, that this people may know that Thou, Lord, art God, for Thou didst turn their heart backward.' Then the fire of God fell, and consumed the burnt-offering, and the wood, and the stones, and the dust, and licked up the water that was in the trench. And when all the people saw it, they fell on their faces; and they said: 'The Lord, He is God; the Lord, He is God.' And Elijah said unto them: 'Take the prophets of Baal; let not one of them escape.' And they took them; and Elijah brought them down to the brook Kishon, and slew them there." (I Kings 18:31–40)

Elijah was successful in temporarily turning the hearts of the Northern Kingdom back to God. However, successes such as these were sporadic and an overwhelming number of Israelites followed aimlessly after their woeful leaders.

Another example of the decay in leadership of the Israelite kings is found in Ahab's successors. Moab started up with King Ahaziah who was badly hurt in an accidental fall—but instead of turning to the prophet Elijah, he asked the god of Akron whether he would recover! Such was the decadence and disgraceful conduct that brought destruction and exile without a trace of these monarch's ancestors.

Brighter Moments in Judah

The Kingdom of Judah had its brighter moments. All told, there were eight good kings from their ranks. Among the standouts are Hezekiah and Josiah, who reigned for 29 and 31 years, respectively.

According to tradition, Hezekiah could have been the anointed Messiah in more favorable times. Even so, he initiated a tremendous spiritual revival by taking down the high places of idolatry in the nation, unifying Judah and Israel to celebrate the Passover together, and refusing to serve Sanherib, the world conqueror who forced 10 tribes of Israel into exile.

Sanherib stood outside the walls of Jerusalem with his mighty Assyrian army of 185,000 officers poised for an invasion. He was determined to crush the last Jewish resistance offered by King Hezekiah. During the night before the scheduled morning of attack, a heavenly angel struck the Assyrian camp, slaying every one of its 185,000 officers and compelling Sanherib to flee to his homeland.

> **The Sages Say**
>
> How did Hezekiah and his people bring off the victory over Sanherib and his mighty army? The Talmud teaches, "The oil of Hezekiah subdued the yoke of Sanherib." Which oil? The oil that burned in the synagogues and houses of learning for the people to study Torah even at night. Hezekiah motivated his people to greater dedication in Torah study, the Talmud continues, by placing a sword at the entrance of each house of learning and proclaiming: "Whoever fails to study Torah should be impaled with this sword!"

When Hezekiah fell sick, the prophet Isaiah came to tell him he would die. The Talmud relates that this punishment reflected Hezekiah's refusal to sire children whom he prophetically saw would become wicked.

Rebuked by the prophet, Hezekiah agreed to marry and have children. He prayed to God, who responded through Isaiah, "I have heard your prayer, I have seen your tears: behold, I will heal you." Hezekiah asked for a sign that he would be healed—namely, that the shadow would return backward 10 degrees (explained by commentators that the sun stood still for 10 hours). He lived 15 more years, but he made the mistake of showing delegates of Babylon all the Temple treasures. As a result, Isaiah told him that God would allow Babylon to carry the Tribe of Judah away into exile after Hezekiah's days.

As for Josiah, Scripture says that the character of his reign was good. He followed in the steps of his ancestor, King David, and was obedient to the Lord.

Josiah was all of eight years old when he was coronated. When he was 20 years old, he began to clean up Judah and Jerusalem. He destroyed the heathen altars and the shameful idols on the hilltops. He, too, started a religious revival and gathered Jews from the kingdoms of both Judah and Israel to celebrate Passover in a grand fashion, the likes of which they had not seen since the days of Samuel. He rid the cities of the tribes of Manasseh, Ephraim, Simeon, and Naphtali of their idols, as well. Later, he set up a collection system for contributions for the Temple, and paid carpenters and masons to repair the Sanctuary from the damage and neglect by the earlier Kings of Judah.

This noble king was a fierce warrior to boot. When King Neco of Egypt led his army against the Assyrians, and warned King Josiah not to interfere while his army passed through Judah, Josiah refused to turn back. He led his army into battle against Egypt at the valley of Megiddo. The enemy archers struck King Josiah with their arrows and fatally wounded him. He died in Jerusalem, and was buried there. All of Judah mourned for him, including Jeremiah the prophet.

The Least You Need to Know

- The Book of Kings begins with the death of King David and the transfer of power to his son, Solomon.

- King Solomon, who contributed three books of Scripture, was blessed with wisdom from above and built a magnificent Temple in Jerusalem.

- Solomon's kingdom was split as a result of his marriage to foreign wives who caused even the wise Solomon to stray.

- A bevy of kings followed Solomon; those who followed his direct line were called the Kings of Judah and comprised two southern tribes. The Kingdom of Israel comprised the 10 northern tribes and was made up of a number of personalities. The majority kings from both camps were generally wicked and caused the nation to stray.

14

The Mighty Prophet: The Book of Isaiah

In This Chapter

- Chastising the people
- Having prophetic visions
- Consoling the downtrodden
- Finding the final redemption and Messianic Age

Isaiah, one of the greatest (if not the greatest) of the prophets, came at a critical time for the Jewish people. Not only was the Northern Kingdom collapsing at the hands of the Assyrians, but Jerusalem was also under siege. As such, Isaiah's words were delivered with a special urgency. He offered the staunchest reprimands as well as the greatest consolations and praise.

Isaiah's prophecies touched on a number of themes, including Israel's eventual restoration and a new age of prosperity. In the pages ahead, we explore some of his prophecies, including those that allude to one of the central themes of all prophetic writings—the coming of the Messiah.

Isaiah the Man and His Visions

Not much is known about Isaiah himself. Some sources say he was a member of Judean aristocracy and that he was married and had two children. The Bible notes that he was the son of a man named Amoz. The Talmud mentions that he was from the House of David, that he received the oral tradition from the prophet Amos and the elders of the Sanhedrin, and that the prophet Micah was among his disciples.

Isaiah's ministry was lengthy, spanning some 80 years and covering the reigns of four kings: Uzziah, Yotam, Achaz, and Hezekiah. It also extended into the reign of King Menashe, Hezekiah's son, who murdered the great man because he couldn't bear to hear his prophecies.

> **It Is Written**
>
> According to Jewish tradition, most of the prophets recorded their prophetic writings at the end of their lives. However, because Isaiah was murdered, he couldn't record his own prophecies. There are differences of opinion on who did write them. Some sources say his students did. Other sources credit three different authors writing them during three different periods that spanned as many as 200 years.

In his long career as prophet and leader, Isaiah foretold many major events, including the downfall of the Southern Kingdom of Judah at the hands of the Babylonians. He also predicted that the royal lineage of Judah would be induced into servitude in the palace of Babylonian kings. The Book of Daniel confirms this last prophecy.

Of all the books in Jewish Scripture, Isaiah probably receives the most attention apart from the Five Books of Moses. Not only do other books of the Hebrew Bible rely on the prophet's writings, they are also frequently quoted in the Christian New Testament.

Christian churches have traditionally interpreted certain verses from the Book of Isaiah as predicting events associated with Jesus' life, death, and second coming. As will be noted later in this chapter, these interpretations go solidly against traditional Jewish beliefs. However, they will be discussed here.

Isaiah's prophecies fall into three main categories:

- Prophecies of condemnation, found in chapters 1 through 35
- Prophecies of history, found in chapters 36 through 39
- Prophecies of comfort, found in chapters 40 through 66

Some of these visions allude to one of the central themes of all prophetic writings—the coming of the Messiah. For the purposes of our discussion here, I'll approach these passages and their potential meanings from a Jewish perspective.

I Condemn Thee!

The Book of Isaiah begins with prophecies of condemnation, which take the form of dire warnings for the prophet's own people in Judah: "'Hear, O heavens and give ear, O earth, For God has spoken; Though I brought up and raised My children, They have rebelled against me.' The ox knows its owner, and the donkey its owner's trough; But Israel does not know, My People does not understand." (Isaiah 1:2–3)

The country had become morally and spiritually corrupt. People were returning to ritualism and neglecting their God. But through Isaiah's words, God encouraged repentance. However, the people of Israel, who knew full well that they would be rewarded if they followed the commandments of the Torah, and would be punished if they failed, refused to obey God's law.

Lord Knows
The prophet's words here closely resemble those of an earlier leader. Like Moses before him, Isaiah wasn't sure prophecy was his calling. He would soon be convinced otherwise.

Isaiah aimed his first message of condemnation at his own countrymen in Judah. He then moved from local to regional judgment as he made a series of proclamations against neighboring countries—Babylon, Assyria, Philistia, Moab, Damascus (Syria), Ethiopia, Egypt, Edom, Arabia, Jerusalem (Judah), and Tyre.

That Isaiah does not consider his people unredeemable is found in two verses of hope and conciliation: "And I will restore their judges and their advisors as in the beginning, following which He will call you (Jerusalem) a righteous and loyal city. Zion will be redeemed with justice, and its inhabitants with the merit of charity." (Isaiah 1:26–27)

Isaiah Becomes a Prophet

Within these condemnations are also some lovely verses that relate to the beginning of Isaiah's prophetic career: "And one (*seraph*—angel) would call to the other, 'Holy, holy, holy! The Lord of Hosts! His presence fills all of the earth!'" (Isaiah 6:3)

It Is Written

Isaiah's prophetic career began with a vision of winged angels praising God. It represents one of the truly magnificent moments of divine revelation and a source of inspiration and transcendence that forms a responsive section of the Jewish daily prayer services.

A conventional interpretation of this verse renders the three occurrences of the word 'holy' as references to God. But the repetitive use of the word could also symbolize the different realms in which God is praised—in the upper realm where the angels and souls dwell; the second to the realm where the planets and celestial spheres exist; and the third, to the earthly realm where humans reside.

Isaiah, however, quickly followed this sublime thought with this harsh pronouncement: "And I said, woe is me, I am going to die, for I am a man of defiled lips dwelling amongst a people of defiled lips." (Isaiah 6:5)

This is a very strange reaction to Isaiah's life-altering communication with God. What could he possibly mean?

As mentioned, Isaiah felt inadequate for his appointed role. So God had to take radical measures to insure his involvement: "Then one of the seraphs flew over to me with a live coal, which he had taken from the altar with a pair of tongs. He touched it to my lips and declared, 'Now that this has touched your lips, your guilt shall depart and your sin shall be purged away." (Isaiah 6:6–7)

A Rabbinic interpretation of this verse goes something like this: To qualify as a prophet, Isaiah must learn to be the people's advocate, not just their disparager. Isaiah's atonement and purification can only be accomplished by divine means. An angel literally takes a live coal from the altar on high and places it in Isaiah's mouth. The coal does not burn Isaiah's mouth because of his exceptional nature as God's chosen prophet. This "divine mouthwash" helps mold the prophet's personality into a pliant messenger of the Almighty. He is ready for the next step.

God now asks, "whom shall I send, and who shall go for us?" (Isaiah 6:8) In other words, who is willing to rebuke the Jewish nation? It wasn't going to be a pleasant job. In fact, it would include much suffering and persecution. Isaiah himself said of it: "I submitted my body to those who smite and my cheeks to those who pluck; I did not hide my face from humiliation and spittle." (Isaiah 50:6)

In essence, Isaiah was agreeing to a suicide mission with the realization that he was opening himself up to ridicule. He ultimately relented and volunteered his services: "and I said: 'here I am! send me!'" (Isaiah 6:8) He was willing to suffer all the persecution and suffering involved in carrying out this mission for his love of God and His people.

At the Service of Kings

Isaiah spoke both of events that were portentous for the Messianic period, or End of Days, and of visions that had immediate consequences for his own generation. Two of the latter concerned two of the kings to whom he ministered. They both involve very specific predictions that are historically accurate. One of them, read correctly, dispels a myth concerning the origin of Jesus.

Around the year 732 B.C.E., the House of David faced imminent destruction at the hands of two warring kingdoms: the Northern Kingdom of Israel, led by King Pekah, and the Kingdom of Syria (Aram), led by King Rezin.

Isaiah recorded that the House of David and King Ahaz were gripped with fear. Out of pity, God sent him to reassure King Ahaz that divine protection was at hand. These two hostile armies would fail in their attempt to conquer Jerusalem.

God even provided a sign—the special birth of a child to a young woman known to Ahaz. It would be an omen from God that the siege would be lifted and that Jerusalem would continue as before: "Therefore the Lord Himself shall give you a sign: behold, the young woman shall conceive, and bear a son, and shall call his name Immanuel. Curd and honey shall he eat, when he knoweth to refuse the evil, and choose the good. Yea, before the child shall know to refuse the evil, and choose the good, the land whose two kings thou hast a horror of shall be forsaken." (Isaiah 7:14–16)

This prophecy has been mistranslated to reinforce the Christian belief in the virgin birth of Jesus. In Matthew 1:20–23 is found this mistranslation from Isaiah: "Therefore the Lord himself shall give you a sign; behold, a virgin shall conceive and bear a son, and shall call his name Immanuel." (Isaiah 7:14)

How did this happen? The original Hebrew text of Isaiah uses the word "almah," which refers to a young woman of marriageable age, not the word "bethulah," which means virgin. However, the author of Matthew used the Septuagint, the Greek translation of the Hebrew Scriptures. It inaccurately used the Greek word "parthenos" for "almah," thereby strongly implying virginity.

The actual text of Isaiah, however, makes no reference to a virgin becoming pregnant other than by normal means.

Lord Knows
Some modern translations of the Bible, which are based on the original Hebrew text, replace the word "virgin" with the more accurate translation "young woman."

In addition to the mistranslation, there are a couple more reasons why this passage cannot possibly refer to Jesus:

◆ The prophecy was completely fulfilled during the days of Ahaz and Isaiah—more than 700 years before the birth of Jesus.

◆ Isaiah 7:15 says "Curd and honey shall he eat when he knoweth to refuse the evil and choose the good." Would the Messiah or God need to choose good and refuse evil?

◆ The entire notion of a virgin birth is inconclusive. There's no way to really ascertain a person's sexual status except by taking that person's word for it.

This is merely one of many such misappropriations of Scripture that are used to advance the agenda of a religious movement outside the pale of Judaism. We will examine another passage that has been taken out of context later in this chapter.

The Day of the Lord

Isaiah also took on Judah and Jerusalem, describing what would happen in the future. In his words, a glimpse at what to expect from the true Messiah when he accomplished his divinely ordained tasks can be found.

"The prophecy of Isaiah ... The mountain of the Temple of the Lord will be firmly established ... They shall beat their swords into plowshares and their spears into pruning hooks; a nation will not lift up a sword against another nation, and they shall no longer study warfare." (Isaiah 2:1–4)

Some put great emphasis on the element of the end of all war and killing in the world, which certainly is contained within the prophecy of Isaiah, and according to Jewish tradition, one of the job descriptions given to the Messiah.

> **Lord Knows**
>
> In verses 2:1–4 of Isaiah can be found the prophecy of world peace, which is inscribed on important monuments throughout the world.

However, this prophecy would be incomplete without paying attention to the second message that emerges—which contains another inevitable Messianic portent: "And it shall come to pass in the last days, that the mountain of God's house shall be established above all mountains and shall be exalted above all hills, and all nations unto it shall stream. And many peoples will go and say, 'Come, and let us go up to the mountain of the Lord, to the house of the God of Jacob, and He will teach us of His ways, and we will walk in His paths. For out of Zion shall go forth the Torah, and the word of God from Jerusalem.'" (Isaiah 2:2)

This last prophetic line about Jerusalem does not merely foretell that it will be a center of world peace. Rather, just as Jerusalem has been the center of the Nation of Israel, so will it be the international center for all those seeking God. Isaiah seemed to be predicting that people from all nationalities and persuasions would see Jerusalem as the address for drawing out spirituality. Just as in the days of the wise Solomon, nations would seek their values of justice and morality specifically in Jerusalem.

> **It Is Written**
>
> In humankind's imperfect state, Jerusalem has been the flash point of ancient hostilities and gut-wrenching bloodshed. But Jerusalem is also a major religious center for a very large segment of the world's population. Isaiah inspired humankind with the hope that one day all people would accept not only its centrality but also its proper role as the site of the Third Temple and the place from which the sparks of authentic spirituality and Torah wisdom would light up the world.

Prophecies of History

In the historical part of Isaiah, the prophet looks back to the Assyrian invasion of Judah in 701 B.C.E. and anticipates the coming Babylonian invasion of Judah.

The historical section of Isaiah is often described as an interlude between the two meatier parts of the book. It tells the same story that is also relayed in similar detail in the books of Kings and Second Chronicles.

In Isaiah 13:19–20, he predicted that Babylonia would be destroyed like Sodom and Gomorrah and would remain uninhabited forever. Did this come true? One merely needs to visit the ancient city of Babylon in Iraq for validation. It is nothing but a mound that only archaeologists, jackals, and the curious visit today.

This prophecy, and many like it found in the Book of Isaiah, confirms the credibility of Isaiah as God's messenger, and of Scripture in general.

Prophecies of Comfort

The final part of Isaiah offers comfort via God's promise of hope and restoration. It speaks of the basis for this hope being the sovereignty and majesty of God. The message is one of Israel's eventual restoration, God's justice expanding to other nations, and a new age of prosperity. Isaiah also discussed the coming of the "servant of the Lord" who would usher in an era of great peace and happiness for the people of Israel.

> **Lord Knows**
>
> Of the 216 verses in these nine chapters, 115 speak of God's greatness and power.

The Restoration of the Holy Land

"Do not be afraid, for I am with you; I will bring your children from the east and gather you from the west. I will say to the north, 'Give them up!' and to the south, 'Do not hold them back.' Bring my sons from afar and my daughters from the ends of the earth." (Isaiah 43:5–6)

Isaiah foresaw that the people of Israel would return to their homeland from the east, the west, the north, and the south. From that time, a succession of empires conquered the Land of Israel and forced its people into exile. This led to a worldwide scattering of Jews. But during the past century, millions have returned to Israel, as Isaiah boldly predicted:

- **From the east:** Many Jews living in the Middle East moved to Israel during the 1900s. After Israel reclaimed independence in 1948, more Jews moved to their ancient homeland after being forced out of various Arab countries in which they had been living for centuries. Over 140,000 of them came from Iraq alone.

- **From the west:** During the mid-1900s, hundreds of thousands of Jews living in the West (Europe and the United States) began moving to Israel to escape various persecutions.

- **From the north:** Hundreds of thousands of Jews living in the former Soviet Union have moved to Israel since the 1970s and continue to do so.

- **From the south:** From 1949 to 1951 thousands of Yemenite Jews were airlifted to Israel. During the 1980s and 1990s, Israel struck a deal with Ethiopia's government to allow Ethiopia's Jews to move to Israel. On the weekend of May 25, 1991, the largest airlift of people in history brought 14,500 Ethiopian Jews to Israel.

Isaiah's prophecy was also correct in saying that the north (Soviet Union) and the south (Ethiopia and Yemen) would have to be persuaded and coerced into allowing their Jews to emigrate to Israel. The United States pressured the former Soviet Union for years before it agreed to allow its Jews to leave. And Ethiopia had to be paid a ransom to allow its Jews to leave.

Isaiah's prophecy was also correct in saying that the Jews would return "from the ends of the earth." Isaiah said that many centuries before the Jews had been scattered to the ends of the earth. During the past 100 years, Jews living as far east as China, as far west as the West Coast of the United States, as far north as Scandinavia, and as far south as South Africa, Australia, and South America have moved to Israel.

The Coming of the Messiah

Chapters 49–57 concentrate on the theme of the coming of the Messiah. In them are contained what are known as "Servant Songs," so called because in them, the prophet foretells the glorious redemption of the righteous remnant of Israel who is repeatedly identified as God's servant, or Suffering Servant, if you will.

In chapters 52 and 53, Isaiah describes the Almighty's servant-nation who, after a vicious and virtually nonstop repressive exile, is vindicated and redeemed—even in the eyes of her former oppressors.

"So shall he startle many nations; kings shall shut their mouths because of him; for that which has not been told them they shall see, and that which they have not heard they shall understand. Who has believed what we have heard? And to whom has the arm of the Lord been revealed?" (Isaiah 52:15–53:1)

Isaiah's words here describe the astonished reaction of gentile kings at the End of Days as they behold the virtuous remnant of the Jewish people exalted and triumphant.

In the next seven verses, these kings of nations continue to speak as they mournfully express their heartfelt confession. Their words bear witness to the realization that, as a result of their peoples' iniquities, the Nation of Israel had to bear the brunt of harsh decrees and treatment throughout its protracted and bitter exile: "Surely he has borne our misery and carried our sorrows; yet we esteemed him stricken, smitten by God, and afflicted. But he was wounded from (or as a result of) our transgressions, he was bruised from our iniquities;

Lord Knows
Skeptical reactions to the Messianic Age is a common theme throughout the writings of the prophets and is clearly accentuated in this chapter.

upon him was the chastisement that made us whole, and with his stripes we are healed." (Isaiah 53:4–5)

Evangelical Christianity claims these passages refer to Jesus as the "Suffering Servant" who dies for the transgressions of humankind. Not only does this interpretation cut against Jewish theology—in context—it clashes with the real message contained within. That message is: In the past, these world leaders would have concluded that the Jews were stricken and smitten by God because they stubbornly refused to embrace the ways of their nations. In other words, they "brought it on themselves." But the words of Isaiah and his Messianic redemption have illuminated the truth. Israel suffered as a result of the destructive haughtiness, greed, and avarice of these very oppressive anti-Semitic regimes.

The Least You Need to Know

◆ The Book of Isaiah, one of the longest in Scripture, contains some of the most often quoted passages and prophecies, some of which have been fulfilled.

◆ Isaiah served as a prophet for some 80 years, spanning the reigns of Uzziah, Yotam, Ahaz, and Hezekiah and into the reign of a fifth King, Menashe, the son of Hezekiah.

◆ Isaiah, even while rebuking the people, inspired them with hope and praise, similar to the style of Moses. Some sages believed that Isaiah's prophecy was comparable to the level of Moses.

◆ Many passages of Isaiah are known to contain messages about the Messianic Age. Several of them have been misquoted or mistranslated over the years. Read in context, these passages do not point to any particular individual who fits the description of the Messiah.

The Great Persuader: The Book of Jeremiah

In This Chapter

- Assisting a righteous king
- Opposing false prophets
- Dealing with death threats
- Destroying Jerusalem
- Consoling the people

What's the difference between a true prophet and a false one? Among other factors and in most cases, true prophets are scolders. They don't hesitate to point out blemishes and defects. False prophets flatter people with sweet talk and fail to identify their shortcomings.

In the prophet Jeremiah's time, Israel had both types. Jeremiah, a giant in spirit who minced no words to reprove the wayward, was definitely in the first group.

A Boy Prophet

Jeremiah was an intense, emotional man, and his emotions and intensity are clearly evident in the book that bears his name. His book can be difficult to read and follow as it's not a historical recollection. Instead, it's a collection of sermons that Jeremiah preached over a 20-year period, sprinkled throughout with the prophet's thoughts (in the form of poetic oracles) and reactions to what was going on around him.

 It Is Written _____

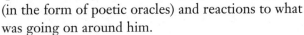 Jeremiah's prophecies began in approximately 627 B.C.E. during the reign of King Josiah and continued through the reigns of three of Josiah's successors: Jehoiakim, Johoachin, and Zedekiah. It also includes the fall of Jerusalem to Nebuchadnezzar in 586 B.C.E.

Jeremiah's prophetic career began with these inspiring words from God: "Before I formed you in the womb I knew you; Before you were born I sanctified you; And I ordained you a prophet to the nations." (Jeremiah 1:5)

Being just a young lad at the time, Jeremiah put up a bit of a protest, telling God that he "... cannot speak, for I am a youth." (Jeremiah 1:6) But God told Jeremiah not to worry and not to be afraid, as "... I am with you to deliver you ...." (Jeremiah 1:8)

Of all the prophets charged to chastise the Jewish people for their headlong plunge to self-destruction, Jeremiah was challenged more than anyone before or since. Starting his task when he was just a young man, he devoted his entire life to cajoling and coaxing a people to change its ways or face the consequences.

The book that bears his name contains a number of parables, sermons, and lessons, and is organized as follows:

- ♦ Jeremiah's call to prophecy (Jeremiah 1:1–19)
- ♦ Jeremiah's prophecies to Judah (Jeremiah 2:1–45:5)
- ♦ Jeremiah's prophecies to the Gentiles (Jeremiah 46:1–51:64)
- ♦ Jerusalem's fall (Jeremiah 52:1–34)

Prophecies for a Fallen People

As Jeremiah notes in the opening lines of this biblical book, the word of the Lord came to him during the reign of King Josiah of Judah. Josiah, who you might remember from the chapter on Kings, was one of Judah's few righteous kings. However, he inherited a strongly idolatrous kingdom when he was just eight years old. Thanks to Jeremiah's fiery sermons, which convinced the Judeans to accept Josiah's reign, the young king eventually became the first king to rule all 12 tribes since Solomon.

With Jeremiah's assistance, by the time of Josiah's eighteenth year in power, he destroyed all the centers of paganism and all visible signs of idolatry were gone.

Despite his idealism and efforts to restore Israel to its monotheistic roots, Josiah fails. His death is rather tragic, for he makes a silly blunder that appears to reflect his immaturity. The Pharaoh of Egypt requested to be given a harmless pass through his kingdom with his army, with the intent of attacking his Assyrian foe. Pharaoh Neho, as he was called, reassured Josiah that he meant him no harm: "What have I to do with you, king of Judah? I do not march against you this day, but against the kingdom that wages war with me." (II Chronicles 35:21)

> **It Is Written**
>
> Josiah is credited with restoring the Temple and its service to its previous glory. Ironically, it made Jeremiah's task even harder because the people insisted that the Temple should offer them refuge and inoculate them from exile, despite their private worship of idols.

Josiah decided to prevent this crossing, and he was "heedless of Neho's words from the mouth of God." (II Chronicles 35:22) According to tradition the "mouth of God" reference is to Jeremiah, who warned sternly against this confrontation. Thus ignoring the advice of Jeremiah, he goes into battle against the immense Egyptian army at Meggido, and is impaled with 300 arrows! His last words were, "God is the righteous and I had made a mistake."

> **It Is Written**
>
> After Josiah's death, Jeremiah lost his standing at court and was no longer in favor with the country's political and religious leaders. At various times he was arrested and was prohibited from speaking in public. Many wrongfully considered him a traitor as he lobbied against fighting the Chaldeans.
>
> Although no specific reason is given, Jeremiah repeatedly warned King Zedekiah about revolting against Babylon and the Chaldeans (Jeremiah 27:12–15). Through Jeremiah, God warned the king that he was a weak leader, that his armies were inferior to the Chaldeans, and that they would not prevail in battle.

Everyone mourned Josiah's passing. And they had every right to, as they faced some difficult times ahead. Josiah's successors were vassals of Egypt, and "did what was displeasing to the Lord." That combination made the country both spiritually and physically weak. The tragic result came 22 years later with the conquest by Babylon and the destruction of the Temple. Most of Josiah's story is found in II Chronicles 34:1–36:27.

Opposing False Prophets

Idolatry returned after Josiah's death, and with it, more false prophets. Jeremiah opposed them with all his strength. For his efforts, he was arrested, imprisoned, and disgraced publicly.

Jeremiah saw in the nation's recidivism the sealing of its doom. It would be only a scant 22 more years until Nebuchadnezzar captured Jerusalem and carried King Jehoiachin into exile. Yet even this did not deter Jeremiah from gently prodding the people to return to their roots and loyalty to God and His Torah. He even suggested that true penitence would eventually lead to their final redemption: "Return, rebellious children, says the LORD, for I am your Master; I will take you, one from a city, two from a family, and bring you to Zion.

I will appoint over you shepherds after my own heart, which will shepherd you wisely and prudently. When you multiply and become fruitful in the land, says the LORD, They will in those days no longer say, 'The ark of the covenant of the LORD!' They will no longer think of it, or remember it, or miss it, or make another. At that time they will call Jerusalem the LORD'S throne; there all nations will be gathered together to honor the name of the LORD at Jerusalem, and they will walk no longer in their hardhearted wickedness. In those days the house of Judah will join the house of Israel; together they will come from the land of the north to the land which I gave to your fathers as a heritage." (Jeremiah 3:14–18)

Jeremiah's efforts to make his message resonate with the masses were frustrated by the proliferation of dubious leaders who promised peace and prosperity. False prophets who insisted that night was day and day was night opposed Jeremiah. These charlatans thwarted Jeremiah's best efforts to rally the nation: "The prophets prophesy lies, The priests rule by their own authority, And my people love it this way. But what will you do in the end?" (Jeremiah 5:31)

Jeremiah squarely placed the judgment not only on lying prophets but on the ones who flocked after them. These false prophets who spoke upon their own authority appealed to the fools. And the greatest tragedy was who there were so many fools for these prophets to deceive! As mentioned, they spoke what the people wanted to hear and Jeremiah was powerless to dissuade them despite his best efforts: "Small and great alike, all are greedy for gain; prophet and priest, all practice fraud. They would repair, as though it were nothing, the breach of my people: 'Peace, peace!' they say, though there is no peace." (Jeremiah 6:13–14)

As though it was naught: The false assurances of well that were given by priests and prophets could not reduce the harm that universal materialism and corruption had wrought upon the people. God's message through Jeremiah became quite graphic and calamitous: "Therefore, beware! Days will come, says the LORD, when Topheth and the Valley of Ben-hinnom will no longer be called such, but rather the Valley of Slaughter. For lack of space, Topheth will be a burial place. The corpses of this people will be food for the birds of the sky and for the beasts of the field, which no one will drive away. In the cities of Judah and in the streets of Jerusalem I will silence the cry of joy, the cry of gladness, the voice of the bridegroom and the voice of the bride; for the land will be turned to rubble." (Jeremiah 7:32–34)

> ### Lord Knows
>
> The Valley of Ben-hinnom (also known as Gey'hinnom) was a location south of Jerusalem where the cult of Molech still flourished. Molech was a Canaanite god who was worshipped by passing one's child through fire—basically sacrificing it.

Thus Jeremiah warned the people of Judah, informing them: "If you do not repent of your sins and return to God, the armies of Babylon will destroy the city of Jerusalem and this temple, and you will become their slaves!" He even rebuked the Jews who pretended to know God but denied Him by their actions.

At this juncture, Jeremiah warned that they should abandon placing their false hopes in "flesh and blood" and turn to God. That would be the only thing that would save them. This is what the Lord says: "Cursed is the one who trusts in man, who depends on flesh for his strength and whose heart turns away from the Lord … The heart is deceitful above all things and beyond cure. Who can understand it? 'I the Lord search the heart and examine the mind, to reward a man according to his conduct, according to what his deeds deserve.'" (Jeremiah 17:5, 9–10)

You would think that over the course of 24 years, the people would get the message and mend their ways. But the people of Judah and their king despised Jeremiah for raining on their parade, and the vast majority of them did not heed the prophet's warnings. In fact, when the priests heard what Jeremiah said, they arrested him, whipped him, and put his feet in chains for the day. The priests could not believe that God would allow their enemies, the Babylonians, to enter Jerusalem and destroy the city and the Temple that had stood for more than 400 years. As such, they were incensed with Jeremiah because predicting the destruction of Jerusalem was so discomfiting to them and grated on their nerves.

Death Threats from the Masses

As mentioned, Josiah was one of the most God-fearing kings to rule Judah. His son Jehoiakim (608 B.C.E.), however, was another story. He was young—25 when he ascended to the throne—and he only reigned for 11 years. But it was 11 years of doing evil in the eyes of God.

The people of Judah didn't fare well under Jehoiakim. In chapter 26 of Jeremiah, we see just how far gone they were: "In the beginning of the reign of Jehoiakim, son of Josiah, king of Judah, this message came from the Lord: Thus says the Lord: 'Stand in the court of the house of the Lord and speak to the people of all the cities of Judah who come to worship in the house of the Lord; whatever I command you, tell them, and omit nothing. Perhaps they will listen and turn back, each from his evil way, so that I may repent of the evil I have planned to inflict upon them for their evil deeds. Say to them: Thus says the Lord: If you disobey me, not living according to the law I placed before you and not listening to the words of my servants the prophets, whom I send you constantly though you do not obey them, I will treat this house like Shiloh, and make this the city which all the nations of the earth shall refer to when cursing another.' Now the priests, the prophets, and all the people heard Jeremiah speak these words in the house of the Lord. When Jeremiah finished speaking all that the Lord bade him speak to all the people, the priests and prophets laid hold of him, crying, 'You must be put to death!'" (Jeremiah 26:1–8)

The noble and courageous prophet was prepared to die for his allegiance to God and his mission. Jeremiah didn't preach to ruffle feathers, to pick a fight, or to stir a ruckus in town. He preached what he did with the hope that Judah would snap out of its sinful rebellion and the people would return to God in repentance.

Fortunately, more reasonable men raised their voices with a history lesson and Jeremiah was spared: "At this, some of the elders of the land came forward and said to all the people assembled, 'Micah of Moresheth used to prophesy in the days of Hezekiah, king of Judah, and he told all the people of Judah: Thus says the LORD of hosts: Zion shall become a plowed field, Jerusalem a heap of ruins, and the temple mount a forest ridge. Did Hezekiah, king of Judah, and all Judah condemn him to death? Did they not rather fear the LORD and entreat the favor of the LORD, so that he repented of the evil with which he had threatened them? But we are on the point of committing this great evil to our own undoing.'"

There was another man who prophesied in the name of the Lord—Uriah, son of Shemaiah, from Kiriath-jearim. He prophesied the same things against this city and land as Jeremiah did. When King Jehoiakim and all his officers and princes were informed of his words, the king sought to kill him. But Uriah heard of it and fled in fear to Egypt. Thereupon King Jehoiakim sent Elnathan, son of Achbor, and others with him into Egypt to bring Uriah back to the king, who had him slain by the sword and his corpse cast into the common grave. But Ahikam, son of Shaphan, protected Jeremiah, so that he was not handed over to the people to be put to death.

> **It Is Written**
>
> Ahikam was one of King Josiah's officials and father of Gedaliah, Jeremiah's friend, who was governor of Judah after Nebuchadnezzer deported Zedekiah to Babylon.

It was yet another call to repentance, warning Judah that they ought to heed the message of the prophets rather than ignore it. So what was the reaction to Jeremiah's less-than-happy message? "The priests, the prophets and all the people seized him and said, 'You must die! Why do you prophesy in the Lord's name that this house will be like Shiloh and this city will be desolate and deserted?'" (Jeremiah 26:8)

Jeremiah merely spoke the truth. He reported nothing but what God gave him to say. And of all the people who should object, who was leading the charge? The prophets and the priests in the Temple. The so-called representatives of the Almighty were the ones leading the death threats against Jeremiah, simply because they didn't like the implications of what he was saying—change or pay the consequences.

Jerusalem's Destruction

Jeremiah's words of warning went unheeded for almost 40 years. The disloyal priests of the Temple, who served their supporters rather than the truth, disputed him at every turn. The masses, always hungry for reassurance and outraged at Jeremiah's refusal to pat them on their backs, demanded he be put to death, as the prophet Uriah had been.

King Tzedekiah, who was now in control of the kingdom, disobeyed Jeremiah and burned the scroll of his prophecies. When Jeremiah refused to be silenced, the king had him thrown into a dungeon, where he remained until Nebuchadnezzar had his way with the holy city of Jerusalem. Even while setting fire to its ramparts, the charlatans "prophesied" that the conqueror would soon return the Temple's looted treasures and go down in defeat.

In the end, the king, the priests, the people, and the false prophets found out who had proclaimed the true word of God. They found out because everything that Jeremiah had announced concerning the destruction of Jerusalem came to pass. The last chapter in the Book of Jeremiah tells it all: "So in the ninth year of the reign of Zedekiah, [king of Judah] ... Nebuchadnezzar king of Babylon marched against Jerusalem with his whole army. They camped outside the city and built siege works all around it. The city was kept under siege ... By the ninth day of the fourth month the famine in the city had become so severe that there was no food for the people to eat. Then the city wall was broken through ... [Thus the soldiers captured the king of Judah] ... He was taken to the king of Babylon ... where he pronounced sentence on him. There at Riblah the king of Babylon slaughtered the sons of [the king of Judah] before his eyes ... Then he put out Zedekiah's eyes, bound him with bronze shackles and took him to Babylon ... [Then Nebuchadnezzar, king of Babylon and his soldiers] set fire to the temple of the Lord, the royal palace and all the houses of Jerusalem. Every important building he burned down. ... and broke down all the walls around Jerusalem. Nebuzaradan the commander of the guard carried into exile some of the poorest people and those who remained in the city, along with the rest of the craftsmen and those who had gone over to the king of Babylon. But Nebuzaradan left behind the rest of the poorest people of the land to work the vineyards and fields. So Judah went into captivity, away from her land!" (Jeremiah 52:4–21)

By the Waters of Babylon

Jeremiah seemed to also have had a premonition about what would befall the people centuries into the future and offered them consolation: "By the waters of Babylon, there we wept and there we sat down; Hung our harps on the willow trees; Zion yet we remembered thee! Then our captors required of us; 'Sing a song of Zion now!' How could we sing the Eternal's song by the waters of Babylon?

Let my right hand forget her skill, if Jerusalem I forget thee; if I fail to remember thee, let my tongue cleave unto my mouth! But we thought of Jerusalem when we sat near Zion's streams; far above even our greatest joy, we remembered Jerusalem." (Psalms 137:1–2)

In the end, Jeremiah tasted the bitter cup of vindication, as Jerusalem was leveled and he was set free, not by his own people but by the conquerors. Still obsessed by his love for Israel, Jeremiah wept and grieved for his tormented brethren as they were led in chains into exile. He encouraged them, charging them that they should bear their ordeal in a hostile, foreign land with courage, because they would become the groundwork upon which the new nation would be built.

Jeremiah bemoaned his own fate; and recorded those words in another book— Lamentations. One can imagine his dismay at why he was chosen to not only foretell the horrors but to witness them, and even to be at the mercy of the very people he was trying to save. But there is no doubt that the exiles in Babylon found strength in his prophecy that there would be redemption and glory 70 years after the destruction. Jeremiah did not live to see his prophecy fulfilled, but many of those who had heard his prophecies were among the ones who returned with Ezra and Nehemiah to inaugurate the Second Temple and restore it to a measure of its previous glory.

The Least You Need to Know

◆ The Book of Jeremiah records the dire predictions and prophecies that went unheeded and eventually culminated in the destruction of the First Temple in Jerusalem and the exile of its inhabitants to Babylonia.

◆ Jeremiah, following the prophet Isaiah, began to prophesy during the reign of the righteous King Josiah. He spanned a period of more than 40 years until the reign of Zedekiah, an evil king of Judah.

◆ Jeremiah's prophecies, while containing the spirit of doom, also contain inspiring and hopeful passages.

◆ Jeremiah's words contained consolation for the Jewish people that they would be restored to their homeland following a 70-year sojourn in Babylon.

Chapter 16

The Prophet of Hope and Rebuke: The Book of Ezekiel

In This Chapter

- ◆ Prophet of exile
- ◆ A divine chariot
- ◆ Dry bones
- ◆ End of Days and the Third Temple

The Book of Ezekiel contains very specific and often graphic prophecies. He offers both bad and good news. The later visions speak to both the immediate restoration of the Jews to their land and the Final Redemption and building of the Third Temple, including detailed blueprints of its structure.

Ezekiel occupies a distinct and unique position among the Hebrew prophets, as he was the first prophet to receive his communications from God outside of Israel. Along the way, he witnessed the destruction of Jerusalem and the Temple, the downfall of the monarchy, and the expulsion of his people to Babylonia.

Prophet of Exile

There are but a few scattered references to Ezekiel's life contained in the book that bears his name. He must have been born exactly at the time of the religious revolution led by King Josiah. He was the son of Buzi, a priest of Jerusalem, and consequently a member of the Zadok family. He was among the aristocracy whom Nebuchadnezzar carried off to be exiled in Babylonia after the first capture of Jerusalem.

Scripture notes that Ezekiel, whose prophecies extended more than 22 years, held a prominent place among the exiles and was frequently consulted by the elders.

Ezekiel stands in the middle between two periods of Jewish history. He drew his inspiration to recap the lesson from one period and helped blaze a redemptive path for the exiles as they journeyed to the other.

Lord Knows

Ezekiel's name in Hebrew means "God strengthens," or "may God strengthen (this person)." A Talmudic tradition teaches that the original Book of Ezekiel was buried with the prophet in his tomb and left there to be reveled in the last days. Hostilities in Iraq have increased interest in his tomb, which is near the modern city of Hilla, not far from the ancient city of Babylon and 60 miles south of Baghdad.

The Divine Chariot

Not only was Ezekiel unique in being the first prophet to receive his communication primarily outside the Land of Israel, his inauguration to divine inspiration came in a most awesome fashion.

"The Word of the Lord came unto Ezekiel the Cohen the son of Buzi in the Land of the Chaldeans by the River Chebar; spirit of prophecy came strong upon him. And I looked and behold, a whirlwind came out of the north, a great cloud, and a fire imploding within itself, and a brightness was about it, and out of the midst thereof came like the *Chashmal*, out of the midst of the fire." (Ezekiel 1:3–5)

The symbolism of whirlwind, cloud, fire, and something called the Chasmal are often interpreted as Ezekiel's own journey through his mind to remove certain impediments to pure divine infusion. The clamor of wind, cloud, and fire all represent impure levels of turbulence that Ezekiel needed to quell. Perhaps this was a description of a meditative exercise that readied this neophyte prophet for communication with God at the highest level.

The Sages Say

The term *Chashmal* might refer to an angelic being (Talmud) or a form of "lightning" within the fire. The commentators point out that this word is a compound one made up of "Chash" and "Mal," the former connotes silence and the latter, speech or word. It is interesting to note that in modern Hebrew, Chashmal means electricity and electronic mail (e-mail) is the silent process of words being transmitted through electrical currents.

The book continues: "Now as I beheld the Chayot (angelic beings), behold one wheel (of the Chariot) at the bottom hard by the Chayot, at the four faces thereof. The appearance of the wheels and their work was like unto the color of a beryl; and the four had one likeness; and their appearance and their work was as it were a wheel within a wheel. When they went, they went toward their four sides; they turned not when they went. As for their rings, they were high and they were dreadful; and the four had their rings full of eyes round about. And when the Chayot went, the wheels went hard by them; and when the Chayot were lifted up from the bottom, the wheels were lifted up." (Ezekiel 1:16–19)

Tower of Babel

The word **Maaseh** means "action," and the word **Merkava** comes from the root Rochev meaning "to ride," and hence means a "chariot" or "riding vehicle."

What Ezekiel is describing is the Divine Chariot (in Hebrew, *Maaseh Merkava*), one of the most esoteric visions in biblical Scripture.

Metaphorically, the concept of riding involves traveling and leaving one's natural place. When Ezekiel says that God "rides," the implication is that He leaves His natural state where He is absolutely unknowable and inconceivable, and allows Himself to be "visualized." However, whatever the nature of this visualization really is, it cannot imply beholding the essence of the divine, for Moses was already instructed by God "No one can see Me and live." (Exodus 33:20)

Ezekiel's vision, which came as the Temple was about to be destroyed, signaled the end of a thousand-year period of prophecy.

Whatever Ezekiel's vision actually symbolized, the Talmudic sages put a great restriction on how it could be studied and understood. In fact, as a result of its mystical nature, graphic content, and wording that contradicted the Torah, the entire Book of Ezekiel had to be saved from being "filed away." Some of the passages that the sages found most objectionable are found in chapters 16 and 23, where the prophet constantly repeats a metaphor of harlotry to describe Jerusalem's behavior.

Ezekiel is the only prophet to use explicit sexual language in describing the profanation of Jerusalem and the Temple by its people. Only through the wise contemplation and reconciliation of these difficult passages by the Talmudic sage Rabbi Chananiah were Ezekiel's words saved for inclusion in the canon of Jewish Scripture.

It Is Written

Throughout the period of the prophets, the Kabbalah was guarded by the master prophets and transmitted to select disciples. During this time, the Sanctuary, and later the First Temple, served as the focal point for all prophetic experience. When the Temple was about to be destroyed, the prophet Ezekiel was shown a vision that was to signal the end of a thousand-year period of prophecy. This vision is known as Maaseh Merkava, the Workings of the Chariot. Although referring specifically to the opening chapter of the Book of Ezekiel, the term Maaseh Merkava is also one general appellation for the entire Kabbalistic tradition.

Mysticism and mystical teachings have been a part of Judaism since the Revelation at Mount Sinai. Scripture itself contains many stories of mystical experiences, from visitations by angels to prophetic dreams and visions. Details of these events have been passed down by experienced Torah scholars from generation to generation, hence the moniker "Kabbalah," which essentially means "to receive." The subjects discussed in secret esoteric writing such as the Book of the Zohar include the existence of the soul and when it becomes attached to the body, heaven and purgatory, the wandering souls and reincarnation, among others. These teachings also fill in deeper meanings of Biblical passages.

Prophecy in Exile

Ezekiel's prophecies speak of the sins of Judah prior to the calamity of the Temple destruction. After the disaster, they take on a note of comfort and future redemption.

In the first three chapters, Ezekiel is sent on a mission to reprimand the Jewish people and is given a vision of a scroll of lamentations. The third chapter finds him symbolically "eating" the scroll; absorbing the message he is given.

He is told that the people will not listen to his words of rebuke. Then, in chapter 4, he is given a bevy of symbolic "exercises" concerning the impending conquering of

Jerusalem: "Now you, son of man, take a brick for yourself and place it before you, and engrave upon it a city, Jerusalem … And you shall lay siege upon it and build around it a stone-throwing catapult, and you shall pour over it a siege mound, and you shall place camps upon it and place villages around it. And you shall take yourself an iron skillet and make it an iron wall between you and the city and direct your face toward it, and it will be in the siege and you shall besiege it; that is a sign to the house of Israel … And to the siege of Jerusalem you shall direct your face, and your arm shall be bared, and you shall prophesy about it. And behold, I have placed ropes upon you, and you shall not turn from side to side until you complete the days of your siege." (Ezekiel 4:1–8)

> **It Is Written** _____
>
> Ancient Babylonia, which covers most of modern-day Iraq, is rich in biblical history. The Tower of Babel was in Iraq. Abraham was from Ur, which is in southern Iraq. Isaac's wife Rebecca was from Nahor, which is in Iraq. Jonah's prophecy was directed to the inhabitants in Nineveh—which is in Iraq. Assyria, which is in Iraq, conquered the Ten Tribes of Israel. Amos cried out in Iraq! Babylon (Iraq) destroyed Jerusalem. Daniel was in the lion's den in Iraq! Three prophets were sent into fire in Iraq. Belshazzar, King of Babylon, saw the "writing on the wall" in Iraq. Nebuchadnezzar, King of Babylon, carried Jews captive into Iraq. And of course, Ezekiel prophesied in Iraq.

Ezekiel also predicts the severity of a famine that would befall the people: "And you, take yourself wheat and barley, and beans and lentils, and millet and spelt. You shall place them in one vessel, and prepare them for yourself for food; the number of days that you lie on your side, three hundred and ninety days you shall eat it …. And as barley cakes you shall eat it, and they shall bake it with human excrement before their eyes. And the Lord said, 'So will the children of Israel eat their bread unclean among the nations where I shall drive them.'" (Ezekiel 4:9–13)

As a result of their deprivation, the residents of Judea could not use wheat or barley in their bread. Instead, they would have to use inferior grains such as millet.

In chapters 5–9 Ezekiel continues to prophesy concerning the doom of destruction primarily as a result of the Israelites' idolatrous practices: "And behold, there was the glory

> **It Is Written** _____
>
> It was well known that beans, lentils, and millet (one of the oldest cereal grains known to humans) were only baked into bread during severe famines.

of the God of Israel, like the appearance that I saw in the plain. Then He said to me, 'Now lift your eyes northward,' and I lifted my eyes northward, and behold from the north of the gate of the altar was this image of jealousy at the entrance. And He said to me, 'Do you see what they are doing? The great abominations that the house of Israel is doing here are to cause Me to distance Myself from upon My sanctuary; and you will yet return and see great abominations.' Then He brought me to the entrance of the court, and I saw, and behold, a hole in the wall. And He said to me, 'Son of man, dig now in the wall,' and I dug in the wall, and behold, an entrance. And He said to me, 'Come and see the evil abominations that they are doing here.' And I came and saw, and behold, every form of creeping thing and animal of detestation and all the idols of the house of Israel, engraved on the wall around and around!" (Ezekiel 8:4–10)

The vision continued as Ezekiel actually beholds angels of destruction who are assisting the Almighty in the destruction of the defiled Temple of Solomon. This image was so shocking to the prophet that he feared the end of the Jewish people was at hand: "And the glory of the God of Israel lifted itself from upon the cherub upon which it had been, to the threshold of the House, and He called to the man clothed in linen, upon whose loins was the scribe's tablet. And the Lord said to him, 'Pass through the midst of the city, through the midst of Jerusalem, and you shall mark a sign upon the foreheads of the men who are sighing and moaning over all the abominations that were done in its midst.' And to these, He said in my ears, 'Pass through the city after him and smite; let your eye spare not and have no pity. Old man, young man, and maiden, young children and women, you shall slay utterly, but to any man upon whom there is the mark you shall not draw near' ... And He said to them, 'Defile the House and fill the courts with the slain [and] go out,' and they went out and smote in the city. And it came about when they smote, that I remained, and I fell on my face and cried out, and I said, 'Alas, O Lord God, are You destroying the entire remnant of Israel when You pour out Your fury on Jerusalem?'" (9:1–8)

There will be consolations, but the litany of woe and desperation associated with the next nine chapters to follow must have cast serious doubts in the mind of the great prophet about being assigned this horrific mission.

In the next nine chapters, Ezekiel ...

- has a second vision of the divine chariot.

- perceives God's glory withdrawing from the Temple.

- is shown more symbols of the exile and King Zedekiah's flight.

- prophesies about destruction in other cities of Israel.

- gives assurances that all the prophecies will be fulfilled.

- denounces false prophets and soothsayers.

- chastises the leaders of Israel for harboring idolatrous notions in their hearts.

- compares Israel to an ungrateful adulteress or harlot.

Warnings of further divine justice are found in chapters 18 through 24. Chapter 24 is itself a historical account of the actual destruction. The chapter ends with Ezekiel's mourning for his wife and the symbolism found there. He is also charged with the responsibility of offering consolation and words of comfort to exiles as they arrive in Babylon.

The tone of the book takes an interesting turn in chapters 25 through 35 as it transitions from harsh rebuke of the Jewish people and premonitions about their exile to vengeance against their oppressive neighbors. In these verses we find vivid portrayals of the doom that is to befall Ammon, Moab, Edom, Sidon, the Philistines, and Egypt and its Pharaoh. Chapter 34 offers a hint of the Messianic era for the first time in Ezekiel's words: "I will take them out from among the nations, and I will gather them from the lands and bring them to their land, and I will shepherd them to the mountains of Israel, by the streams and in all the dwellings of the land. On good pasture I will pasture them, and on the mountains of the height of Israel will be their dwelling; there they will lie in a good fold and graze on fat pastureland upon the mountains of Israel. And I shall put up over them one shepherd and he shall feed them, namely My servant David; he shall feed them, and he shall be their shepherd. And I, the Lord, shall be to them for a God, and My servant David [will be] a prince in their midst; I, the Lord, have spoken. And I shall make with them a covenant of peace, and I shall abolish the wild beasts from the land, and they will dwell securely in the desert and grow old in the forests." (Ezekiel 34:12–14, 24–25)

This theme waxes even stronger in chapter 36, which contains passages that many contemporary authorities believe applies to the miraculous rejuvenation of the Land of Israel in the last century.

Contrast these words with Ezekiel's pronouncement of what might be expected when God remembers his outcast flock and returns them to their borders: "And you, the mountains of Israel, will produce your branches, and you will bear your fruit for My people Israel because they are about to come. For behold I am for you, and I shall turn to you, and you will be tilled and sown. And I shall multiply men upon you, the whole house of Israel in its entirety, and the cities will be settled, and the ruins will be built up. And I shall multiply upon you man and beast, and they will be fruitful and multiply, and I shall settle you as in your early days, and I shall make you better than your beginnings, and you will know that I am the Lord. And I shall cause man to walk upon you, My people Israel, and they will inherit you, and you will be to them for an inheritance, and you will no longer continue to be bereaved of them." (Ezekiel 36:8–12)

Raising the Dry Bones

"The hand of the Lord came upon me, and carried me out in the spirit of the Lord, and set me down in the midst of the valley, and that was full of bones." (Ezekiel 37:1)

Every "the hand of the Lord" in a prophecy is an expression of compulsion, meaning that the spirit would compel the prophet to go to a place that the spirit desired.

"Then He said to me; 'Son of man, can these bones become alive?' And I answered, 'O Lord God, You [alone] know.' And He said to me, 'Prophesy over these bones, and say to them, "O dry bones, hear the word of the Lord." So says the Lord God to these bones; "Behold, I will cause spirit to enter into you, and you shall live! And I will lay sinews upon you, and I will make flesh grow over you and cover you with skin and put breath into you, and you will live, and you will then know that I am the Lord."'" (Ezekiel 37:3–6)

There is a dispute as to how to understand these verses. One opinion holds that Ezekiel actually pulled this miracle off. Another opinion is that the entire account in chapter 37 is a metaphor for the Jewish people. This latter opinion is supported by the verse that follows: "Then He said to me, 'Son of man, these bones are all the house of Israel. Behold they say, "Our bones have become dried up, our hope is lost, we are clean cut off to ourselves."'" (Ezekiel 37:11)

There is intimation and an example of the entire house of Israel in their exile, for they say, "Our bones have become dried up from the troubles; our hope is lost, and what further hope can we have for salvation?" To support the first option, one may explain: "All of these were of Israel, and because you revived them now, they say, Our hope is lost, and we shall not come to life once again when the dead are resurrected."

Finally, reunification of the lost Ten Tribes of Israel with the two tribes of Judah and Benjamin is predicted: "And you, son of man, take for yourself one stick and write upon it, 'For Judah and for the children of Israel his companions'; and take one stick and write upon it, 'For Joseph, the stick of Ephraim and all the house of Israel, his companions.' And bring them close, one to the other into one stick, and they shall be one in your hand." (Ezekiel 37:16–17)

End of Days and the Third Temple

Much is made of the concept of "a war to end all wars" in theological literature. The Hebrew apocalypse, where the destruction of evil is in the form of Gog of Magog, is first depicted in Ezekiel.

"Then the word of the Lord came to me, saying: 'Son of man, set your face toward Gog, [toward] the land of Magog, the prince, the head of Meshech and Tubal, and prophesy concerning him. And you shall say, 'So said the Lord God: Behold, I am against you, Gog, the prince, the head of Meshech and Tubal. And I shall unbridle you, and I shall put hooks into your jaws and bring you forth and all your army, horses and riders, all of them clothed in finery, a great assembly, with encompassing shield and buckler, all of them grasping swords. Persia, Cush, and Put are with them; all of them with buckler and helmet. Gomer and all its wings, the house of Togarmah, the utmost parts of the north and all its wings, many peoples with you. Be prepared and make ready for yourself, you and all your assembly who are gathered about you, and you will be to them for a guardian. For many days you will be remembered; at the end of the years you will come to a land [whose inhabitants] returned from the sword, gathered from many peoples, upon the mountains of Israel, which had been continually laid waste, but it was liberated from the nations, and they all dwelt securely.'" (38:1–8)

How exactly this encounter is supposed to pan out isn't clear. Nor does it necessarily have to transpire to usher in the new Messianic Age.

Whatever the case may be, the last 10 chapters to the end of the Book of Ezekiel close with words of profound comfort. His message teaches the exiles, who felt they were dry bones with no part in the future of Israel, that indeed they would share in the glorious future. The message of comfort includes the reconciliation of the Lost Ten Tribes with Judah and Benjamin (which according to tradition have always remained intact), a future Messiah descended from David, and the rebuilding of the Temple. Ezekiel spoke in very exact terms of height and length in measurements of this Third Temple. This makes for a heightened sense of reality to identify with. It gives us the blueprint in which to place our hopes for a redeemed world.

The Least You Need to Know

♦ Ezekiel was both a priest and prophet who lived during the transition of Jewish exile from Israel and resettlement in Babylonia.

♦ The Book of Ezekiel contains very esoteric, even erotic passages that present difficulties to the rabbis in considering inclusion of it in the official canon.

♦ The content, although very damning of the behavior of the inhabitants of Jerusalem, contains words of consolation and hope of return to a rebuilt city.

♦ Ezekiel was shown a vision of the Messianic Age, the Divine Chariot, the apocalypse, and the structure of the future Third Temple in Jerusalem. Some of these visions were not shown to any other prophet.

Part 4

The Minor Prophets

The Minor Prophets, or, as they're known in Hebrew, the *Trei Asar* ("The Maker's Dozen") were anything but minor in the scope of their visions. Many of these luminaries prophesied alongside their better-known colleagues, such as Jeremiah, Isaiah, and Ezra, and their words are considered as important, if not more so, than their earlier counterparts.

Sitting in Judgment

In This Chapter

- The gentlest prophet
- Joel the judgmental
- Sins exposed
- Prophetic visions
- A prophet and his whale

From visions of menacing locusts darkening the Judean countryside (Joel), to glistening raindrops upon grass (Micah); and from images of lions roaring in the forest (Amos), to the chaff floating away from the threshing floor and smoke out of the sunlight (Hosea)—the prophets you'll read about next used every tool in their spiritual arsenal to goad the masses to repentance.

Their timeless words have made an indelible imprint on the daily liturgy of the Jewish people. We also sample some of them in the pages that follow.

Hosea, the Gentle Prophet

Hosea, whose name means "salvation," is often described as the gentlest of the prophets. Tradition tells us that he enjoyed considerable longevity as a prophet, and communicated God's word to his people for 90 years.

Gomer, the Immoral Wife

The Book of Hosea opens with the story of the prophet and his family. Like most of the prophets, Hosea was married, but there's a twist here. God literally commanded Hosea to marry an immoral woman. According to Scripture, Gomer, Hosea's wife, abandoned him and took a series of lovers.

> **It Is Written**
>
> Very little is known about Hosea. Geographic references in the Book of Hosea put him in the Northern Kingdom of Israel. It is believed that he ministered between 750 to 730 B.C.E., which was a period of great wealth for both kingdoms.

To drive the point home even further, Gomer bore Hosea three children. God appropriately gave them names as signs to His wayward people—Jezreel, which means "God Scatters," Lo-Ruhamah, which means "Not Pitied," and Lo-Ammi, which means "Not My People."

But there's more to the story here. Let's return to the beginning of the story and take a look at the verses that open the Book of Hosea: "Go, take yourself a wife of harlotry and children of harlotry; For the land has committed great harlotry by departing from the Lord." (Hosea 1:2)

In Hosea, the prophet's relationship with his wife parallels and reflects the sins of Israel. As Gomer prostituted herself in her relationship with her husband, so, too, have the people of Israel prostituted themselves away from the Almighty. As such, the story of the prophet and his wife is typically taken allegorically, not literally.

> **Lord Knows**
>
> There is more than one take on the details of Hosea's marriage to Gomer. Some sources say that Gomer was already a prostitute with children when Hosea married her. Some hold that Gomer's prostitution was spiritual rather than moral, and that her immorality reflected her worshipping idols. Still others hold that Gomer was a chaste woman when she married Hosea, and that God's describing her as adulterous is a prophecy that reflects her character and future actions.

A Faithful Husband

God will ask Hosea to divorce the depraved Gomer, even though divorce was traditionally considered a last resort. This, too, symbolizes God's distancing himself from the nation to which He was once betrothed. Yet, throughout the Book of Hosea, there are also conciliatory words.

Hosea never gives up on Gomer. In fact, God even tells him to go to Gomer and take her back. The prophet pays 15 shekels of silver for his former wife and tells her: "… You shall stay with me many days; you shall not play the harlot, nor shall you have a man …." (Hosea 3:3)

Here again, the prophet's words are parallel with Israel's future: "Afterward the children of Israel shall return, seek the Lord their God and David their king, and fear the Lord and His goodness in the latter days." (Hosea 3:5)

So, too, does God never give up on His people. When his greatness is acknowledged, He showers His people with blessings. Among them is the greatest blessing of them all: "… I will say to those who were not My people, you are My people! And they shall say, "You are my God." (Hosea 2:23)

The rest of Hosea, which consists of Hosea's public preaching, further illustrates the similarities between Hosea's experience with his wife and God's experience with Israel. In it are all the dynamics of a typically stormy relationship—heartbreak, rejection, anger, efforts to reconcile, and so on.

Hosea concludes his visions with two themes central to Jewish thought—repentance and prayer serving in place of animal offerings: "Take with you words, and return unto the Lord; say unto Him: 'Forgive all iniquity, and accept that which is good; so will we render in place of bullocks—the offering of our lips.'" (Hosea 14:2)

It is from this verse that the sages of Israel extracted the concept that God accepted the "offering of our lips," at a time when the Jewish people could no longer bring the designated sacrifices to the Temple in Jerusalem.

To reflect the "offering of our lips," on the Sabbath preceding Yom Kippur, the Day of Atonement, these verses from the last words of Hosea are publicly read in synagogue:

> "I will be as the dew unto Israel;
>
> He shall blossom as the lily,
>
> And cast forth his roots as Lebanon."
>
> "His branches shall spread,
>
> And his beauty shall be as the olive tree,
>
> And his fragrance as far as Lebanon." (Hosea 14:6–7)

Legend has it that Hosea died in Babylon before Ezra led many Jews back to Israel to help complete the Second Temple. He requested that his remains be interred in the Holy Land. Because the path was long and dangerous, Hosea didn't want his fellow

Jews to endanger themselves. He asked that his casket be tied to a camel and that the beast be allowed to wander in the direction of Israel. Wherever the camel stopped would be his burial site.

Miraculously, the camel traveled hundreds of miles until it arrived in the Galilean city of Sefad. The Jews who lived there buried him in their cemetery.

Lord Knows

The words of Hosea find their way into the liturgy of not only Yom Kippur, but every day. When a Jewish man straps on Tefillin for his morning prayers, he meditates on a passage from Hosea that emphasizes his close relationship with God: "And I will betroth you unto Me forever; yea, I will betroth you unto Me in righteousness, in justice, in loving kindness, and in compassion and I will betroth you unto Me with faith, and you will know that I am the Lord." (Hosea 2:21–22)

Judgments from Joel

The Book of Joel begins with a dire, unannounced disaster that has struck the Southern Kingdom of Judah. It's an ugly swarm of black locusts, and it destroys everything in sight. But it's nothing like what the future holds, according to Joel, who takes the opportunity to proclaim God's message: "Its like has not been from eternity, and after it there will never again be, until the years of generation after generation." (Joel 2:2)

The Sages Say

Exodus 10:6 said the plague of locusts in Egypt was the worst that ever was and ever will be. Joel seems to contradict Scripture by saying the plague of locusts that will come will be mother of all locust plagues. How could a prophet of God disagree with something explicit in the Torah? The simple explanation, given by Abarbanel in his Torah commentary, is that Joel was speaking about locusts in Israel. The statement about what happened in Egypt remains true to this day.

Joel wanted his people to avoid such harsh judgment and implored them to avert this dire prediction. He warned them that self-mortifications, such as beating their chests, meant nothing if such actions weren't heartfelt; "Tear your hearts and not your clothes." (Joel 2:13)

True penitence means change, Joel told the people. The reward for soul-searching hard work comes at the end of his short-recorded prophecy: "For, behold, in those days, and in that time, when I shall bring back the captivity of Judah and Jerusalem … So shall ye know that I am the Lord your God, dwelling in Zion My holy mountain; then shall Jerusalem be holy, and there shall no strangers (invaders) pass through her any more. And it shall come to pass in that day, that the mountains shall drop down sweet wine, and the hills shall flow with milk, and all the brooks of Judah shall flow with waters; and a fountain shall come forth of the house of the Lord, and shall water the valley of Shittim. Egypt shall be desolation, and Edom shall be a desolate wilderness, for the violence against the children of Judah, because they have shed innocent blood in their land. But Judah shall be inhabited forever, and Jerusalem from generation to generation. And I will hold as innocent their blood that I have not held as innocent; and the Lord dwelleth in Zion." (Joel 4:1,17–21)

Amos, the Exposer of Sins

Amos prophesied during the reign of Kings Uzziah of Judah and Yeravam ben Yoash and was a contemporary of Isaiah, Hosea, and Micah. Tradition has it that he was extremely wealthy and humble, so humble that he denied he was worthy of prophecy; "Neither a prophet, nor son of a prophet am I!" (Amos 7:14)

Like his colleagues, Amos didn't mince words when chastising his people. He was particularly vocal against the wealthy who evidently did not know what to do with their riches. These few opulent Israelites were so rich that they owned not just one house, but two, three, or four.

Lord Knows
Midrashic sources identify the etymology of Amos's name as an adjective for "one who stutters."

Blinded by their riches, thinking God had prospered them for their righteousness, they ignored the terrible oppressions they were inflicting on the poor and weak. God wasn't pleased with such selfishness and promised severe punishment for their miserliness and greed: "I will not turn away its punishment, because they sell the righteous for silver, and the poor for a pair of sandals. They pant after the dust of the earth which is on the head of the poor, and pervert the way of the humble." (Amos 2:6–7)

"Hear this word, you cows of Bashan, who are on the mountain of Samaria, who oppress the poor, who crush the needy, who say to your husbands, 'Bring wine, let us drink!'" (Amos 4:1)

"Woe to you ... who lie on beds of ivory, stretch out on your couches, eat lambs from the flock and calves from the midst of the stall; who chant to the sound of stringed instruments, and invent for yourselves musical instruments like David; who drink wine from bowls, and anoint yourselves with the best ointments." (Amos 6:3–6)

Had their transgressions ended with mere self-indulgence and no more, their crime would have been grievous enough. However, they extended their wrongdoings into court bribes, corruption, and extortion. They held in disdain the very wise leaders who tried to correct them: "They hate the one who rebukes in the gate, and they abhor the one who speaks uprightly …. For I know your manifold transgressions and your mighty sins. You afflict the just and take bribes; you divert the poor from justice at the gate." (Amos 5:10,12)

It Is Written

In ancient Israel, public meetings and court trials were held at the city gate where everyone could witness the proceedings and litigants would be able to have their disputes adjudicated conveniently and punctually. When some of them were rebuked for the way that they lived, for their social attitudes, for their immorality, or for their lack of spirituality, the hedonistic Israelites would typically malign or assault their critics rather than repent. Bribery, obstruction of justice, and attacks on law-abiding citizens were common occurrences in Amos's time.

Like other books of the prophets, Amos ends on a positive note. First, however, he passes harsh judgment of exile and death on reprobates who refused to heed his warnings: "For, lo, I will command, and I will sift the house of Israel among all the nations, like as corn is sifted in a sieve, yet shall not the least grain fall upon the earth. All the sinners of My people shall die by the sword, that say: 'The evil shall not over-take nor confront us.'" (Amos 9:9–10)

Then comes the good news: "In that day will I raise up the tabernacle of David that is fallen, and close up the breaches thereof, and I will raise up his ruins, and I will build it as in the days of old; That they may possess the remnant of Edom, and all the nations, upon whom My name is called, says the Lord that doeth this. Behold, the days come, says the Lord, that the plowman shall overtake the reaper, and the treader of grapes him that sows seed; and the mountains shall drop sweet wine, and all the hills shall melt. And I will turn the captivity of My people Israel, and they shall build the waste cities, and inhabit them; and they shall plant vineyards, and drink the wine thereof; they shall also make gardens, and eat the fruit of them. And I will plant them upon their land, and they shall no more be plucked up out of their land which I have given them, says the Lord thy God." (Amos 9:11–15)

Obadiah's Visions

As a descendant of Esau, Obadiah is the only convert to Judaism to have his prophecy included in the official canon. Obadiah seems to be the earliest of the Minor Prophets by some 75 years, but he is placed after Amos because he too prophesied concerning his ancestral nation:

> "For the violence done to your brother Jacob,
>
> Shame shall cover you,
>
> And you will be cut off forever."
>
> "In the day that you stood aloof,
>
> In the day that strangers carried away his substance;
>
> When strangers stood at its gates,
>
> And they cast lots for Jerusalem;
>
> You were as one of them."
>
> "And the House of Jacob shall be a fire,
>
> And the House of Joseph a flame,
>
> And the House of Esau for stubble ..." (Obadiah 1:10–11,18)

These verses (and one that follows) allude to Edom's behavior during the Babylonian exile when Esau's descendents offered their assistance in driving the final nails into the Jewish coffin. Obadiah said, "And don't stand by the crossroads to finish off refugees." (Obadiah 1:14) Tradition teaches that this passage refers to the treacherous strategy of the Edomites during the first exile. They would station themselves a short distance behind the Babylonian army and wait in ambush for the Jewish refugees. They reasoned that if the Jews win we'll say we're here to help them and if the Babylonians win we'll help them kill the remaining Jews.

This dubious brotherhood with Edom has proven to be a bane to Jewish existence. Due to their duplicitous nature, they've often tried to pass for true brothers waiting to assist Jews in their time of distress. This subterfuge only provided them a pretext to eradicate any trace of the Jewish people, should the situation arise. Obadiah's last words spell out their ultimate fate—that they will be displaced in favor of the returning Jewish population from all over the globe and God's kingdom shall prevail: "And the returning host of the house of Israel, who are with the Canaanites as far as 'Tzorfas'/France, And the Exile of Jerusalem from as far as 'Sepharad'/ Spain, shall inherit the cities of the Negev (southern Israel); And saviors shall ascend Mount Zion, To judge the mountain of Esau, And the Lord shall have the Kingdom." (Obadiah 1:20–21)

Obadiah was instrumental in saving 100 other prophets from persecution at the hands of Jezebel, the wife of Ahab. It is for that reason that he was meritorious to receive prophecy.

> **Lord Knows**
>
> The sages identify Obadiah as the prophet who served as overseer of the royal household in the time of King Ahab (875 to 853 B.C.E.), and was a student of Elijah the Prophet. His book is the shortest of all the 24 books of Jewish Scripture, and contains only one chapter consisting of 21 verses.

Jonah and the Whale

Jonah, the son of Amittai, prophesied in the days of Jeroboam II. Although he is most famous for the book that bears his name and tells of his miraculous sojourn in the belly of a big fish (maybe a whale), he prophesied the extent to which Jeroboam II would restore the boundaries of the Northern Kingdom, "from the entering of Hamath unto the sea of the plain." (II Kings 14:25) He is said to have attained a very advanced age (more than 120 years).

According to Talmudic sources, the holy spirit descended on Jonah while he participated in the festivities of the last day of the holiday Succot. His wife is mentioned as an exemplar of a woman voluntarily assuming duties not incumbent on her, for she is remembered as having made the pilgrimage to Jerusalem on the "regel" or bi-annual pilgrimage festival. However, what is most remarkable about Jonah is the story of his divine mission to rebuke and rally the inhabitants of the great city of Nineveh (modern Iraq) to repentance.

Here is that story in a nutshell: "Now the word of the Lord came unto Jonah the son of Amittai, saying: 'Arise, go to Nineveh, that great city, and proclaim against it; for their wickedness is come up before Me.' But Jonah rose up to flee unto Tarshish from the presence of the Lord; and he went down to Joppa, and found a ship going to Tarshish; so he paid the fare thereof, and went down into it, to go with them unto

Tarshish, from the presence of the Lord. But the Lord hurled a great wind into the sea, and there was a mighty tempest in the sea, so that the ship was like to be broken." (Jonah 1:1–4)

Jonah, when told to deliver a message of impending doom to the city of Nineveh, fled to Joppa to catch a ship. We are told he was reluctant to fulfill his mission because he knew the non-Jewish city of Nineveh would repent while his own people were wallowing in sin.

At any rate, he was too late, for the vessel on which he had intended to take passage had sailed two days before. God, however, caused a divergent wind to arise and the ship was driven back to port. At this Jonah rejoiced, regarding it as an indication that his plan would succeed, and in his joy he paid his passage-money in advance—contrary to the usual custom, which did not require its payment until the conclusion of the voyage.

> **The Sages Say**
>
> According to the Talmudic commentator Rashi, Jonah even paid the full value of the ship, amounting to 4,000 gold denarii. But all this happened to teach him the fallacy of his conclusion that God could be evaded, for the contrary wind affected his ship only; all others on the sea at that time proceeded uninterruptedly on their courses.

A storm overtook Jonah and the passengers. After the sailors' prayers to their idols—as well as their efforts to turn about and lighten the ship—had proved futile, the crew was finally compelled to believe Jonah's statement that this calamity had befallen their craft on his account, and assented to his petition to be thrown overboard. Praying that they might not be held accountable for his death, they first lowered him far enough for the waters to touch his knees. Seeing that the storm subsided, they drew him back into the ship, whereupon the sea at once rose again. According to legend, they repeated this experiment several times, each time lowering him deeper, but taking him out again. Each time led to the same result, until finally they threw him into the sea.

> **Lord Knows**
>
> The Book of Jonah is read in its entirety on the holiest day of the year—Yom Kippur. This teaches just how valuable the lesson of heeding God's Will is, and the power of prayer and of repentance.

After three days, Jonah saw the folly of his actions in trying to escape a divine task and the fish spat him out onto dry land. Jonah tried to take refuge from the oppressive sun under a certain tree. An enormous gourd suddenly appeared growing next to him that formed shade. Before its appearance, Jonah was tortured by the heat and by insects of all kinds; his clothes had been burned by the heat of the belly of the fish; and he was tortured again after the worm caused the gourd to wither. This brought Jonah to pray that God should be a merciful ruler, not a strict judge. He eventually fulfilled his task, the city of Nineveh repented, and many lessons are culled from this story.

The Least You Need to Know

- The Minor Prophets used every tool in their spiritual arsenal to goad their people to repent.

- Their writings contain passages teaching moral lessons and also predict future Messianic events.

- Many of the writings of the Minor Prophets are incorporated into the Jewish prayer book and are read weekly in synagogues.

The Visionaries

In This Chapter

- ◆ The prophet of the poor
- ◆ Nahum the Poet
- ◆ Habakkuk, God, and Faith
- ◆ Zephaniah and the Day of the Lord

The prophets you learn about in this chapter belong to a direct line of prophets who began prophesying in 600 B.C.E. and extended until approximately 450 B.C.E. Though these prophets are also referred to as the Minor Prophets, this simply reflects the length of their recorded works, which is relatively short when compared to other prophetic writings. The content of their works, however, is as influential to the Jewish nation they serviced as any of the writings of the Major Prophets.

Micah, Prophet of the Poor

Micah lived at the same time as Isaiah in Judah and Hosea in Israel. He was from a small village called Moresheth-Gath, located 22 miles southwest of Jerusalem.

Micah's prophetic ministry was during the days of Jotham, Ahaz, and Hezekiah, all kings of Judah. In Micah's day, Judah was prosperous. Her people were worldly and materialistic. Outwardly, they were very religious. Sacrifices were offered, but they were just forms to be observed. But inner devotion to God was lacking. Micah reprimands the people for not applying the timeless principles of their religion to everyday life: "Wherewith shall I come before the Lord, and bow myself before God on high? Shall I come before Him with burnt offerings, with calves of a year old? Will the Lord be pleased with thousands of rams, with ten thousands of rivers of oil? Shall I give my first-born for my transgression, the fruit of my body for the sin of my soul? However, it has been told thee, O man, what is good, and what the Lord does require of thee: only to do justice, and to love kindness, and to walk humbly with thy God." (Micah 6:6–8)

> **Lord Knows**
>
> Very little is known about the prophet Micah. His name is a shortened form of Micaiah, meaning "Who is like God?" He is sometimes called the "prophet of the poor" as he might have belonged to the peasant class.

The sages of the Talmud mention that the last verse contains three primary objectives of God's requisites to His People. They taught that God conveyed 613 commandments to the Jewish people through Moses and the Torah. Micah came and established the entire Torah on three principles, namely, doing justice, loving kindness, and walking humbly with God.

Not only did Micah face a nation that didn't want to adhere to these commandments and major principles of moral living, they tolerated many false prophets who flattered the nation and gave in to its whims: "If a man walking in wind and falsehood do lie: 'I will preach unto thee of wine and of strong drink;' he shall even be the preacher of this people." (Micah 2:11)

"Thus says the Lord concerning the prophets that make my people to err; that cry: 'Peace,' when their teeth have any thing to bite; and who puts not into their mouths, they even prepare war against him. Therefore it shall be night unto you, that ye shall have no vision; and it shall be dark unto you, that ye shall not divine; and the sun shall go down upon the prophets, and the day shall be black over them. And the seers shall be put to shame, and the diviners confounded; yea, they shall all cover their upper lips; for there shall be no answer of God." (Micah 3:5–7)

Witchcraft and idolatry were practiced along with the worship of God. Judges and other government officials were corrupt. They took bribes and perverted justice. The poor were oppressed. Micah minced no words speaking out against these evils.

Like Jeremiah, Micah made a number of prophetic proclamations about imminent exile and restoration. He specifically made the following accurate predictions:

- The destruction of Samaria (fulfilled in 722 B.C.E.)

- The destruction of Jerusalem (fulfilled in 586 B.C.E.)

- The Babylonian captivity of Judah (fulfilled in 605 to 536 B.C.E.)

- The return of Judah from Babylonian exile (fulfilled in 535 B.C.E.)

Micah's greatest premonition—world peace, the rebuilding of the Temple, and the restoration of the Davidic throne—has not yet come to be. If one had to choose a Messianic prophecy to serve as an inspiration, it would be difficult to find one more splendid than this: "But in the end of days it shall come to pass, that the mountain of the Lord's house shall be established as the top of the mountains, and it shall be exalted above the hills; and peoples shall flow unto it. And many nations shall go and say: 'Come ye, and let us go up to the mountain of the Lord, and to the house of the God of Jacob; and He will teach us of His ways, and we will walk in His paths'; for out of Zion shall go forth the law, and the word of the Lord from Jerusalem. And He shall judge between many peoples, and shall decide concerning mighty nations afar; and they shall beat their swords into plowshares, and their spears into pruning hooks; nation shall not lift up sword against nation, neither shall they learn war any more. But they shall sit every man under his vine and under his fig tree; and none shall make them afraid; for the mouth of the Lord of hosts has spoken. For let all the peoples walk each one in the name of its god, but we will walk in the name of the Lord our God forever and ever. In that day, says the Lord, will I assemble her that halted, and I will gather her that is driven away, and her that I have afflicted; And I will make her that halted a remnant, and her that was cast far off a mighty nation; and the Lord shall reign over them in Mount Zion henceforth forever." (Micah 4:1–7)

The last three verses from the Book of Micah form part of a unique Rosh Hoshana (Jewish New Year) observance called Tashlich. On this holy day, pious Jews walk to a body of water where they make a symbolic "casting away of sin." These are the passages recited: "Who is a God like unto Thee, that pardons iniquity, and overlooks transgression of the remnant of His heritage? He retains not His anger forever, because He delights in mercy. He will again have compassion upon us; He will subdue our iniquities; and Thou wilt cast all their sins into the depths of the sea. Thou wilt show faithfulness to Jacob, mercy to Abraham, as Thou hast sworn unto our fathers from the days of old." (Micah 7:18–20)

Lord Knows

Micah also hinted to the origins of the Messianic Davidic King: "But you, Bethlehem Ephrath, who are little to be among the thousands of Judah, out of you shall come forth to Me that is to be ruler in Israel; whose goings forth are from of old, from the beginning of time." (Micah 5:1) The author of Matthew claimed that from this verse the Messiah would be born in Bethlehem of Judah and that Jesus was that man. This verse indeed refers to the Messiah, a descendant of David. Because David came from Bethlehem, Micah's prophecy speaks of Bethlehem as the Messiah's place of origin. Actually, the text does not necessarily mean the Messiah would be born in that town, but that his family originated from there. From the ancient family of the house of David will come forth the Messiah, whose eventual existence was known to God from the beginning of time.

Nahum the Poet

Nahum lived about 2,600 years ago. He was a native of Elkosh (about 20 miles southwest of Jerusalem) and lived around the time of the evil Judean King Menashe.

Nahum's short book consists almost entirely of a prophecy of Nineveh's destruction, and is believed to have been written about two years before Nineveh was destroyed in 612 B.C.E. At the time, Nineveh was the capital of the Assyrian empire, which was one of the most powerful empires of the ancient world. In Jonah's time, about 150 years before its destruction, Nineveh embarked on a remarkable national repentance. Nonetheless, the Assyrians conquered the Kingdom of Israel in about 722 B.C.E. The conquest was cruel and devastating.

Nahum explains that because of Assyria's pride and cruelty in their destruction of Israel, and because of their idolatry, treachery, superstition, and injustice, their empire would be destroyed as punishment. Nahum is quite vivid and direct in conveying this message: "But Nineveh hath been from of old like a pool of water; yet they flee away; 'Stand, stand;' but none looks back. Take ye the spoil of silver, take the spoil of gold; for there is no end of the store, rich with all precious vessels. She is empty, and void, and waste; and the heart melts, and the knees smite together, and convulsion is in all loins, and the faces of them all have gathered blackness. Behold, I am against thee, says the Lord of hosts, and I will burn her chariots in the smoke, and the sword shall devour thy young lions; and I will cut off thy prey from the earth, and the voice of thy messengers shall no more be heard." (Nahum 2:9–11,14)

"Yet was she carried away, she went into captivity; her young children also were dashed in pieces at the head of all the streets; and they cast lots for her honorable men, and all her great men were bound in chains." (Nahum 3:10)

In 612 B.C.E., a coalition of Babylonians, Scythians, and Medes conquered Nineveh. "Nothing can heal your wound; your injury is fatal. Everyone who hears the news about you claps his hands at your fall, for who has not felt your endless cruelty?" (Nahum 3:19)

Nahum's writings about the destruction of Nineveh are often poetic in style. In them, he shares a message of hope and comfort, as befits his name—which is synonymous with consolation. He teaches that God is slow to anger, is good, and offers good tidings to those who want His blessings.

It Is Written

As Micah predicted, Nineveh, which is located in Iraq, is nothing more than an archeological site and was never rebuilt.

Habakkuk, God, and Faith

Habakkuk's name means "embrace." It is found twice in the book that bears his name. He was a student of Isaiah the Prophet and enjoyed longevity that extended until Daniel was thrown in the lion's den.

Habakkuk prophesied between 612 B.C.E. and 606 B.C.E. We know this because he spoke of the Chaldeans (Babylonians) being God's instrument to punish his people. Babylon did not become a world power until it conquered Nineveh in 612 B.C.E. Babylon invaded Judah in 606 B.C.E. and took many of its citizens into captivity. This was the fulfillment of Habakkuk's prophecy.

He also authored a very bold supplication to beseech the Almighty to answer his prayers: "I will stand upon my watch, and set me upon the tower, and will look out to see what He will speak by me, and what I shall answer when I am reproved. And the Lord answered me, and said: 'Write the vision, and make it plain upon tables, that a man may read it swiftly.'" (Habakkuk 2:1–2)

Tradition has it that Habakkuk uttered these words alluding to a perplexing issue he had with why the righteous suffer and the wicked prosper. He wanted a clear answer from Above. So he took a stick and drew a circle in the ground. He placed himself in that circle and stood in the middle (for example "stood upon my watch"). He insisted that he wouldn't move until God answered him and that he would accept whatever that explanation would be. God accommodated the prophet: "For the vision is yet for the appointed time, and it declares of the end, and doth not lie; though it tarry, wait for it; because it will surely come, it will not delay. Behold, his soul is puffed up, it is not upright in him; but the righteous shall live by his unyielding faith." (Habakkuk 2:3–4)

He is given a vision to wait for the end (alluding to the Messianic Age) when all will be clear. Habakkuk also intones an immortal line that has found its way into Jewish liturgy and thought, "but the righteous shall live by his unyielding faith." Strange and unfathomable are the ways of God and many challenges and questions arise as a result. Habakkuk is taught that with all the efforts and strivings a person extends in this world—holding on to one's faith is the greatest attribute of them all.

Zephaniah and the Day of the Lord

The Book of *Zephaniah* is the only time in all the prophetic books that an author traces his genealogy. We find his lineage traced all the way back to King Hezekiah. Making such a connection is indicative of the righteousness of Hezekiah and the publicizing of prophecy being found in the royal family. He prophesies in the time of Josiah who sets a number of national reforms that turn Israel around. He also mentions the destruction of Nineveh that occurred circa 612 B.C.E.

Zephaniah taught that a period of divine judgment was inevitable and pointed to the "coming day of the Lord." He envisioned a frightful final judgment upon the nation of Judah and the nations of the world. It was a shocking decree that would wreak more havoc on the earth than at the time of Noah's deluge: "The word of God which came unto Zephaniah the son of Cushi, the son of Gedaliah, the son of Amariah, the son of Hezekiah, in the days of Josiah the son of Amon, king of Judah. I will utterly consume all things from off the face of the earth, says the Lord. I will consume man and beast, I will consume the fowls of the heaven, and the fishes of the sea, and the stumbling blocks with the wicked; and I will cut off man from off the face of the earth, says God." (Zephaniah 1:1–6)

> **Tower of Babel**
>
> The name **Zephaniah** means "Hidden of God." It is possible that this moniker described the nature of his prophecy, which contained matters hidden by God until their final revelation.

With a sense of urgency in delivering his message, Zephaniah provided more graphic details: "The great day of the Lord is near; it is near and hastens greatly, even the voice of the day of God, wherein the mighty man cries bitterly. That day is a day of wrath, a day of trouble and distress, a day of waste and desolation, a day of darkness and gloominess, a day of clouds and thick darkness, a day of the horn and alarm, against the fortified cities, and against the high towers. And I will bring distress upon men that they shall walk like the blind, because they have sinned against God; and their blood shall be poured out as dust, and their flesh as dung.

Neither their silver nor their gold shall be able to deliver them in the day of God's wrath; but the whole earth shall be devoured by the fire of His jealousy; for He will make and end, yea, a terrible end, of all them that dwell in the earth." (Zephaniah 1:15–18)

Delivering such a gloomy forecast, Zephaniah addressed humankind as a whole. The metaphor of the "fire of His jealousy" illustrates that the people will have become callused to the evil in their society and turned to "competing" forces of power. Their silver and gold, one of those forces of power, will not bail them out on the day of God's wrath. We've seen that in our own society, where extremely wealthy individuals suffer the ravages of illness, terror, and natural disasters—just as the poor do.

The third and last chapter of Zephaniah's short vision gets better. The message is that it's not too late to turn back to God, to seek righteousness and humility.

Though He exacts judgment on the nations, He promises to help turn them back to Him. Moreover, these nations will no longer worship a motley set of foreign gods, rather the one omnipotent God Almighty: "Therefore wait ye for Me, says the Lord, until the day that I rise up to the prey; for My determination is to gather the nations, that I may assemble the kingdoms, to pour upon them Mine indignation, even all My fierce anger; for all the earth shall be devoured with the fire of My jealousy. For then will I turn to the peoples a pure language that they may all call upon the name of God, to serve Him with one consent." (Zephaniah 3:8–9)

Perhaps the vision of turning the people of the earth to one "pure language," is a rescinding of the curse of the Tower of Babel when God broke their unity by confounding their language. There are a few more details of Zephaniah's prophecy that will only be revealed when the Final Redemption occurs. We are taught that God will also bless the Jews and bring the remnant back to Jerusalem (My holy mountain). And there will be justice, humility, peace, and plenty in the land.

However, as a harbinger for that glorious moment in time, the prophet concludes his vision with a prediction of the restoration of the Jewish people to their land: "In that day shalt thou not be ashamed for all thy doings, wherein thou hast transgressed against Me; for then I will take away out of the midst of thee thy proudly exulting ones, and thou shalt no more be haughty in My holy mountain. And I will leave in the midst of thee an afflicted and poor people, and they shall take refuge in the name of God. The remnant of Israel shall not do iniquity, nor speak lies, neither shall a deceitful tongue be found in their mouth; for they shall feed and lie down, and none shall make them afraid." (Zephaniah 3:11–13)

"Sing, O daughter of Zion, shout, O Israel; be glad and rejoice with all the heart, O daughter of Jerusalem. God has taken away thy judgments, He has cast out thine enemy; The King of Israel, even the Lord, is in the midst of thee; thou shalt not fear evil any more. In that day it shall be said to Jerusalem: 'Fear thou not; O Zion, let not thy hands be slack. The Lord thy God is in the midst of thee, a Mighty One who will save; He will rejoice over thee with joy, He will be silent in His love; He will joy over thee with singing. At that time will I bring you in, and at that time will I gather you; for I will make you to be a name and a praise among all the peoples of the earth, when I turn your captivity before your eyes, says the Lord.'" (Zephaniah 3:14–17,20)

The prophet Zephaniah's essential message, however it is played out, inspires hope and confidence that Israel will be restored to its homeland and prominence, the nations will respond positively, and everyone will benefit from that new harmony.

The Least You Need to Know

- Micah, Nahum, Habakkuk, and Zephaniah are a direct line of prophets who prophesied one after another for a period of about 150 years.

- Like the other eight books of the Twelve Minor Prophets, these books are short in length, yet contain vivid images of future Messianic events.

- Habakkuk is the shortest of all books of Scripture, consisting of one small chapter of 21 verses. In keeping with his style of brevity, he established the entire Torah on one principle, "but the righteous shall live by his unyielding faith."

- Zephaniah is the only prophet in all the prophetic books who traces his genealogy. He was from the royal family of the kings of Judah. He prophesied about the restoration of the Jewish people to their land and about achieving praise in the eyes of the nations of man.

Chapter 19

The Prophets of Faith and Trust

In This Chapter

- ◆ Haggai's assurances
- ◆ Zechariah's persuasions
- ◆ Malachi's hope for right living

In 538 B.C.E., the Persian King Cyrus issued a decree allowing the Jews to return to their homeland and rebuild their Temple. The three Minor Prophets that you meet in this chapter all lived and served the Jewish people during their return to the land after their 70-year Babylonian exile and during the building of the Second Temple.

The last three Minor Prophets lived at the end of the Age of Prophecy. After their deaths, there have been some people with divine inspiration, but none of them have been considered prophets.

Most prophets brought dire warnings along with words of consolation and hope. The messages of the last three, however, were virtually 100 percent hopeful and conciliatory, even while being laced with chastisement. As their messages were the last divinely transmitted prophecies, they contain concentrated verses of Messianic significance. Let's examine some of them now.

Reassuring the People

The Jews were back in their homeland, but things weren't as they had hoped. Their initial excitement over being allowed to return and rebuild their Temple quickly waned in the face of the desolation of the land. Not only were they faced with an extraordinary struggle to rebuild, they were also surrounded with enemies that opposed their efforts. It was enough to make them want to return to their comfortable digs in Babylon.

Both Haggai and Zechariah were called by God to urge the people to stay the course and reclaim their heritage, which included rebuilding the Temple that the Babylonians had destroyed in about 586 B.C.E. Malachi, who we discuss later in this chapter, ministered to the people after the Temple was rebuilt.

Haggai and Zechariah, along with Zerubbabel, the governor of Judea, were central figures in the rebuilding project.

Haggai's Encouragement

Haggai began communicating his prophecy around 520 B.C.E., after the initial work to rebuild the Temple had ceased. He addressed his messages to Zerubbabel and to Joshua the High Priest. Haggai attributed a recent drought to the peoples' refusal to rebuild the Temple, which he saw as key to Jerusalem's glory. He also drew a link between Judah's poverty and dejected state of affairs and the corrupt indifference regarding the Temple: "You looked for much, but indeed it came too little; and when you brought it home, I blew it away. Why? Says the Lord of hosts. Because of My house that is in ruins, while every one of you runs to his own house. Therefore the heavens above you withhold the dew, and the earth withholds its fruit. For I called for a drought on the land and the mountains, on the grain and the new wine and the oil, on whatever the ground brings forth, on men and livestock, and on all the labor of your hands." (Haggai 1:9–11)

Haggai's words have their intended effect. The work began anew and the Temple was completed. This Temple was not as glorious as the first, but God, through Haggai, said it would eventually become so: "'… and I will shake all nations, and they shall come to the Desire of All Nations, and I will fill this Temple with glory,' says the

Lord of hosts. 'The silver is Mine, and the gold is Mine,' says the Lord of hosts. 'The glory of this latter Temple shall be greater than the former,' says the Lord of hosts. 'And in this place I will give peace ...'" (Haggai 2:7–9)

The Sages Say

It is not certain that Haggai was ever in Babylonia. He might have lived continuously in Jerusalem along with a small community of expatriates. Judging by the length of his book, his public ministry was rather brief. Zechariah, the leading prophet of those times, indicated that Haggai was probably near his end when he made his exhortations to the people.

According to Talmudic sources, although Haggai's ministry might have been short, it was quite fruitful. He is credited with instituting a number of religiously oriented legal decisions, organizing the priestly service into 24 rotating groups, and regulating the wood contributions brought to the Temple.

The Blessings of Obedience

Having encouraged the people to complete the work that God asked of them, Haggai then turned to the priests and questioned them on the laws of purity.

He asked them the following two questions: "If a man is carrying sacrificial flesh in a fold of his garment, and with that fold touches bread, meat, wine, oil or other food, will the latter become holy ... If someone defiled by a corpse touches any of these, will it become defiled, as well?" (Haggai 2:12–13)

The priests could only know the answers from an oral tradition, as they are not in the Torah. It would be that same oral tradition that would allow them to recall or re-learn many of the laws of Temple service that had fallen to disuse since the destruction 70 years earlier. But God, through Haggai, had something else in mind by posing these questions.

God basically told Haggai to ask the priests if holiness is transferred from a holy to a neutral object. To this, the priests answered "no." He then asked if defilement is transferred from a person defiled by a corpse to a neutral object. The priests answered "yes."

Haggai didn't really need to know the answers to these questions. He asked them to get the priests' attention to what was really on his mind—the rebuilding of the Temple, which was of utmost importance.

A Most Significant Prediction

At the end of his brief book—only Obadiah is shorter—Haggai makes his most significant prediction—the overthrow of the Persian yoke and the establishment of the Kingdom of Israel: "In that day, says the Lord of hosts, will I take thee, O Zerubbabel, My servant, the son of Shealtiel, says the Lord, and will make thee a signet; for I have chosen thee, says the Lord of hosts." (Haggai 2:23)

"In that day," turned out to be the twenty-fourth of Kislev, the day before a later commemoration of Hanukah would be celebrated. On that day, the foundations of the Second Temple were established. Years later it would be the day the priest entered the Temple that had been defiled by the Syrian-Greeks, found a cruse of oil, and lit the Menorah. This event was considered a rededication of the Temple (the word Hanukah actually means dedication) and thus we have a chronological connection between the initial dedication of the Second Temple and its rededication 200 years later.

> **Lord Knows**
>
> Hanukah is a Jewish holiday highlighted by an eight-day candle-lighting celebration. It commemorates the victory of Judah Macabee and his armies over the Syrian-Greek occupiers who defiled the Second Temple in Jerusalem 2,200 years ago.

The completion and dedication of the Second Temple was a time of the Jewish people's greatest joy—comparable to the completion of Solomon's Temple five centuries earlier.

Tradition has it that another Davidic descendent of Zerubbabel would lead the charge of the final construction project on the Temple Mount, ushering in an era of peace and prosperity.

Zechariah's Persuasions

Like his colleague Haggai, Zechariah also focused on persuading the tribe of Judah to resume the rebuilding of the Temple.

Zechariah's prophecies came from visions that showed God's power, His judgment of iniquity, the imperative of pursuing spiritual vigor, and promises of future national redemption, including the promise of the Messiah.

Zechariah's prophecies spoke to a future in which the Jews would again be exiled from their homeland and scattered throughout the world. He said that Jews would be persecuted worldwide, that Jerusalem would become a battleground of nations, and that Jerusalem would become the religious center of the world.

"Shout and rejoice, O Daughter of Zion, for I am coming—And I will dwell within you, says the Lord." (Zechariah 2:14)

Zechariah proclaimed an impending occasion of great joy, for God's presence was returning openly to the Jewish people after a period of departure.

Reference to the historical period in which Zechariah lived is obvious, but there is also a hint that the prophet addressed an exile millennia later that would culminate in another dwelling—the Third Temple. Yet another verse references a future Messianic vision: "And many nations will attach themselves to the Lord ...." (Zechariah 2:15)

It Is Written

Progress had been stopped when the (not-so-good) Samaritans protested. Evidently, they had their own agenda and did not want to see the Jewish nation restored to its previous prominence.

It Is Written

Other prophets envisioned a futuristic unity of the nations under one banner as well. Zephaniah wrote, "For then will I turn to the peoples a pure language that they may all call upon the name of God, to serve Him with one consent." (Zephaniah 3:8–9) Isaiah wrote, "... For My house shall be called a house of prayer for all people." (Isaiah 56:7) Ezekiel wrote, "The nations also will know that I, the Lord, sanctify Israel, when My sanctuary is in their midst forevermore." (Ezekiel 37:26–28) And finally, Zechariah's own colleague Haggai wrote, "'... And I will shake all nations and they shall come to the "Desire of All Nations," and I will fill this Temple with glory,' says the Lord of hosts." (Haggai 2:6)

In another end-of-days vision, Zechariah punctuates the theme of redemption and paints a very rosy picture of how Jerusalem will look after the nations recognize it as the eternal capital of the Jewish state and God's central "dwelling place" on earth. In an interesting expression of wonderment, Zechariah depicts God as being amazed over the specter of Jews gathering from their far-flung communities of refuge in exile to return to their land:

"Thus says the Lord: I will return to Zion and will dwell in the midst of Jerusalem. There shall yet be old men and old women sitting in the streets of Jerusalem ... And the broad places of the city shall be full of boys and girls playing. So says the Lord, if there will be wonder in the eyes of the remnant of this people, it will also be a wonder in My eyes ...." (Zechariah 8:3–6)

Lord Knows

A part of Zechariah is read in synagogue on the Sabbath of the Eight Days of Hanukah. The reason is simple. Zechariah is shown a vision of a "Golden Menorah, with a receptacle on top, and with seven lamps on it, and each lamp had seven pipes attached to the bowl on top. Two olive trees were next to the Menorah, one on the right, and one on the left." (Zechariah 4:2–3)

The Blood of the Covenant

According to Zechariah, the restoration of the Jewish people to their land may not come because of overwhelming merits or great righteousness. In fact, there might not be any mitigating factors that will hasten the redemption. Nonetheless, the prophet reassured them there would be that "ace in the hole," that would bail them out: "Rejoice exceedingly, daughter of Zion … for your king shall come to you, righteous is he … because of the blood of your covenant shall I send forth your prisoners out of the pit wherein there is no water." (Zechariah 9:9,11)

Water is used as a metaphor throughout Scripture. The sages of Israel say it refers to Torah. The implication of Zechariah's words, according to Nachmanides, is that in the "pit of exile," where "there is no water," means that Torah will be forgotten from the midst of the Jewish people. The only merit that will remain to their credit, he adds, is the merit of *Brit Milah*, or ritual circumcision.

Tower of Babel

Brit Milah (Lit. "covenant of circumcision") is a commandment performed by removal of the foreskin from the male reproductive organ. The ritual circumcision of a Jewish child normally takes place on the eighth day of his life. It is frequently referred to simply as a *brit or bris.*

In the post-Holocaust era, many of the prophecies of Scripture regarding the pre-Messianic period have been realized. Unfortunately, Torah knowledge and observance, though in an upswing in recent times, has been forgotten by large segments of the Jewish population. However, the vast majority, even those most alienated from Torah observance, still maintain the mitzvah of *Milah.* Zechariah provides consolation that "because of the blood of your covenant shall I send forth your prisoners," will yet be fulfilled.

Armageddon and Final Redemption

As we have seen throughout this guide, prophetic events cast their shadows into the present and serve as harbingers of things to come. Zechariah repeats a divine vision hinted to elsewhere in Scripture: "For I will gather all nations against Jerusalem to battle." (Zechariah 14:2)

It Is Written

The rising tide of almost universal animosity against the State of Israel, which is the new form of anti-Semitism, is seen by many as a sure sign of the Armageddon (war to end all wars). Zechariah himself alludes to this: "I will make Jerusalem and Judah like an intoxicating drink to all the nearby nations that send their armies to besiege Jerusalem. On that day I will make Jerusalem a heavy stone, a burden for the world. None of the nations who try to lift it will escape unscathed." (Zechariah 12:1–3) The Second Book of Kings seems to predict a similar scenario: "… And there was great indignation against Israel: and they (enemy nation) departed from him, and returned to [their own] land." (2 Kings 3:27)

After this frightful Armageddon, the final confrontation preceding the time of the Messiah, in which the enemies of Israel make one last-ditch effort to destroy her, God will come to her rescue. The prophet contributes yet another image of what will happen next.

"And the Lord shall become the King over all the earth; On that day shall the Lord be One, and His Name be One." (Zechariah 14:9)

Zechariah's words have been immortalized by inclusion into every prayer book found among the Jewish people. This prayer called "Alenu," which concludes most prayer services, expresses a deep yearning for that glorious future event where truth and God-consciousness will finally prevail.

Malachi and Right Living

The last of the Minor Prophets, Malachi prophesied after the Temple was rebuilt. His intense love for God and the people of God moved him to speak with great urgency in the streets and marketplaces.

Interestingly, by this time the Jews had become apathetic about spiritual matters in general and the Temple in particular. They had also adopted many practices alien to the spirit of the Torah. This is reflected in the opening passages of Malachi, which contain a stern rebuke addressed to the priests who had despised the name of God, and who departed from His pure worship and the covenant: "A son honors his father, and a servant his master; if then I be a father, where is My honor? and if I be a master, where is My fear? Says the Lord of hosts unto you, O priests, that despise My name. And ye say: 'Wherein have we despised Thy name?' Ye offer polluted bread upon Mine altar. And ye say: 'Wherein have we polluted thee?' In that ye say: 'The table of God is contemptible.' And when ye offer the blind for sacrifice, is it no evil! And when ye offer the lame and sick, is it no evil! Present it now unto thy governor; will he be pleased with thee? or will he accept thy person? And now, I pray you, entreat the favor of God that He may be gracious unto us! ... this hath been of your doing ... will He accept any of your persons? Says the Lord of hosts." (Malachi 1:6–9)

> **The Sages Say**
>
> According to Rabbinic tradition, Malachi represented the last of the true prophets. After him, the Talmud records that the gift of prophecy was given to (holy) fools and madmen.

Through Malachi, God accused the priest and the people of not showing Him proper honor, of bringing Him blind and lame sacrifices, and of not even measuring up to the nations in service to the Lord. To this, the people essentially had no response.

To embellish the point, Malachi portrayed a debate between God and the People of Israel. It was delivered in Malachi's typical question-and-answer style, and began with God going first: "I have loved you, says the Lord, But you said, 'How have You loved us?' Was not Esau the brother of Jacob? says God, 'and I loved Jacob!' But I hated Esau, and made his mountains a desolation, and gave his inheritance to the jackals of the wilderness." (Malachi 1:2–3)

God also accused the people of being disloyal to their wives: "... Because the Lord has been witness between you and the wife of your youth, against whom you have acted treacherously, though she is your companion, and the wife of your covenant." (Malachi 2:14)

Judaism looks with disfavor upon divorce; however, it is not prohibited and even accommodates couples who for whatever reason cannot find domestic bliss by giving them a legitimate out. This is through a *get* (bill of divorcement). The rabbis of the Talmud considered marriage a holy contract, invoking this verse from Malachi, and viewed the dissolution of marriage an unwholesome act. The sages add, "Even the Altar of God sheds tears when anyone divorces his wife."

In one final rebuke, God declared that the Jews had not observed the laws of tithing, which required them to donate one tenth of their produce to the Levites. Malachi proclaimed in God's name that tithing was essentially a test of one's steadfast faith and trust in God's "capability" to provide and bestow. The sages even suggested that this might be the only Torah observance with which one is allowed to "test" God: "Bring the whole tithe into the storehouse, that there may be food in my house and test me, says the Lord, in this, if I will not open the windows of Heaven, and pour you out a blessing, That shall be far more than sufficient." (Malachi 3:10)

In the very last chapter of prophecy, Malachi addresses the people as a whole and warns them of the coming of the God of Judgment and great day of reckoning that will precede the return of Elijah the Prophet and the advent of the Messiah: "Behold, I will send you Elijah the Prophet, Before the coming of the great and terrible Day of the Lord." (Malachi 3:23)

In this generation we are witnessing the first signs of a thirsting for the word of God that many of the prophets hinted at.

The phenomenon is known as the *Baale Teshuva* Movement where many Jews, both young and old, have been turned on to the traditions of their ancestors. They have abandoned the hedonistic and material icons of modern society and thrown their lot with the God of Israel. Conventional wisdom would suggest that it is the fathers or elders who will initiate the reach out to bring back the wayward youth. Although that may be true, we have also witnessed just the opposite, a phenomenon that strongly supports Malachi's last words: "And He shall turn the heart of the fathers to the children, and the heart of the children to the fathers …." (Malachi 3:24)

The Sages Say

"For the priest's lips should keep knowledge, and they should seek the law from his mouth; for he is the messenger of Lord of hosts." (Malachi 2:7) It is from this verse that the sages of the Talmud derive a litmus test for selecting a Torah teacher, rabbi, or mentor. "If he behaves like a 'messenger of the Lord of hosts,' then 'seek the law from his mouth.'" (Talmud)

Tower of Babel

Baale Teshuva literally means "One of Return." It is the term for someone who either never observed Torah law, or left the fold and is now a penitent Jew.

The Least You Need to Know

♦ Haggai, along with the prophet Zechariah, and Zerubbabel—the governor of Judea from the line of David, was a central figure in rebuilding the Temple. Haggai drew a link between Judah's poverty and dejected state of affairs and the corrupt indifference regarding the Temple.

♦ Like his colleague, Haggai, Zechariah's main message was to persuade the tribe of Judah to resume the rebuilding of the Temple that had been destroyed by the Babylonians.

♦ Zechariah hints to an Armageddon, or final military confrontation, with the words, "For I will gather all nations against Jerusalem to battle." (Zechariah 14:2)

♦ Malachi was the last of the prophets to experience and record true prophecy. He made reference to the return of Elijah the Prophet and a time when "Fathers will return to their sons," meaning the youth will motivate their elders to return to Torah observance.

Part 5

Writings Part I: The Poetical Books

The books of Psalms, Proverbs, and Job all deal with profound insights into how to deal with life's vicissitudes, challenges, and sufferings. During times of war, tranquility, and at any other time, Jews have turned to these books for inspiration and instruction on how to cope and how to succeed in the game of life.

Chapter 20

God's Songbook: The Book of Psalms

In This Chapter

- Meditating with a lonely young man
- Singing songs of praise
- Playing the songs of the Levites
- Letting everyone praise God

When King David wrote and published the Book of Psalms, it became an instant bestseller. And it hasn't left the Jewish all-time bestseller list ever since!

Psalms is arguably the most universally utilized book of the 24 books that comprise the Jewish Bible. From the womb to the tomb, there is a Psalm for every person and every occasion.

Peaceful Meditations from a Lonely Young Man

David's beginning was a bit shaky, to say the least. As a boy he was mistakenly considered an illegitimate child who was born from a prohibited union between a Jew and a Moabite. In the aftermath of the curious (and embarrassing) circumstances of David's birth, he was shunned by his father and older brothers and forced to live apart from them for approximately 25 years. He shepherded the family flocks—living for the most part in painful isolation.

Among the sheep and the fields, David learned to ease his suffering and heal the deep wounds of rejection by drawing close to God through two of his profound gifts—music and poetry. Unencumbered by the clamor of family and public affairs, he developed an original form of self-expression and eventually shared that gift with humanity in a big way.

Lord Knows

David's life, in a certain way, parallels the history of his people. The fear of pursuit (Saul), flight into the wilderness (his son, Absalom), and the privations of exile mirror a similar fate of the Nation of Israel for more than 2,000 years. The peaceful meditations in the verdant pastures of his youth honed David's skills as a deep thinker and communicator. But it would take more than that to become a paradigm of prayer and lover of God and to have one's intimate thoughts repeated by millions of people over the millennia. Like Israel, David needed the challenge of vengeful enemies, internal intrigues, and epic military encounters to develop an unwavering trust in God and the fortitude to withstand every test of life.

Through the centuries, David's perceptive words have resonated with humankind in virtually every circumstance. His lyrics of petition, praise, and thanksgiving have become the staple of the Jewish prayer book and a significant component of Western religion for many centuries.

Although it is generally accepted that King David published Psalms (*Tehillim*, in Hebrew), a number of them seem to have been transmitted from earlier periods. In fact, one Talmudic tradition attributes publication of some of the Psalms to 10 elders, or famous personalities:

Elder	Psalms
Adam	92
Malchi-tzedek	110
Abraham	89
Moses	90–100

Elder	Psalms
Heman	88
Yeduthun	39,62,77
Asaph	50,73–83
Assir ben Korach	42,49,78,84–85,88
Elkanah ben Korach	42,49,78,84–85,88
Aviassaph ben Korach	42,49,78,84–85,88

The Nature of David's Songs

The two main forms of songs found in Psalms are a *mizmor* and a *shir*. These two words converge in Psalm 30, one of the most upbeat and magnificent songs that David composed in anticipation of the dedication of the Temple (that he laid the cornerstone for), and that serves as an introduction to the daily morning prayers found in Jewish prayer books.

What is the difference between mizmor and shir? What are they altogether? Why is this phrase appropriate for daily initiation into prayer? And what is the connection to the Temple dedication? Here's what Rabbi Abraham Isaac Kook (1865 to 1935), the first chief rabbi of Israel and a preeminent Talmudic scholar had to say:

Tower of Babel

The sages define a **mizmor** as the musical outpouring of the soul, and a **shir** as song and poetry.

"Heartfelt emotion, emanating from the depths of the soul, lies hidden in the crevices of life. When these feelings burst forth, they cannot be composed into words and expressed by speech. Without thought, we happily hum a tune. We give voice to our emotions through *zemer*, in the notes of a tune or melody. This is *mizmor*, the musical outpouring of the soul. As our feelings expand and become more revealed, they connect with our powers of thought and cognition. They reach the treasury of language and speech. This is the level of *shir*, song and poetry. We can now articulate the outburst of emotion using our mental faculties of reason and language. When we join together *mizmor shir*, we link our emotional and intellectual sides. First *mizmor*, musical expression from the depth of emotion and outpouring of the soul. Then comes *shir*, poetic expression from holy meditation and thought. When we enter our house of prayer, we need to aspire to the sublime ideal of *mizmor shir*. We should fully awaken our emotional and intellectual potential for praise and joy. These two holy faculties achieved their greatest expression when the place most suitable for spiritual elevation was completed—at the dedication of the holy Temple in Jerusalem."

Songs of Praise

Virtually every Jewish prayer service, custom, and practice uses King David's Psalms as the cornerstone of praise. The common theme running through them all is praise of God. From the Exodus from Egypt when Moses led a spontaneous singing of praise to God at the splitting of the Red Sea to the miracles of Hanukah, the people have used song to acknowledge the deliverance and salvation of God.

Lord Knows
The dictionary definition of the word *psalm* is "sacred song" or "hymn." The Greek *psalmos* is from *psallein*, meaning "to play the harp."

Psalm 145 is perhaps the most recited of the psalms. It is generally identified by its first word Ashrei, meaning "fortunate." Religious Jews have recited it three times a day for hundreds of years. It inaugurates the afternoon prayers and the sages teach that the one who recites it with particular fervor and proper intent is assured a portion in the World-to-Come.

This psalm also attains special status for possessing two qualities found nowhere else together in Psalms:

♦ Beginning with the first truly significant word "Aromimecha" (I will extol), the first letter of each stanza follows the order of the Hebrew alphabet with the exception of the letter "nun."

♦ It contains inspiring testimony to God's attribute of mercy with the words "You open Your hand and sustain the desire of every living being." This is not spoken as a request of God to sustain us, rather as a statement of fact and ecstatic praise that this is so.

The consummate Song of Praise goes like this:

1 [A Psalm of] praise, of David. I will extol Thee, my God, O King; and I will bless Thy name forever and ever. **2** Every day will I bless Thee; and I will praise Thy name for ever and ever. **3** Great is the LORD, and highly to be praised; and His greatness is unfathomable. **4** One generation shall laud Thy works to another, and shall declare Thy mighty acts. **5** The glorious splendor of Thy majesty, and Thy wondrous works, will I retell. **6** And men shall speak of the might of Thy tremendous acts; and I will tell of Thy greatness. **7** They shall utter the fame of Thy great goodness, and shall sing of Thy righteousness. **8** The LORD is gracious, and full of compassion; slow to anger, and of great mercy. **9** The LORD is good to all; and His tender mercies are over all His works. **10** All Thy works shall praise Thee, O LORD; and Thy saints shall bless Thee. **11** They shall speak of the glory of Thy kingdom, and talk of Thy might; **12** To make known to the sons of men His mighty acts, and the glory of the majesty of His kingdom. **13** Thy kingdom is a kingdom spanning all eternities,

and Thy dominion endures throughout every generation. **14** The LORD supports all that fall, and raises up all those that are bowed down. **15** The eyes of all wait for Thee, and Thou gives them their food in due season. **16** Thou open Thy hand, and satisfy every living thing with favor. **17** The LORD is righteous in all His ways, and gracious in all His works. **18** The LORD is close unto all them that call upon Him, to all that call upon Him in truth. **19** He will fulfill the desire of them that fear Him; He also will hear their cry, and will save them. **20** The LORD preserves all them that love Him; but all the wicked will He destroy. **21** My mouth shall speak the praise of the LORD; and let all flesh bless His holy name forever and ever.

The five psalms that follow this one are also recited daily as part of what's known as *Hallel*, which means "the highest level of praise." It also connotes a prayer of adoration and thanks incorporating several passages of Psalms recited on most festivals such as Passover, Succot (Feast of Booths), Shavuot (Feast of Weeks or Pentecost), Rosh Chodesh (New Moon), and Hanukah.

Lord Knows

The old joke surrounding Jewish holidays is, "Nu, we were oppressed, we fought, we won, so let's eat!" However, these commemorations lack content if they are not acknowledged with heartfelt joy and gratitude for all our salvations and deliverances from Above. David's Psalms provide the vehicle to convey these praises and thanks.

It Is Written

Adam, the first man, might have been the first to compose a psalm of praise. He was inspired to do so when he realized that his sin had been forgiven and the Sabbath had come as a form of protection. King David captured this notion when he wrote Psalm 92, "A Psalm, A Song for the Sabbath Day. It is good to thank God and to sing praise to Your exalted name."

In addition to the occasions mentioned previously, some rabbis rule that it is incumbent upon Jews to chant some of King David's Hallel songs of thanksgiving for the miraculous recreation of the State of Israel in 1948 and the deliverance of the State and the reuniting of the Jewish people and land with their holy city and singular capital—Jerusalem—that miraculously occurred in the aftermath of the Six Day War of 1967.

Songs of the Levites—Songs of Ascent

After Solomon built the Temple, the Levites no longer had to transport the Tabernacle, which was their major role as defined in the Torah. Instead they began to play a liturgical role in the Temple as singers and musicians.

Many of the psalms were sung by the Levites in the Temple, most notably those that begin with the words Shir HaMa'alot (A Song of Ascents). The Levites sang them as they stood on the steps of the sanctuary leading up to their platform, and they still play a role in regular prayer service today.

The Sages Say

What inspired David to compose the 15 Songs of Ascent? The Talmud relates that when King David excavated the deep cisterns beneath the altar, the waters of the deep came up and threatened to flood the world. He prayed or placed something in the holes and the water receded too much. Thereupon he was inspired to recite 15 Songs of Ascent, and the waters returned to their normal level.

Psalm 126, which is actually known as the Shir HaMa'alot, is customarily said on Shabbat, Rosh Chodesh (New Moon), Passover, Succot (Feast of Booths), and Shavuot (Feast of Weeks or Pentecost), as part of grace after meals. This short hymn portrays a valuable message to Jews in Israel and the Diaspora. It speaks of the restoration of Zion, holy festivals, and includes a direct reference to the Temple in Jerusalem: "A Song of Ascents. When God will bring back the captivity of Zion, we will be like them that dream. Then our mouth will be filled with laughter, and our tongue with singing; they among the nations will say: 'The Lord has done great things with these.' God has done great things with us; we are rejoiced. Turn our captivity, O Lord, as the streams in the desert. They that sow in tears shall reap in joy. He who bears the measure of seed, walks along weeping, but he shall return with joy, bearing his sheaves."

This Shir HaMa'alot is a song of hopeful praise, as it begins with the Jews returning to Jerusalem "as if in a dream," filled with laughter and singing, and is traditionally sung with a joyful melody and with very expressive and pleasing words.

The phrase "then our mouths will be filled with laughter and our tongue with singing," is particularly idealistic. Moreover, David's lyrics emphasize a longing he had that the nations of the world would one day look in awe and recognition of the great things God has done for them and for the people of Israel—making them indeed a "light unto the nations."

In many Jewish communities, it is customary at the beginning of the Jewish New Year to recite a cycle of the Shir HaMa'alot Psalms at Shabbat afternoon time. Here's a taste of what they're all about:

> Psalm 120: "Shir HaMa'alot, A Psalm of the Elevation, In my distress I called to the Lord and God answered me."

> Psalm 121: "Shir LaMa'alot, I turn my eyes to the mountains, from where will my help come? My help comes from the Lord, maker of Heaven and Earth."

> Psalm 122: "Shir HaMa'alot, Our feet stood at your gates, Jerusalem, Jerusalem built like a city twinned together … There where the seats of judgment sat … Pray for the peace of Jerusalem for quietude for those who love her For the sake of my family and friends I speak about her peace For the sake of the house of God I ask for her to know goodness."

Let All Souls Praise God

King David penned and composed not only the words but also the tunes (most lost by now) on his famous harp of 10 strings. His work expressed praise that not only incorporated the mouth and tongue but one's entire being.

Liturgical melodies are used by many faiths as an aid to create the proper mindset. Jewish prayers and prayer services have traditional melodies associated with them. They no doubt trace their origins to the Levites and King David.

Their purpose, among others, is to increase one's focus on what one is doing and help block out extraneous thoughts. Many find it useful to move while praying. Traditional Jews routinely sway back and forth during prayer, apparently a reference to Psalm 35, where David proclaims, "All my limbs shall declare, 'O Lord, who is like You?'" Some might find it a bit distracting, but for others it engages more of their primary senses in the act of communing with and praising God.

King David has another psalm, however, that not only engages individual limbs in praising the Lord, but inspires all of creation to get into the act. Here are some excerpts from Psalm 104:

"Bless the Lord, O my soul. O Lord my God, Thou art very great; Thou art clothed with glory and majesty. Who covers Thyself with light as with a garment, who stretches out the heavens like a curtain; Who lays the beams of Your upper chambers in the waters, who makes the clouds Thy chariot, who walkest upon the wings of the wind; Who makes winds Thy messengers, the flaming fire Thy ministers … the waters stood above the mountains. At Thy rebuke they fled, at the voice of Thy thunder they hasted away … Who sends forth springs into the valleys; they run between the mountains; They give drink to every beast of the field, the wild asses quench their thirst. Beside them dwell the fowl of the heaven, from among the branches they sing. Who waters the mountains from Your upper chambers; the earth is full of the fruit of Thy works … And wine that makes glad the heart of man, making the face brighter than oil, and bread that satiates man's heart … Who appoints the moon for seasons; the sun knows his going down … the young lions roar after their prey, and seek their food from God. The sun arises, they slink away, and couch in their dens … In wisdom hast Thou made them all; the earth is full of Thy creatures. Yonder sea, great and wide, therein are creeping things innumerable, living creatures, both small and great. There go the ships; there is leviathan, which Thou hast formed to sport therein. All of them wait for Thee, that Thou may give them their food in due season … May the glory of God endure forever; let God rejoice in His works! Who looks on the earth, and it trembles; He touches the mountains, and they smoke. I will sing unto God as long as I live; I will sing praise to my God while I have any being. Let my musing be sweet unto Him; as for me, I will rejoice in the Lord. Let sinners cease out of the earth, and let the wicked be no more. Bless the Lord, O my soul. Hallelujah."

> **Lord Knows**
>
> Several psalms have been incorporated into the services and rituals of other religions. For example Psalm 23: "the Shepherd's Prayer" (without question the most famous of the entire 150) is used at Christian funerals. The popular hymn "Bringing in the Sheaves" is based on Psalm 126.

There are many Jews who recite the entire Book of Psalms once a month, a few each day, or all of them on the Sabbath morning before the new moon. Psalms are recited during crises and in the face of extremely dangerous times such as warfare (most often

Psalms 121 and 130). As mentioned, they envelope Jewish life from the womb (or eight days later at the ritual circumcision) to the tomb, for Psalm 91 is repeated seven times until the coffin has been escorted to the gravesite from the chapel—where Psalm 23 is usually recited during the brief ceremony before interment.

Psalms for All Occasions

Traditions handed down through the centuries prescribed psalms for literally every occasion and circumstance, including the following:

◆ Supplications on behalf of an ill person

◆ For visiting a gravesite

◆ Conveying blessings for miracles and rescues

◆ Rescues from danger

◆ Supplicating for miracles

◆ Asking for blessings for a long journey

◆ Asking for general thanksgiving

◆ For help in troubled times

◆ For repentance

◆ For peace

◆ For business success

There are even special psalms for divine guidance, for recovery from illness, or the birth of a child. On the eve of each Sabbath, there is a short service to welcome the Sabbath "queen" into our midst and pious Jews sing psalms even after the Sabbath departs. Many don't lie down to sleep each night until they recite psalms. There are even psalms to atone for sexual and other sins.

King David requested of God that his Book of Psalms be received by Him as a replica of Torah itself, and that those who endeavored to plumb its depths should receive equal reward and esteem in this world and in the next as those who study the Bible and the Talmud. His wish was fully granted and his lifeworks and contributions to the spiritual and physical survival of the Jewish people were acknowledged and honored by God, sealing for all time to come the name of King David under the term *magen david* (the Shield of David), which God assigned as the guardian of the future of His people and covenant.

Until the advent of his scion, the Messiah the son of David, this seal would not be broken and the dynasty of David's throne was sworn for eternity. This is just reward for the physical wars he fought on Israel's behalf and for the spiritual wars he waged and recorded for our benefit in his Book of Psalms.

The Sages Say

In Rabbinical literature, David is equated to Moses, "Who is the best of the prophets and who is the best of kings? The best of the prophets was Moses; the best of the kings was David. For you find that whatever Moses did, David did. Moses took Israel out of Egypt, and David took Israel out of the bondage of the kingdoms ... Moses gave Israel the Five Books of the Torah, and David gave Israel the Five Books of Psalms."

The Least You Need to Know

◆ King David is generally considered the author of the 150 chapters of Psalms, although there might have been as many as 10 elders or biblical personalities who contributed some of them.

◆ The young David lived among the sheep as his family's shepherd where he began his "career" of praising God through song and poetry. His personal experiences, which were fraught with pain and suffering and perseverance, are reflected in the individual psalms.

◆ Psalms has become a mainstay of the Jewish prayer book, and religious Jews recite tens of them on a daily basis. There are subtle differences between the poetic and melodious varieties of David's Psalms.

◆ There is a psalm for every occasion in Judaism. Whether it is a circumcision celebration or funeral service, psalms from the "womb to the tomb" surround a religious Jewish person.

Chapter 21

Wise Sayings: The Book of Proverbs

In This Chapter

- ◆ Discovering Solomon the wise
- ◆ Fearing the Lord and seeking wisdom
- ◆ Reading his allusions and parables
- ◆ Learning life lessons

Tradition has it that Solomon composed more than 3,000 proverbs. Many of them—some 800, in fact—are found in his Book of Proverbs.

It's hard to even think of Solomon's name without imagining the pithy witticisms and profound parables that he left behind in this biblical book. Through them, Solomon imparts his amazing wisdom—the gift he requested from God—and tells his people how to deal with everyday life. That and more are found in this chapter about Solomon's proverbs.

Solomon Says

As you might recall, Solomon asked God for wisdom, and God granted his wish. But Solomon wasn't your ordinary wise man. His knowledge was so deep and wide that people traveled long distances to hear him speak. He also brought great prosperity and glory to Israel until the waning years of his reign. No one could be better equipped to write a book of wisdom than this remarkable man.

In the beginning verses of Proverbs, Solomon speaks of three different types of wisdom that are essential to acquire and that he himself possessed: "… to know wisdom and moral instruction; to comprehend the words of discernment." (Proverbs 1:2)

According to the Talmudic sages, these three components represent practical wisdom, moral instruction, and divine knowledge. They encompass all facets of a person's intellectual pursuits in this world.

All Solomon's proverbs contain one of these three elements and sometimes more. Likewise, the consummate seeker of wisdom strives to combine the divine with the mundane, as mediated by study.

As mentioned, Proverbs contains instruction on how to live life. These pearls of wisdom are arranged as follows:

◆ The Purpose of Proverbs. (1:1–7) Here, Solomon introduces himself as author and states the theme and purpose of the book.

◆ Proverbs to the Youth. (1:8–9:18) This is a series of 10 teachings, each beginning with the words "My son."

◆ Proverbs of Solomon. (10:1–24:34) This is a series of mostly one-liners on such themes as money, speech, and so on.

◆ Proverbs of Solomon Copied by Hezekiah's Men. (25:1–29:27) This is a second collection of Solomon's proverbs, copied and arranged by "the men of Hezekiah." They further develop the themes found earlier in the book.

◆ The Words of Agur and King Lemuel. (30:1–31:31) The Talmud mentions that Solomon was known by seven names; among them are Agur and Lemuel. The last chapter is arranged as a 22-verse acrostic that portrays a virtuous wife.

We will now sample a few selections of Solomon's wisdom found in these various sections of his book.

It Is Written _____

Proverbs is considered a wisdom book, not a historical book. Some sources debate whether Solomon wrote all the proverbs himself or whether he gathered and edited some proverbs other than his own. A verse in Ecclesiastes—a book that Solomon penned in his later years—seems to support his using other sources: "He pondered and sought out and set in order many proverbs." (Ecclesiastes 12:9)

Proverbs itself refers to the "words of the wise." (Proverbs 22:17, 24:23) As wise men of the times often went to hear each other speak, it's certainly plausible that Solomon did so, and perhaps borrowed and elaborated on certain wise sayings he heard others speak. However, traditional Jewish sources believe there is no doubt that Solomon wrote all Proverbs. The only issue is whether he had time to publish them before his death.

From Father to Son

As mentioned, after Solomon opens his book, he launches into a series of teachings that read as a father's kind words to his son. However, Solomon's true intent was for readers to process his words in a way that applied to their own lives. He goads wisdom-seeking readers to begin the task of seeking wisdom by first applying the quality of listening: "Let the wise listen and the insightful take heed and increase in learning, and the man of understanding may attain unto wise counsels." (Proverbs 1:5)

After oriented, the way is open and a path has been shown to walk in an upright way. The gist of this teaching is that every single person who is inclined to open their channels of learning through listening will discover an upright path before the Creator.

There is one other prerequisite Solomon emphasizes to achieve this goal: "The fear of Heaven is the beginning of knowledge; but a fool denigrates despise wisdom and discipline." (Proverbs 1:7)

Here, Solomon is stressing that it is extremely difficult to acquire religious knowledge—or any

The Sages Say _____

The great Vilna Gaon was Rabbi Eliyahu of Vilna, 1720–1797. ("Gaon" means genius and no person personified this title more.) Rabbi Eliyahu was probably the most influential Jewish leader in modern history. He noted that when one comes to read a book of wisdom, the extent to which the book will actually impart wisdom depends on the wisdom of its author.

true discipline, for that matter—without fear of God. Establishing a foundation of being awestruck by the Great Designer in the design, and recognizing that even one's ability to reason and intellectualize comes from Him is where it all begins.

Solomon then proceeds to a series of lessons on a variety of themes. Many are saturated with graphic allusions. For example, Solomon tells the son to be faithful to his own spouse by ... "Drink[ing] water from your own cistern, And running water from your own well. Should your fountains be dispersed abroad, Streams of water in the streets? Let them be only your own, And not for strangers with you." (Proverbs 5:15–17)

Solomon seemed to have a parable suited for every occasion. One of his favorite subjects was animals. He felt that if one merely gazed downward, there would be much to be learned from these critters. One can even learn from the lowly ant in his teaching on laziness: "Go to the ant, thou sluggard; consider her ways, and be wise; which having no chief, overseer, or ruler, provides her bread in the summer, and gathers her food in the harvest." (Proverbs 6:6–8)

What can be learned from an ant? Rashi comments that the ant is the paradigm worker; it carries far more than its weight compared to other creatures. More significantly, it has a great work ethic and integrity. It will forage without having to take orders from a superior, will not stop until there is enough for the winter, and will keep its grimy paws off someone else's haul!

Solomon had a loathing for sloth and laziness. He pursued it relentlessly. Recognizing the evil of laziness and the greatness of the loss that results from it, he said, "A little sleep, a little slumber, a little folding of the hands to rest, and like a wanderer, your poverty will come." (Proverbs 6:10)

The lazy man, though not actively evil, produces evil through his very inactivity. Solomon punctuates this notion, "Also he who slackens in his work is a brother to the Destroyer." (Proverbs 18:9) Though he is not the Destroyer himself who commits the evil with his own hands, he becomes guilty by association—in fact, he is like his blood brother.

Returning to the ant and a few of her little friends, Solomon said: "There are four things that are little upon the earth, but they are exceeding wise: The ants are a people not strong, yet they provide their food in the summer; The rock-badgers are but a feeble folk, yet make their houses in the crags; The locusts have no king, yet go they forth all of them by bands; The spider thou canst take with the hands, yet she is in kings' palaces." (Proverbs 6:25–28)

Busy ants, independently swarming locusts, and crafty spiders allow us to take a look at our own lives and realize the wisdom the Creator imparted to His creation. As the sages commented, in case we are unable to learn proper conduct from human example, God provides us with ample specimens to learn from.

On adultery again (Solomon must not have felt he drove the point home strongly enough the first time): "My son, keep your father's command, and do not forsake the law of your mother. Bind them continually upon your heart; tie them around your neck. When you roam, they will lead you; When you sleep, they will keep you; and when you awake, they will speak with you. For the commandment is a lamp, and the law is light; reproofs of instruction are the way of life, To keep you from the evil woman, From the flattering tongue of a seductress, Do not lust after her beauty in your heart, Nor let her allure you with her eyelids. For by means of a harlot a man is reduced to a crust of bread; and an adulteress will prey upon his precious life." (Proverbs 6:20–26)

It Is Written

King Solomon's exhortation against immorality is a theme found in the Torah itself, as it states, "Do not stray after your hearts and after your eyes, after which you stray." (Numbers 15:39) The sages take this as a prohibition for men to lust after women, even with one's eyes. In that spirit, Jewish tradition encourages women to avoid wearing provocative clothing that is alluring and that might lead to immodest behavior.

Lessons for Life

What can be considered the middle section of Proverbs contains a series of biblical one-liners. They begin with proverbs that contrast the godly with the wicked:

- "A wise son makes a glad father, but a foolish son is the grief of his mother." (Proverbs 10:1)

- "He who deals with a slack hand becomes poor, but the hand of the diligent makes one rich." (Proverbs 10:4)

- "He who gathers in summer is a wise son, but he who sleeps in harvest is a son who causes shame." (Proverbs 10:5)

- "Hatred stirs up strife, but love covers all sins." (Proverbs 10:12)

♦ "The righteous eats to the satisfying of his soul: but the belly of the wicked always lacks." (Proverbs 13:25)

Encounters between the righteous and wicked and rejoicing over the fall of the wicked are grist for Solomon's mill of moral teachings here. There are more than 70 verses in Proverbs that speak to this subject. Here is just one more: "A muddy spring, a dirtied source, is the righteous who breaks down before the wicked." (Proverbs 25:26)

Doesn't sound too rosy for the righteous, does it? Solomon is informing us, however, of the qualities of an upright person, for when a good person falls into the hands of the wicked and breaks down before him, his defeat is only temporary; he is confident that in a short while he will be delivered from his hands, "Though the righteous falls seven times, he will rise again." (Proverbs 24:16) In the end, he will return to his superior position and regain his prestige. To what does Solomon compare this? To a well-trampled muddy spring, but whose muddiness is only temporary—in no time at all, the water will become clear once more. In fact, it will not even show its previous murkiness.

There is an interesting paradox found in this same chapter (24) concerning how one should respond to the eventual downfall of one's enemy: "Rejoice not when your enemy falls, and let not thy heart be glad when he stumbles; Lest God see it, and it displease Him, and He turn away His wrath from him." (Proverbs 24:17–18)

Yet another verse teaches just the opposite: "When the wicked perish, there is jubilation." (Proverbs 11:10)

So which one do we follow? Some explain that the former verse is referring to one's personal enemy, but not to "wicked people" in general, over whose downfall one should rejoice—as the latter verse suggests. Other commentators explain that this simply means not to have public rejoicing in the streets, but it's certainly fair to rejoice privately in one's heart or home. It's a natural human response to feel elation over the defeat and subjugation of one's mortal enemy.

Lord Knows

Proverbs, we are told by the rabbis, was the second of three books written by King Solomon. In his youth, he penned the eternally optimistic (and deeply symbolic) "Song of Songs." During midlife he wrote this book, replete with parables and analogies offering sound guidance and practical advice. In his waning years, perhaps after having "seen it all," Solomon wrote the somewhat cynical Ecclesiastes.

Solomon on Education

Solomon spares no ink to promote the necessity not to "Spare the rod," if we don't want to spoil the child. In his milieu, he was clearly an advocate of physical discipline in raising wise children.

Today, many parents reject a physical response to misbehavior but still claim that we do not discipline or punish our children well enough to teach them the consequences of their actions. In fact, lack of parental guidance has led to the situation that Solomon bemoaned and graphically warned against: "The eye that mocks at his father, and despises to obey his mother, the ravens of the valley shall pick it out, and the young vultures shall eat it." (Proverbs 30:17)

Contrast this with a hand's-on approach to rearing children, where Solomon advises a tailor-made system of education and parenting as opposed to the cookie-cutter variety: "Train a young lad according to his method (or path), so that when he grows older he will not deviate from it." (Proverbs 22:6)

Successful child rearing involves much attention to the way we are taught how to adapt to life's many hurdles, tests, and challenges. In the Solomonic system of education, instruction consists of a means of training our charges how to deal with life, even how to stumble properly, and not about just stuffing them with knowledge. How to recover from making mistakes and adapting to life's ups and downs, successes and failures is at least as important as acquiring factual knowledge. Finding just the right path for each child should be the goal of any skilled parent or educator. In this fashion, Solomon promises, "he (or she) will not deviate from it."

The Wise Woman

Solomon ends with the famous tribute to the righteous woman. These are some of the most beautiful verses in all Scripture; they are reprinted here in their entirety.

These passages have been interpreted allegorically by many commentators as alluding to everything from the *Shechinah*, or Divine Presence, to Torah wisdom, and even the soul. Regardless, the fact that Solomon penned this

> **Tower of Babel**
>
> The term **Shechinah** is derived from the verb "lishkon" which means "to rest" or "to dwell." Hence, the idea is that God causes His Presence to be experienced in this world through the vehicle of the Shechinah.

most sublime poem using the woman of valor as the subject is a testament to the lofty spiritual qualities of women.

"Who can find a virtuous wife? For her worth is far above rubies. The heart of her husband safely trusts her; so he will have no lack of grain.

She does him good and not evil, all the days of her life.

She seeks wool and flax, and willingly works with her hands.

She is like the merchant ships, she brings food from afar.

She also rises while it is yet night, and provides food for her household, and a portion for her maidservants.

She considers a field and buys it; from her profits she plants a vineyard.

She girds herself with strength, and strengthens her arms.

She perceives that her merchandise is good, and her lamp does not go out by night.

She stretches out her hands to the distaff, and her hand holds the spindle.

She extends her hand to the poor, yes, she reaches out her hands to the needy.

She is not afraid of snow for her household, for all her household is clothed with scarlet.

She made for herself luxurious bedspreads; linen and purple wool are her clothing.

Her husband is distinctive in the councils, when he sits with the elders of the land.

She makes a cloak and sells [it], and delivers a belt to the peddler.

Strength and majesty are her raiment, and she joyfully awaits the last day.

She opens her mouth with wisdom, and the teaching of kindness is on her tongue.

She anticipates the ways of her household, and does not eat the bread of laziness.

Her children have risen and praised her; her husband, and he extolled her:

'Many women have amassed achievement, but you surpassed them all.'

Grace is false, and beauty vain; a woman who fears God, she should be praised.

Give her the fruits of her hands; and let her be praised in the gates by her very own deeds."

Writing in the fourteenth century, the Spanish sage Rabbi Israel al-Nakawa explains this biblical poem as follows: "If a man is fortunate enough to have found a good wife, he will never miss anything. Though he may be poor, he should consider himself rich. A good wife is one who manages her husband's affairs correctly, helps him to the best of her ability, gives him her honest advice, and does not urge him to spend more than is necessary. She intelligently supervises the needs of the home, and the education of their children … She does not act snobbish toward her husband's family even if she happens to come from a more refined environment … Marriage is not a one-sided affair. The man has obligations as well as the woman … A man should sacrifice his personal needs in order to provide more abundantly for his wife and children. Above all, he should treat his wife with love and sympathy, for she is part of him. He must never abuse her …." (Menorath HaMaor—"Lamp of Illumination")

> **Lord Knows**
>
> There is a time-honored custom for married Jewish men to chant the concluding verses of Proverbs in the presence of their wives at the Sabbath evening meal. Its content is a tribute to the price-less contributions she makes to her husband, home, and domestic tranquility.

The Least You Need to Know

- ◆ Solomon wrote thousands of parables that represented practical wisdom, moral instruction, and divine knowledge.

- ◆ Solomon used many vivid metaphors, including animals, to make his point.

- ◆ His proverbs contain profound truths and practical advice for successful living.

- ◆ Solomon was big on the subject of contrasting the righteous and wicked. He also exhorted his readers to take child rearing and education seriously.

Righteous Suffering: The Book of Job

In This Chapter

- ◆ Taking on Satan
- ◆ Having friends or foes?
- ◆ Being a pious fool?
- ◆ Receiving God's consolation

The Book of Job is the story of an exceptionally righteous man who is made to suffer for no apparent reason. His tragic suffering evokes some powerful questions. Should the totally righteous suffer? What purpose does such suffering serve? How does the righteous suffering contrast with the wicked that prosper?

These questions have to be one of mankind's most elusive mysteries since time immemorial. Several answers are presented and fiercely debated throughout the chapters of the Book of Job.

The lesson of the Book of Job is that man's sufferings are a test of his fidelity to God. Job's life is a lesson for everyone to learn regarding the appropriate way to accept suffering.

The Mysterious Job

Of all the characters in the Bible, Job is among the most enigmatic. There's even some doubt as to whether he even existed. Those who doubt his existence hold his story as nothing more than a moral teaching.

Among those who believe he isn't a fictional character, there is general agreement that he was not Jewish and that he lived in the time of Abraham. In fact, there is a Talmudic tradition that he was a colleague of Abraham and eventually married one of Jacob's daughters.

The Sages Say

The prophet Ezekiel, in the book that bears his name, specifically mentions Job, which lends credence to his actual existence. Nonetheless, the great Talmud sage Resh Lakish expressed the view that Job never existed and that the story is simply a poetic comparison or parable. Although the authorship of the Book of Job is not known with certainty, the sages of Israel believe none other than Moses wrote it.

One thing we know for sure, the story of Job's life closely parallels that of Abraham—namely, he had faith, was fabulously rich, left his homeland, and was steadfastly faithful to God despite many hardships and tests.

The Book of Job consists of three parts: a prologue, a poem in dialogue form, and an epilogue. In the original Hebrew, the language is very esoteric, sometimes very difficult to translate, and its literal meaning even more difficult to understand. There is one character, an antagonist—the Satan, who figures most prominently in the story. His motivations and function are immediately revealed in the opening chapter.

Lord Knows

Judaism views the concept of Satan quite differently than Christianity and considers its role to strengthen man's moral compass by leading him into temptation. Curiously, the Satan of Job is mainly interested in getting him to blaspheme God in response to his incomprehensible suffering. In Talmudic literature, the word *ha-Satan* is understood as an entity that was transformed into the *yetzer hara*—the evil inclination—and not as some rogue angel who has fallen from grace and acts independent of God.

According to traditional Jewish commentators, Job's chief complaint was that although man is driven to sin by the *yetzer hara*—or the evil inclination—which is a part of God's creation, he is still subject to punishment.

The sages point out that God also created divine law which man can follow to subdue evil inclinations. In fact, chapter 32 enumerates the virtues of a subdued evil inclination specified by Job: a blameless family life, consideration of the poor and weak, charity, modesty, generosity, and hospitality to strangers.

Most of the Book of Job is discussions and debates in the form of a dialogue between Job and his friends. Each of these characters presents a unique approach to Job's plight. On the one hand Job is a believer, a man of intense faith and devout service. However, he cannot accept that a merciful, compassionate God would consent to the dreadful suffering meted out to him at the hands of the Satan, or anyone else, for that matter.

The very foundations of religion and divinity are tested in a combat zone of what appears to be relentless and gratuitous human afflictions. The issues are hotly debated and advanced between Job and his three friends: Eliphaz, Beldad, and Tzofer. Finally, Job finds balm for his wounds in the wisdom of Elihu.

Provoking Satan

Job is minding his own business as a righteous, prosperous family man with a large family of fourteen sons and seven daughters. Then, for no apparent reason, God said this to the Satan: "Have you seen my servant Job, that there is none like him in the earth, who fears God and shuns evil?" (Job 1:8)

The Satan wants to rain on Job's parade and levies a stern protest to God: "Haven't you made a hedge around him, and around his house, and around all that he has, on every side? You have blessed the work of his hands, and his substance is increased in the land. But put forth your hand now, and touch all that he has, and he will renounce you to your face." (Job 1:10–11) Satan believed that Job's righteousness was due entirely to his happy and successful life. If his riches, family, and health were withdrawn, he would surely abandon his faith.

God then did something that's somewhat unbelievable. He permitted the Satan to afflict Job in any way he wished, but not to take his life: "The Lord said to Satan, 'Behold, all that he has is in your power. Only against his soul do not send forth your hand.'" (Job 1:12)

Given such license, the Satan wasted no time in reducing Job into the most pitiful hard-luck, riches-to-rags case imaginable: "… There came a messenger to Job, and said, 'The oxen were plowing, and the donkeys feeding beside them, and the Sabeans attacked, and took them away. Yes, they have killed the servants with the edge of the sword, and I alone have escaped to tell you.' While he was still speaking, there also came another, and said, 'The fire of God has fallen from the sky, and has burned up the sheep and the servants, and consumed them, and I alone have escaped to tell you.' While he was still speaking, there came also another, and said, 'The Caldeans made three bands, and swept down on the camels, and have taken them away, yes, and killed the servants with the edge of the sword; and I alone have escaped to tell you.' While he was still speaking, there came also another, and said, 'Your sons and your daughters were eating and drinking wine in their eldest brother's house, and behold, there came a great wind from the wilderness, and struck the four corners of the house, and it fell on the young men, and they are dead. I alone have escaped to tell you.' Then Job arose, and tore his robe, and shaved his head, and fell down on the ground, and worshiped. He said, 'Naked I came out of my mother's womb, and naked shall I return there. The Lord gave, and the Lord has taken away. Blessed be the name of the Lord.' In all this, Job did not sin, nor charge God with wrongdoing." (Job 1:14–22)

Eventually Job's very flesh was afflicted with boils and disease and he was bedridden. His wife, who bore witness to these inhuman tragedies, responded in a most human way. She suggested Job use the only weapon of retaliation, his tongue, and "let God have it:" "Then his wife said to him, 'Do you still maintain your integrity? Renounce God, and die!'" (Job 2:9)

Job's response was almost as paranormal (that is, angelic) as his wife's was natural: "But he said to her, 'You speak as one of the foolish women would speak. What? Shall we receive good at the hand of God, and shall we not receive misfortune?' In all this Job didn't sin with his lips." (Job 2:10–11)

Lord Knows

Job's words are the basis for several Jewish traditions. One of them is based on the words "Naked I came out of my mother's womb, and naked shall I return there. The Lord gave, and the Lord has taken away. Blessed be the name of the Lord." These verses help form the text of a service called Tzidduk HaDin, where mourners for loved ones at the cemetery acknowledge the ultimate righteous judgment of God over their loss. The verse "Shall we receive good at the hand of God, and shall we not accept misfortune?" alludes to this concept as well, namely one blesses over misfortune just as he does over good tidings.

Job's Friends

When Job's three friends heard of all this evil that had come on him, they each came from very distant locations to sympathize and comfort him: "And when they lifted their eyes afar off, and knew him not, they lifted up their voice and wept; and they rent every one his coat, and sprinkled dust upon their heads toward heaven. And they sat down with him on the ground for seven days and seven nights, and none spoke a word to him; for they saw that his suffering was great." (Job 2:12–13)

After the first few chapters that introduce us to Job and the details of his tragedy, the book transitions into a group of eight speeches or responses of Job. Each time one of Job's friends spoke, he responded. Job's answers to his "comforters" show that he carried mixed feelings about God and his experience. He laments his lot, he requests to die, and indicates that he is really struggling with his sorry fate.

When Job does open up in front of his dear colleagues, he seems to be taking things so hard that he curses God in his heart, but does not express it on his lips. However, his friends are a bit shocked when Job curses the day he was born: "After this, opened Job his mouth, and cursed his day. And Job spoke, and said: Let the day perish wherein I was born, and the night wherein it was said: 'A man-child is brought forth.' Let that day be darkness; let not God inquire after it from above, neither let the light shine upon it." (Job 3:1–4)

The Sages Say _____

The story of Job and his three friends is remarkable as you continue reading. In fact, the Talmud tells us that not only did they travel from different parts of the world, but they arrived together at the exact same time to console him. Being this wasn't the age of telecommunications, exactly how did they all receive the tragic news about Job at the same time?

According to one commentary in the Talmud, Job and his comrades had crowns upon which their faces were engraved. When misfortune or sorrow befell any of them the image of that person's face would miraculously turn sad on all their crowns. This was a distress signal and the friends would come to help. Many enigmatic passages found in the Talmud are interpreted symbolically—this one might be no exception. Perhaps these crowns were a metaphor for wisdom. They were attached to each other through the bounds of wisdom. Being unselfish and devoted friends allowed them to bond in a way that transcended conventional limitations of time and space. Thus they were able to simultaneously hear Job's distress signal and responded as true friends would.

Bottom line, he does not curse his Maker. Later he will voice complaint again: "I was at ease and He broke me apart, He took me by the neck and dashed me to pieces … His archers surround me … He breaks me again and again, He runs upon me like a giant. Although there is no violence in my hands, and my prayer is pure." (Job 16:12–14,17) He is perplexed that these things have befallen him. Regardless, throughout all this suffering he refuses to blaspheme The Almighty.

Piety or Foolishness

Job's self-control is even more remarkable inasmuch as even Eliphaz, the first of his friends to speak up, seemed to take Job to task for not unburdening his soul of all his grief and verbally retaliating against God. The implication is that Job's blind faith and simplistic fear of Heaven is actually seen as a liability and not a praiseworthy virtue: "Then answered Eliphaz the Temanite, and said: If one venture a word unto thee, wilt thou be weary? But who can withhold himself from speaking? … Is not your fear of Heaven, the folly of your hope and simplistic way?" (Job 4:1–2,6)

Job and then his friends devoted much time to finding a rational explanation for his misfortune. With the exception of Elihu, they could find none, and therefore they concluded that Job could not have been as righteous as they had previously thought. They reasoned that God doesn't gratuitously punish someone. Nonetheless, this must have caused considerable discomfort to Job and his friends would be taken to task for their actions. Above all, friends should be sensitive to pain and suffering of each other, and it was bad timing for them to imply that God might have justifiably afflicted Job.

Job rejected their deduction, knowing full well that he had done everything in his power to be a loyal servant to God. After his friends took leave of him and God Himself paid Job a visit, he took the opportunity to question God about what had befallen him. The book then turns into a series of Job's soliloquies, or speeches to himself, concerning his perplexing, mind-numbing calamity.

Eliphaz, along with his other two friends, all eventually fail to console Job and reconcile him with God over this tragedy. In the last chapter, God takes them to task for not only neglecting to comfort and advise their holy brother in the way that he needed to go, but for speaking against their Creator as well: "And it was so, that after God had spoken these words unto Job, God said to Eliphaz the Temanite: 'My wrath is kindled against thee, and against thy two friends; for you have not spoken of Me the thing that is right, as My servant Job has." (Job 42:7)

God Consoles Job

In Job's responses to his friends and speeches to himself, he persisted in his innocence and the unjustness of God's decree. However, rather than sympathize with Job, God took him to task for even questioning His judgment. He rhetorically laid into Job: "Who is this who disgraces [My judgment, which is made with] secret wisdom, with words [which he speaks] without knowledge [of the secret wisdom]? … Where were you when I founded the earth? Tell [Me] if you have knowledge to understand its foundation?" (Job 38:1–4)

God then proceeded to take Job on an eye-opening tour of the universe, showing him the fantastic wisdom with which He fashioned creation. Curiously, despite the fact that God seemed to ignore Job's own personal tragedy in His response, Job was placated and humbled even more: "Behold, I am worthless, so how can I answer You? I place my hand on my mouth. I have spoke once, and I won't respond [again]. A second time, I will not [complain] anymore." (Job 40:4–5)

Job felt ashamed that he ever doubted the workings of his Creator. Awestruck by the divine wisdom he was just shown, he intuited that as smart as man may be, compared to God, his vision of reality was still extremely restricted. That was the lesson, Job ultimately learned, albeit he learned it in a more harsh way than anyone else.

Toward the middle and end of the book, we find Job a man of strengthened faith through his afflictions, which is the best result one can hope for in reaction to the righteous suffering. Some verses indicate that God, communicating to Job through incomprehensible suffering, would eventually be understood, even if that would only happen for Job in the grave: "But as for me, I know that my Redeemer lives, And that He will witness at the last upon the dust, And when after my skin is destroyed, then from my underlying flesh shall I see God; … And my eyes shall behold, and not another's …. (Job 19:25–27)

A Happy Ending

Most tragedies like this one don't merit a happy ending. This one is an exception. Technically, it wouldn't seem to matter as Job passed this test with flying colors. Even the injustices experienced by Job, and his right to vocalize them, were not refuted by God. He could die, never having blasphemed God and as a complete penitent.

Nonetheless, God did not withhold His blessings and granted Job a reversal of his heart-wrenching misfortunes: "And God changed the fortune of Job, when he prayed for his friends; and God gave Job twice as much as he had before. Then came there unto him all his brethren, and all his sisters, and all they that had been of his acquaintance before, and did eat bread with him in his house; and they bemoaned him, and comforted him concerning all the evil that God had brought upon him; every man also gave him a piece of money, and every one a ring of gold. So God blessed the latter end of Job more than his beginning; and he had fourteen thousand sheep, and six thousand camels, and a thousand yoke of oxen, and a thousand she-asses. He had also seven sons and three daughters. And he called the name of the first, Jemimah; and the name of the second, Keziah; and the name of the third, Keren-happuch. And in all the land were no women found so fair as the daughters of Job; and their father gave them inheritance among their brethren. And after this Job lived a hundred and forty years, and saw his sons, and his sons' sons, even four generations. So Job died, being old and full of days." (Job 42:10–17)

With this remarkable conclusion to this book of Scripture we find Job setting an eternal example of a man strengthened of faith through his afflictions—and ultimately vindicated—which is the scenario when the righteous suffer.

The Least You Need to Know

- Job's existence is debated among scholars. Some say he lived in the time of Abraham. Others believe that the entire story of Job was a fabrication to teach a moral lesson.

- The seemingly unfair reality that the righteous suffer is a major theme of the Book of Job. Testing faith and loyalty through pain and suffering is a part of life, and Judaism.

- The Book of Job was written as a series of speeches between Job and his friends who came to console him in his loss; between Job and himself, and between God and Job.

- Job's answers to his "comforters" showed his mixed feelings about God. Yet he never cursed his Maker out loud.

Part 6

Writings Part II:
The Five Scrolls

The Five Scrolls (in Hebrew, the Five *Megillot*) are books that, at first glance, might not seem like they have much in common. But their being grouped together actually makes a lot of sense. These books all address various aspects of human experience and emotion. The story of Esther, for example, expresses rejoicing—over salvation from a notorious enemy— and it is read on the holiday of Purim. Lamentations, on the other hand, evokes a sentiment of mourning and is publicly read on Tisha B'av, the day of Jewish national mourning. The other three are read at other occasions during the year.

Sacred Love Song: The Song of Songs

In This Chapter

- ◆ Readings of love or lust?
- ◆ A love poem to God
- ◆ Passover and public readings
- ◆ The Ten Songs

"Let him kiss me with the kisses of his mouth …" (Song of Songs 1:2)

"Thy two breasts are like two fawns, twins of a gazelle, which feed among the lilies." (Song of Songs 4:5)

Pretty risqué stuff, isn't it? Song of Songs, the first book in Megillah, or Five Scrolls, is full of it. Read one way, the prose in this most unusual book is an amazing love poem, and racy enough to make anyone blush. But there are deeper meanings to the romantic musings penned centuries ago by a love-intoxicated young king.

Solomon's complex originality meets new heights in this work. We will examine this most unique book that "cries out" for explanation.

Sweet Songs from Solomon

Song of Songs is the last of King Solomon's writings included in Jewish Scripture. It's believed the king wrote them early in his reign, roughly around 965 B.C.E. Some critics have rejected his authorship, believing the songs were about Solomon, not written by him, and were collected at a later date. However, there's much about this book that supports the traditional belief that Solomon wrote it.

Solomon might have just stepped up to the plate as king, but he had already amassed a sizeable number of wives—anywhere from around 100 to 1,000, depending on the source. As such, it's somewhat hard to believe that he would devote such lavish attention to just one woman, as he does in these writings. Maybe, just maybe, he isn't.

If you read Song of Songs in a Christian Old Testament, you'll see the woman in Song of Songs identified as The *Shulamite*, and the other players in the love song identified as "The Beloved," "The Daughters of Jerusalem," "Her Brothers," and so on.

Read Song of Songs in a Tanakh, however, and you might see the players identified as "Israel," "Israel to God," "God responds to Israel," "Israel to the nations," and so on. This is the first clue to the deeper meaning of Song of Songs.

Many people read this book at this very basic level, and they delight in the gorgeous prose. But even at its most simplistic level, it's hard to miss the allegory in this book, as it's laden with it.

Tower of Babel

The term **Shulamite** might have been derived from the town of Shunem, located southwest of the Sea of Galilee in the tribal area of Issachar. According to some sources, the Shulamite was a shepherd's wife whose beauty kindled a strong passion in Solomon. He endeavored to win her for his harem, but refrained, avoiding repetition of his father David's indiscretion. Another theory is that the name Shulamite is associated with Avishag (I Kings 1:3), who after David's death became prominent in Solomon's court in Jerusalem.

A Love Poem to God?

Here's what Rashi, one of the most famous commentators, has to say about Solomon's writings: "This song itself, representing the Jewish people, is uttered with her mouth in her exile and in her living widowhood, 'If only the God would kiss her with the kisses of his mouth, as in ancient times; for there are places where they kiss on the back of the hand or on the shoulder, but I (the Jewish people) desire and long for him to conduct himself with me as at first, as a groom to a bride, mouth to mouth …'" (Rashi Commentary to Tanakh)

"… This is its literal meaning and, according to its allegorical meaning, it was said in reference to the fact that He gave them His Torah and spoke to them face to face; and that love is still sweet to them, more than any delight. And he is assuring them that He will once again appear to them to explain the secrets of its (that is, the Torah's) reasons and its hidden intricacies; so they beseech Him to fulfill His word. And this is the meaning of 'Let him kiss me with the kisses of his mouth.'" (Ibid)

In other words, Rashi and other commentators believe that Song of Songs, even taking its literal meaning, is an everlasting allegory of the relationship between God and the Jewish people, cloaked in terms of the love between a man and a woman.

> **The Sages Say**
>
> The sages use the metaphor of betrothal and love to specifically describe the relationship the Jewish people entered with God when they received the Ten Commandments. With this as a historical backdrop, it's easy to understand why Song of Songs is publicly recited on Passover, the holiday that celebrates the liberation of the Jewish people from slavery in Egypt and put the people in a position to receive God's word at Mount Sinai. In some communities, the eight chapters of Song of Songs are recited in unison in synagogue before the evening prayers of each Sabbath night.

Holy of Holies

Judaism regards the marital bond between a man and his wife as potentially holy. The sages of Israel, however, thought King Solomon had gone a bit too far with what appeared to be thoroughly erotic prose and wanted to exclude it from the Hebrew Scriptures. Rabbi Akiva, on the other hand, argued for including it. He said that if all the other books were considered holy, then Song of Songs must be considered the holiest of the holy because all the allegory it contains comes from a holy place.

What is that holy place? King Solomon wrote these words in his youth—about the same time he completed the construction of the First Temple in Jerusalem (833 B.C.E.). The Temple was intended to represent the earthly personification of the Revelation at Mount Sinai.

Solomon's logic was simple—just as God's divine presence descended on that holy mountain, so, too, would it reside in the holy Temple. Therefore, this great edifice would enlighten the Jewish people where the Almighty could transmit His Word to mere mortals. Surely, something to sing about!

These mortals would include gentiles as well. Isaiah spoke of a future time when the third and final Temple would rally all nations of faith to this central location to bask in the divine light. Well, that is precisely what happened in Solomon's time. Dignitaries from all over the globe came to pay tribute to the wisest man on earth. World peace was never as palpable as it was during the 40-year reign of Solomon. Wine flowed like the Tigris River from the barrels of his wine cellar, and every imaginable delicacy was to be had from his royal chefs.

Lord Knows

Jewish tradition teaches that the highest form of relationship between an individual and the Creator is one based on love. Reverence or awe of God is a good thing; it serves as a deterrent for a person to avoid sin and to avoid harming others. Love of one's Maker, however, transcends the level of a relationship based on fear. The gist of this principle is that when a man loves a particular woman, he cannot remove her from his thoughts; so, too, should such intensity be reserved for one's love of God.

Amidst this opulence and extravagance, coupled with the mind-boggling number of wives, one might think Solomon was simply self-indulgent. Nothing could be further from the truth. Great minds such as Rabbi Akiva wouldn't consider Song of Songs as the "holiest of the holy," if its author was anything less than holy himself.

King Solomon had a master plan to unite all pagan nations under the banner of monotheism. His many wives were all princesses and daughters of the most esteemed leaders of the world. His dazzling architectural designs, lavish feasts, and demonstrations of his wisdom and cleverness were all intended for one purpose only—to glorify the King of Kings, God Almighty. It is with this historical backdrop that Solomon's love poetry is best understood.

Song of Songs can be seen as an allegory of a young and beautiful woman who is betrothed and then married by a monarch. Not long after the nuptials, she is unfaithful to him, causing him to banish her from his palace. She now gains the status of "living widowhood," which means as if a widow.

Our king cannot get over his love for his erstwhile bride and behind the scenes, keeps a watchful eye over her, to protect her. When she commits to return to him, and remain faithful, he will take her back in a heartbeat, with a passion and love at full strength.

> **Lord Knows**
>
> In trying to understand God, the writers of Scripture sometimes used anthropomorphic expressions to allow us to relate. "God is a 'man of war,'" and "The eyes of God are upon the land," are a couple of examples. The use of allegory in the Song of Songs is one example of this, and the best indication that its true meaning transcends the scope of mundane comprehension.

Let's take a look at another verse to embellish this point: "Behold, thou art fair, my love; thou art fair; thine eyes are as doves in front of thy braids: thy hair is like a flock of goats that cascades down from mount Gilead." (Song of Songs 4:1)

The Talmudic sage Rabbi Yochanan says that this refers to Israel at Mount Sinai. "They were as a flock that was not faint when they were in front of Mount Sinai. 'In front of your braids' is similar to the concentration of hair in a braid. Similarly, the people of Israel concentrated their thoughts to hear each commandment and were not faint hearted. On the contrary, they were filled with awe, trembling with sweat. The expression 'That cascades down from mount Gilead' refers to Mount Sinai which Israel cascaded from." (Song of Songs Rabbah 4:1)

Near the end of the book we find another enigmatic and somewhat steamy example of Solomon's Scripture, which might very well be interpreted closer to its literal meaning: "O that you were like my brother, who sucked at my mother's breasts! I would find you outside, I would kiss you, and they would not despise me." (Song of Songs 8:1)

To the Jewish people, kissing in public is an act of immodesty regardless of whether between sister/brother, husband/wife, etc. According to traditional sources, this verse is essentially a message from the maiden to her betrothed, similar to: "I long to kiss you in the street, in public, but I am embarrassed lest I be put to shame. If only you would be to me as my infant brother, who still sucks my mother's breasts and whose sister is not ashamed to kiss him in public."

One more glimpse of the allegorical Wisdom of Solomon is found in the same chapter: "His left hand supports my head, and His right embraces me. I bind you with an oath daughters of Jerusalem not to arouse the love until it is desired" (Song of Songs 8:3–4)

King Solomon is understood to depict Israel addressing the nations as if to say despite my bemoaning the long Exile, God's 'left hand' still supports my head, yet His right embraces me in (greater) support. Symbolically, the left, in Jewish thought, alludes to strict judgment, while the right connotes mercy. In this regard, even when God judges His people of Israel He provides a hand to support them. But when He extends His 'right hand' with mercy He not only supports, but also actively embraces.

The Song of All Songs

According to tradition, King Solomon wrote more than 1,000 songs, but Song of Songs stands out from them all. As the sages say, "the whole world is not as worthy as the day on which the Song of Songs was given to Israel; for all the Writings are holy but the Song of Songs is the Holy of Holies." (Tractate Yodayim 3:5)

That said, the concept of song in the Hebrew Bible is quite different from how we customarily understand it.

The significance of composing the appropriate song for the occasion that gives thanks and acknowledges God's benevolence and deliverance cannot be understated. In fact, neglecting or failing to do so could have dire consequences.

In Jewish history, there are only 10 instances where the inspired writings of leaders, prophets, sages, or the general populace qualified for the appellation "song." They are as follows:

- Adam's song, composed when he realized that his sin had been forgiven and the Sabbath had come as a form of protection. King David captured this notion when he wrote Psalm 92, "A Psalm, A Song for the Sabbath Day."

- The song that Moses and the Jewish people sang when they witnessed the splitting of the Red Sea. "Then Moses and the Children of Israel sang this song." (Exodus 15:1)

- The song sung by the Children of Israel when they were given a well of water. This is alluded to as *"Then Israel sang."* (Numbers 21:17)

- The song Moses sang just before he died, *"Give ear O heavens and I will speak ..."* (Deuteronomy 32:1)

- The song sung by Joshua when he performed the miracle of the sun standing still. It is found beginning with the words "Then Joshua spoke." (Joshua 10:12)

- The song attributed to the judges Barak and Deborah, sung when Sisera, the Assyrian leader, was delivered into their hands. (Judges 5:1)

- The song sung by Hannah when she finally gives birth to a son (the prophet Samuel). (I Samuel 2:1)

- The song sung by David in recognition of all the miraculous events in his life. (II Samuel 22:1)

The scroll Song of Songs is counted as the ninth song. The tenth, according to Isaiah, will be sung when the exiled 10 Tribes are finally redeemed and returned to Israel.

The Least You Need to Know

- King Solomon, in Song of Songs, was recapping a 480-year romantic love affair between the Jewish people and God that reached its crescendo with the building of the Temple. He completed the Song of Songs at the same time he completed the Temple.

- Song of Songs was considered by some sages as the most holy of Scripture. Its simple meaning is a poetic allegory of this love affair between God and the Jewish people.

- Song of Songs, which contains prophetic messages, is read publicly in Jewish communities on the Sabbath of the Passover holiday. It is also recited publicly in certain communities each Sabbath night.

- There are 10 songs that were uttered by certain people from the time of Adam until the coming of the Messiah. Solomon's was one of them, and the greatest.

Chapter 24

The Royal Mother: The Book of Ruth

In This Chapter

◆ Chaotic times

◆ Righteous conversion

◆ Matchmaker, matchmaker

◆ An unlikely pair

"For where you go, I will go; where you lodge, I will lodge." These words, or a variation of them, are often part of marriage ceremonies, spoken as words of fidelity between husband and wife. Interestingly, they were originally exchanged between a daughter and a mother-in-law.

What would make a woman speak so earnestly to the mother of her husband? The answer is in the Book of Ruth, which is one of the most inspiring and endearing stories in the Bible. It's also the story of the Bible's most fascinating convert and of the unlikely pairing of two individuals who would become the forebears of the royal family of Israel.

Times of Chaos

The story of Ruth is set in approximately 973 B.C.E., during a period of chaos in Jewish history. These are the difficult days of the Judges, a time marred by rebellion, immorality, and a general social decline. By contrast, Ruth is a godly woman, a paragon of integrity and righteousness. So, too, are Boaz, her future husband, and Naomi, her mother-in-law from a previous marriage. Their story symbolizes the fact that people of faith and conviction can always be found, even when the world seems more corrupt than not.

The authorship of the short Book of Ruth—it only contains four chapters—is traditionally credited to the prophet Samuel. There are a couple of good reasons for this attribution. First, the author of Ruth uses the same biblical Hebrew prose idioms and classical syntax found in the Book of Samuel. Second, the book's setting captures the period of the Judges in a uniform manner that would be very familiar for Samuel. Some argue against the possibility of Samuel as author because they hold to a later date for Ruth for various reasons. What isn't in dispute is the talent of Ruth's author. He crafted a beautiful work containing strong messages about love, devotion, and redemption. It is beloved by Jews and non-Jews alike for its literary beauty and great spiritual value.

It Is Written

In composing the four chapters of Ruth, the author also reveals the origins of the kingship of the House of David. Ruth is a Moabite princess who converted to Judaism, motivated by her love and dedication to her mother-in-law. By marriage, she also becomes King David's great-grandmother.

The action in Ruth takes place in four settings:

- The country of Moab. This is Ruth's homeland, to which she returns with Naomi after both their husbands die.

- A field in Bethlehem. Ruth works in this field, which happens to be owned by her future husband.

- The floor of a threshing room in Bethlehem. Naomi sends Ruth here so she can meet Boaz.

- The city of Bethlehem. Here, Boaz claims Ruth as his own.

When the Judges Judged

The Scroll of Ruth opens with an interesting statement about the state of affairs in the Israelite nation several years before its first king, Saul:

"And it happened in the days when the Judges judged, and there was a famine in the land, and a man went from Bethlehem in Judah to dwell in the fields of Moab." (Ruth 1:1)

Judges were quasi-monarchs who governed the Jewish people from the time of Joshua until their first anointed king, Saul—a period spanning 400 years.

It Is Written

Talmudic writings observe that the statement "when the Judges judged" is a veiled criticism of the judges. God was judging the judges and this judgment was the cause of the famine, an oft-used divine punishment in biblical times.

Elimelech and His Family

The man referred to in the first verses of Ruth is Elimelech of Bethlehem. To escape the famine in Judah, Elimelech moved his wife and sons to Moab. This was enemy territory for the Jews; Elimelech's willingness to expose his family to some danger indicates that the famine was severe.

Sometime after the move—an exact time frame isn't given—Elimelech died, leaving Naomi to dwell in a foreign land with her two sons. They both took Moabite wives—Ruth and Orpah. About 10 years go by, and both men die.

After losing her husband and her sons, Naomi decided she'd had quite enough with Moab. She was convinced that her losses happened because she turned away from her people years earlier, and she was determined to go home, despite the scorn and ridicule she expected to receive upon returning to the Land of Judah.

On the Road to Bethlehem

Naomi left Moab and set out for Bethlehem. She allowed her daughters-in-law to accompany her at first, but something happened. Perhaps Naomi realized that bringing these two Moabite women would not exactly endear her to her former neighbors and kinsfolk. Nor did it bode well for these foreign women. She empathized with them and looked to their future contentment and consolation, which she believed could only be found if they stayed with the familiar surroundings of the fields of Moab.

Either way, she stopped and said: "Go, return each of you to her mother's house. May God deal kindly with you as you have dealt kindly with the dead and with me … She kissed them and raised her voice and she wept." (Ruth 1:8–9)

However, both women remained loyal to this woman with whom they shared a common bond and fate. They insisted on staying together: "And they said to her, '(No), we will return with you to your people.'" (Ruth 1:10)

Naomi, however, was adamant. She wanted the girls gone, and she wanted them gone now.

"But Naomi said, 'Turn back my daughters. Why should you desire to come with me? Have I more sons in my womb that could become husbands to you? Return my daughters; go back, for I am too old to have a husband. Even if I were to say, there is hope for me and even were I to take a husband tonight and eventually bear sons—would you wait for them 'til they were grown? Would you anchor yourselves down for them and not marry anyone else? No, my daughters, I am excessively embittered on account of you for the hand of the Lord has gone against me." (Ruth 1:11–13)

One can almost feel the anguish in Naomi's words. She loved these women, but she also saw them as part of the reason why she lost her sons. God's wrath had been against her by virtue of her sons marrying these non-Jewish women. Notwithstanding their loyalty and righteousness, she again insisted they return to their homeland.

 The Sages Say

Naomi tells her daughters-in-law to turn or go back three times. One of the most famous of the late medieval commentators, Alshich, points out that these words were spoken on the road "to return to the land of Judah," and their intention was not out of simple courtesy to Naomi, but a desire to convert to Judaism. Naomi's response to them forms the basis of a Jewish law, namely to discourage a potential proselyte three times before relenting and welcoming them onboard.

The Righteous Convert

Orpah finally decided to take her mother-in-law's advice. She kissed and embraced her and left. Naomi expected Ruth to follow suit, but she was in for a surprise here.

Instead of deserting Naomi, Ruth affirmed her loyalty to her mother-in-law and her people, in one of the most profound and moving orations in Scripture: "Do not urge me to leave you, to turn back from following you. For where you go, I will go; where you lodge, I will lodge; your people are my people, and your God is my God. Where you die I will die, and there I will be buried. May the Lord do this to me—and more!—If anything but death separates me from you!" (Ruth 1:16–17)

In telling Naomi "Your people are my people," Ruth declared her intention to share a common God with her mother-in-law. Put another way, she was converting to Naomi's beliefs.

From the writings here, we derive another important detail of Jewish law. Ruth said first "Your people are my people," meaning, "I accept to become part of your nation. I accept the same destiny, the same obligation to suffer as part of the Jewish people." It's only after that declaration that she can accept "Your God is My God," for now she can share a common God. After the convert is willing to accept this common destiny, Judaism enthusiastically embraces him/her.

What compelled Ruth to take the plunge? What inspired this noblewoman to sacrifice the comforts of her princely origins to follow this forlorn lady into the great unknown? Simply put, Ruth loved Naomi. She could be a little prickly at times, as many mothers-in-law can be. She saw herself as utterly useless and empty. Her ordeal in Moab, going from riches to rags, was a humbling experience. But in general, Naomi lived up to her name, which means "pleasant."

It was Naomi's personality that Ruth found so evocatively appealing. It was this, not any intellectual evaluation of Judaism's basic truths, that drew Ruth closer to Naomi, and in doing so, closer to Naomi's god.

Lord Knows

If you read an Old Testament translation of Ruth, it might look like Naomi wasn't pleased with Ruth's choice, regardless of why she made it. In the New King James version, the verses note "When she saw that she was determined to go with her, she stopped speaking to her." (Ruth 1:18) In the Stone translation of the Tanakh, the same verse reads "When she saw that she was determined to go with her, she stopped arguing with her."

An Unlikely Match

Ruth and Naomi finally arrived in Bethlehem, where it appeared that Naomi was given a warm welcome. But Naomi deflected the attention, stating that "the Almighty has dealt very bitterly with me. I went out full, and the Lord has brought me home again empty." She also insisted that people quit calling her Naomi, which, as noted, means "pleasant one." Instead, she wanted her new name to be Mara, which means "embittered one."

As it happened, the two women arrived in Bethlehem during harvest season. Virtually penniless, Ruth asked Naomi's permission to go to the fields and gather grain from the forgotten sheaves and individual grains that the owner of the land left behind for the poor.

Lord Knows
Biblical writers often used the word "behold" to draw the reader's attention to something special or out of the ordinary. In Ruth, the word was used to announce Boaz's arrival at his fields. It was clearly providential that Boaz should arrive at his field precisely at the time Ruth was gleaning.

Ruth made an interesting comment here about gathering the grain "in the presence of someone in whose eyes I shall find favor." (Ruth 2:2) Is she looking for a new husband? Keeping herself open for the potential? Either way, it doesn't take long for her to find favor in someone's eyes.

As it turns out, a man named Boaz owned the fields in which Ruth toiled. As the main judge of the time and the head of the Sanhedrin, the Jewish Supreme Court, Boaz was a man of tremendous prestige and admiration. He also happened to be the nephew of Naomi's deceased husband.

When Boaz saw Ruth, he asked who she belonged to. His harvesters told him she was a Moabite woman who arrived in town with Naomi. Impressed with her industriousness and her kindness toward her widowed mother-in-law, Boaz addressed Ruth as "my daughter" and invited her to glean exclusively from his fields where she would not be harassed or molested.

Although much older than Ruth, Boaz was clearly taken with her and continued to ply her with favors. She was invited to drink from the water drawn by his servants. At mealtime, when Boaz would eat with his workers, he included her at the head table. However, her modesty inclined her to stay with the harvesters.

Being a sensitive man and good judge of character, Boaz saw something subtle and sublime in Ruth. He was awestruck by her extraordinarily modest behavior: When she spied grains of barley on the ground, she declined to bend down to pick them up—in spite of the fact that it would have been the easiest and most efficient way of collecting. No, she made a point of sitting down to pick them up. Ruth's refined nature was not lost on the patriarch. He knew she was a keeper, and destined to become his wife.

Matchmaker, Matchmaker

When Ruth arrived home, Naomi asked her where she had worked, so that the "one that took [such generous] notice of you be blessed." Ruth told Naomi about Boaz, whom Naomi immediately recognized as a close relation. In fact, he was a *redeeming kinsman*.

Even with the age difference, both Naomi and Ruth perceived Boaz's actions in the field as a strong indication that he was thinking of taking her as a wife. Doing so perpetuated the memory of Ruth's deceased husband, as a kinsman who would be "redeeming" her and the real property that was part of his estate. In so doing, Boaz would also fulfill the Jewish tradition of *Levirate marriage*.

Boaz, however, seemed to be a bit of a reluctant suitor. By the end of the harvest, he still hadn't made his move. The two women were naturally concerned that fate would pass them by. Naomi feared that once out of sight, Ruth would be forgotten and a Moabite convert, even one as modest and polished as she, was just not that desirable.

Naomi decided to take fate into her own hands with a very audacious and unconventional plan. She told Ruth to bathe, anoint, don her Sabbath finest, and to make an unannounced entry into Boaz's tent.

Boaz was at first startled by Ruth's bold entry. After all, here was a woman who he prized for her refinement and virtue. However, he quickly gathered his composure and proclaimed that Ruth had "made your latest act of kindness greater than the first—that you have not gone after the younger men—poor or rich … Do not fear, all that you request I will do—for all people in the gate of the city know that you are a worthy woman." (Ruth 3:11)

Seemingly, Ruth and Naomi now had their redeemer, the person who would restore to Ruth

> **Lord Knows**
>
> Parts of chapter 3 of Ruth read like a racy soap opera. However, the intentions of these two women were entirely for the "sake of Heaven," and should be understood in that context. They felt that only the most draconian measures might arouse Boaz to take on his obligations to the family of his dead uncle Elimelech. In the end, the plan worked.

and Naomi all that they had lost—marriage and offspring for Ruth, redeemer care for Naomi. But Ruth soon learned that the redeemer responsibility fell on someone other than Boaz. Boaz told her there was another male relative—a *ploni almoni*—someone closer to the family than he was. He told Ruth to stay the night. He would straighten things out in the morning.

> ### Tower of Babel
>
> A **redeeming kinsman** was a male relative on a woman's dead husband's side. In Jewish tradition, when a man passes away without leaving any children, this man would fulfill the precept called *Yibum* or **Levirate marriage** to be performed by a surviving brother. (Deuteronomy 25:5–10) This Torah law obligates one of the male relatives of a man who died before having children to marry his widow. This guarantees the perpetuation of the deceased's memory. **Ploni almoni** means "unnamed, anonymous one." Because this redeemer shirked his duty and didn't marry Ruth, the author of Ruth hid his name.

The Ploni Ploy

The next day, Boaz confronted the other redeemer and convinced him to yield his role. He told the man that Naomi had a plot of land for sale that had belonged to Elimelech, and that they were the only two people who could redeem it.

Ploni had no problem with this part of the deal. A little extra real estate couldn't hurt—so why not. However, when Boaz informed him that he would have to take the Moabite convert as a wife, he demurred. He was not prepared to take such a step. In his defense, he was not so sure of the newly publicized exemption of females in the prohibition against Moabite converts. Boaz, the head of the Jewish Supreme Court and a formidable scholar, had big enough shoulders to support his actions: "When the redeemer (Ploni Almoni) said to Boaz, 'Redeem them yourself,' He drew off his shoe." (Ruth 4:8)

Scripture here emphasizes that it was at one time customary for the people in Israel to transact and consummate business dealings by removing their shoe and handing it to the other person. According to Jewish law, whenever a monetary transaction occurred, such transactions could be consummated by a symbolic barter—even before money or property was presented. In this case, it was Boaz removing his shoe and handing it to Ploni Almoni, to acquire all the rights of redemption concerning Naomi and Ruth.

Boaz had now cleared the way for his marriage to Ruth. He announced this on the spot before those gathered at the gate of the city. The people enthusiastically responded: "We are witnesses. May God place the woman who is entering your house like Rachel and like Leah, both of whom built up the House of Israel. May you prosper in Efrat and be renowned in Bethlehem. And may your house become like the house of Peretz whom Tamar bore to Judah—through the offspring that God will grant you through this young woman." (Ruth 4:11–12)

Indeed, the people spoke almost prophetically. God allowed Ruth to conceive the very same night her marriage to Boaz was consummated. The child's name was Obed. He was the father of Jesse, who in turn was the father of the man who would become the King of Israel.

> ### Lord Knows
>
> The Book of Ruth is read on the holiday of Shavuot, the Pentecost. Shavuot also commemorates the anniversary of the revelation at Mount Sinai, where the Israelites were drawn into their special covenant with God. Converts like Ruth voluntarily entered that covenant to become part of the Jewish community. Shavuot is both the birthday and anniversary of the death of King David.

The Least You Need to Know

- The Book of Ruth recounts the story of the most famous convert in Jewish history.

- Ruth's story takes place during a time of national turbulence for the Israelites, who have yet to coronate a king and are ruled by the Judges.

- Naomi, Ruth's mother-in-law, helped orchestrate the fateful meeting between Ruth and Boaz.

- The Scroll of Ruth is traditionally read in Jewish congregations on the holiday of Shavuot, as this is a time of commemorating the Giving of the Torah at Mount Sinai—a covenant that includes all righteous converts.

Chapter 25

Impending Doom: The Book of Lamentations

In This Chapter

- ◆ Warnings from Jeremiah
- ◆ Weeping for generations
- ◆ Picking up the pieces
- ◆ Readings to the public

It's hard being all alone. Loneliness and isolation are arguably the most painful experiences in the realm of human experience. But for 52 years after the destruction of Solomon's Temple in 586 B.C.E., the Land of Israel—once so full of people and life—was deserted and empty.

Lamentations is a book that literally sobs over what has become of Israel, and specifically the city of Jerusalem, after Nebuchadnezzar and his Babylonian army reduced it to rubble. It is the saddest of the 24 books of the Tanakh, and many people avoid reading it for this reason. But among its anguished verses are glimpses of consolation and hope.

Fulfilling a Prophet's Warnings

Eicha, or Lamentations, according to tradition was written by the prophet Jeremiah as a poetic dirge or lament in the wake of the end of the First Temple era. It contains a vivid description of the destruction of Jerusalem by the Babylonians in 586 B.C.E. According to the Talmud, it also contains hints about the destruction of the Second Temple more than 500 years later in 70 C.E.

Tower of Babel

Eicha means "alas" or an expression of anguish or lament in Hebrew. The English title Lamentations comes from the Greek *threnoi*, a translation of the Hebrew word for "laments."

Interestingly, Lamentations appears directly after Jeremiah in the Christian Old Testament. In the Hebrew Bible, the books are separated—Jeremiah, of course, is placed with the Prophets. Lamentations appears in Writings. Some sources point to this separation as proof that Jeremiah did not write Lamentations. It is a weak argument, and since Jewish tradition holds that Jeremiah is indeed the author, we'll stick with that here.

As discussed in Chapter 14, Jeremiah spent almost 40 years cajoling, pleading with, and warning the Jewish people to change their ways or suffer the consequences. His writings in Lamentations bear witness to the fulfillment of his dire warnings.

What precipitated the fulfillment of Jeremiah's ominous predictions? Is there a connection between the wayward behavior of the Israelites and the exile and depopulation of the Land of Israel? Does this isolation and solitude of the land serve as a suitable punishment for the nation's wrongdoings? These are questions that have perplexed scholars and experts for centuries. Let's examine some potential answers.

The Sages Say

Jeremiah wrote the first four chapters of Lamentations in acrostic fashion. That is, each verse follows the order of the 22 letters of the Hebrew alphabet—the first verse begins with the letter Aleph, the second with the letter Bet, and so on, all the way through the Hebrew alphabet. Why did he do so? We don't know for sure, but the sages of the Talmud offer some possible explanations. One is that doing so reflected the fact that the Jews had transgressed the laws in every way possible—literally from A to Z (or from Aleph to Tav in the Hebrew alphabet).

A Prophet Weeps

The opening line of the Scroll of Lamentations sets the tone for the entire book and reflects Jerusalem's sad state: "Alas—she dwells in isolation. The city that was great with people has become like a widow. The finest among nations, the princess among provinces, has become a tributary!" (Lamentations 1:1)

Throughout Lamentations, Jeremiah refers to Jerusalem as "she." The sages of the Talmud explain this personification by likening Jerusalem to a widow. They stress that her bereavement would be temporary, that she was like a woman whose husband went to a foreign country with every intention of returning to her.

Lord Knows

The famous American humorist Mark Twain confirmed the depiction of Judah as "desolate without inhabitant" when he chronicled his visit to the Holy Land in 1867 in *The Innocents Abroad* or *The New Pilgrim's Progress*, when he wrote, "We traversed some miles of desolate country whose soil is rich enough but is given wholly to weeds—a silent mournful expanse ... We reached Tabor safely ... We never saw a human being along the entire route ... Even the olive and the cactus, those fast friends of a worthless soil, had almost deserted the country ... Jerusalem is mournful, dreary and lifeless ... I would not desire to live here."

Crying Bitter Tears

Jeremiah's next line also hints at another of Lamentations' main themes: "She weeps bitterly in the night ..." (Lamentations 1:2)

In Hebrew, this line actually begins with the words "Bacho Tivkeh," a repetitive phrase that literally means "weeping she shall weep!" The sages of the Talmud view this as a prophetic vision that indicates the Jewish people will weep not just once over the destruction of the First Temple in Jerusalem, but twice—for the second one as well.

There is yet another interesting connection here. The sages point out that the phrase alludes to the episode of the 12 spies who were dispatched by Moses to scout out the Land of Canaan. (Numbers 13) When these men returned from their mission and reported their findings to the Jewish people, the people wept, as it says: "the people wept that night." (Numbers 14:1) They were frightened by the prospect of encountering the inhabitants of the land—whom they perceived as giants.

The night on which the spies delivered their assessment, according to the Talmud, was in fact the Ninth of Av, which is the day observed as the national day of mourning for the Jewish people (more on this later in this chapter).

God finds their action reprehensible and as a result, decrees, "Since you wept a weeping for nothing, I will give you something to weep about." Hence, that night became the time for weeping for generations to come, and the Ninth of Av (Av is the fifth month on the Jewish calendar) remained the "appointed time" for Jewish people to mourn during their 2,000-year exile.

> **It Is Written**
>
> In June 1967, Israeli paratroopers captured the Old City of Jerusalem and made their way to the Wall. Many of the religious soldiers were overcome with emotion and leaned against the Wall spontaneously praying and crying. Far back from the Wall stood a nonreligious soldier who was also crying. His friends asked him, "Why are you crying? What do these old stones mean to you?" The soldier responded, "I am crying because I don't know why I should be crying." Although it's a sad state of affairs when an Israeli soldier has no idea of the significance of recapturing the Temple Wall, the fact that he was weeping with the Temple reflects an organic connection to the lamentations of centuries before.

Jeremiah fills this chapter and the next with more sad portrayals of Jerusalem's ruin. He continues to connect the city's sorry state of affairs to divine retribution for her people's sins and follies, and relates how those who once thought greatly of her now treat her: "Jerusalem sinned greatly, she has therefore become a wanderer. All who once respected her disparage her, for they have seen her disgrace. She herself sighs and turns away." (Lamentations 1:8)

"The Lord consumed without pity all the dwellings of Jacob; in His anger He razed the fortresses of the daughter of Judah down to the ground; He profaned the kingdom and its leaders." (Lamentations 2:2)

The Divine Hand of Retribution

Jeremiah also provided rather graphic descriptions of how Israel was overrun by its enemies: "Judah has gone into exile because of suffering and great servitude. She dwelled among the nations, but found no rest; all her pursuers overtook her in narrow straits." (Lamentations 1:3)

Following the notion that exile came as a result of specific transgressions of the people, commentators identify one of those sins in the Hebrew expression Me'oni, which means "because of suffering." They suggest that Judah went into exile because of the poor (Oni) whom they failed to properly care for. Jeremiah's words subtly allude to this idea that is a form of a *quid pro quo* (measure for measure), a way in which God deals with people.

Now that the Israelites were being led into captivity, the enemy would have no mercy on them. Scripture and Rabbinic teachings inform us that as they marched to the Euphrates River before entering into Babylon, their treatment was particularly barbaric. Nebuchadnezzar's generals took the captives in chains, marched them through the hot sun, cut them to pieces if they stopped to pray, and gave them no respite whatsoever. Jeremiah accompanied them the entire route and tried to comfort and console them.

After they reached the Euphrates, the Babylonian general figured the God of Israel was unlikely to take them back, and so he ordered his troops to let them rest. That is the meaning behind the verse in Psalm 137, "there (by the Rivers of Babylon) we sat and wept," but until there, they were not allowed to sit—walking continuously from the time they left Jerusalem.

> **The Sages Say**
>
> Another expression of their enemy's oppression is found in the verse: "I called for my lovers but they deceived me …." (Lamentations 1:19) Rashi identifies these "lovers" as nations who feigned friendship with the Jewish people. Those erstwhile neighbors were Moab, Ammon, and Egypt. The very notion of calling upon these unreliable allies was sinful and history shows how they suffered for such folly. When the captives were led through the lands of these foes, the Ishmaelites accosted them on the road and pretended to show sympathy. Tradition teaches that they ostensibly offered them food and drink, however they gave them bags filled with nothing more than air. When they placed these bags over their mouths, the hot air entered their bodies and they perished on the spot.

While still in the Land of Israel, Jeremiah warned the people to prepare drinking utensils and kneading troughs to take with them into exile. But they only scoffed at him. Indeed, when it came time to knead their dough, they had no utensils with which to work. So what did they do? They kneaded dough in pits that they dug into the ground. And when they came to eat their bread, it was full of little pebbles.

That is the explanation for Jeremiah's lament "And He ground my teeth in grit." (Lamentations 3:16)

Again we see the divine hand of retribution being meted out tit for tat; they did not share their bread with the poor, and therefore they would eat their bread in poverty—admixed with pebbles.

Acknowledging the Source of Suffering

"I have become a laughing stock to all my people; object of derision all day long." (Lamentations 3:14)

In chapter 3 of Lamentations, Jeremiah's laments take a personal tone. He made the despairs of the people his own. Imagine what a person such as Jeremiah must have felt like, labeled as the "Prophet of Doom," when his exhortations fell on deaf ears, or worse, were relentlessly ridiculed.

> **It Is Written**
>
> According to tradition, when Jeremiah returned to the Holy Land shortly after the destruction, he tore his garments and lamented, "Show me the road the exiled have taken. Which road have those who are about to perish taken? Let me die with them!" When he found that very road covered in blood, he lowered his tear-drenched face to the ground and noticed the footprints of little children who had been walking into captivity. He prostrated himself to the ground and kissed those foot-prints.
>
> When he eventually caught up to the exiles, he embraced them and they wept to-gether. He spoke to them with empathy and reprovement, "if you'd only listened to the prophecy spoken through me by the Almighty, you could have avoided these horrors. Had you wept even once while still in Zion, you would have averted this exile."

Despite suffering a terrible fate, enduring ridicule of his co-religionists, seeing their leaders, his beloved people, and his cherished Temple all destroyed, Jeremiah told the nation: "Of what shall a living man complain? A strong man for his sins! Let us search and examine our ways, and return to God." (Lamentations 3:39–40)

The prophet's question, "Of what shall a living man complain?" is difficult to under-stand. It's the nature of people to complain. Didn't Jeremiah himself experience enough to complain about? And what about the term "living man"? Dead men tell no lies, and they don't complain either. What did he mean?

Jeremiah was sharing a deep insight into the human condition. We all have questions, but such questions do not require us to obsess about always finding answers. Often, the best answer we have is to engage into deep introspection, search the inner recesses of our souls, and return to God. God did not create us to demand answers, or as a great philosopher once quipped, "If I understood God, I would be God!"

Our main objective, according to Jeremiah, is to improve the world and ultimately ourselves. He was also instructing that to survive tragedies and misfortune with our faith intact, we must turn to our own lives for the answers instead of expecting God to reveal all.

Destruction of the Second Temple

In chapter 4, Jeremiah offered a vision of what is to come when he wrote, "Rejoice and exult, O Daughter of Edom (Rome), who dwells in the land of Uz, to you also, will the cup pass, you will be drunk and vomit." (Lamentations 4:21)

Here, according to Talmudic scholars, Jeremiah foresaw the destruction of the Second Temple in 70 C.E. by the Romans. He also predicted the downfall of the Roman Empire (the cup will pass) an allusion to punishment. He also declared: "God will not exile you again," which is taken to mean that the Jews would not be exiled again following the Roman exile.

The cities of Israel are considered in a state of destruction only when other nations rule over them. Today, although the people of Israel rule over the Holy Land, they are promised that there will be no future exiles. Jeremiah's promise that Israel would not have to endure any more exiles, coupled with the imminent termination of their enemy's reign, enhances their sense of consolation that mourners over Zion and Jerusalem have experienced throughout the generations.

Perpetuation of Sin

One of the themes found in Lamentations, as well as in scattered verses throughout Tanakh, is the concept of being held accountable for sins. In fact, the prophets constantly railed against the people to improve their ways, or else. In many verses of Lamentations, Jeremiah found poetic and pithy ways of expressing this theme. However, when it came to the concept of children bearing the sins of their fathers, he was quite blunt: "Our fathers have sinned, they are no more. We (ancestors) suffer for their iniquities." (Lamentations 5:7)

When Jeremiah called attention to the sins for which the Temple would be destroyed, he looked beyond the immediate transgressors. The prophet was suggesting that children are to be held accountable as well. The commentators explain that misfortune is often the result of intermingling of our sins with those of our ancestors for which they were given a pass and not punished for—but their children bear them.

Reading Lamentations

As mentioned earlier, there is a day associated with national mourning for catastrophes affecting the Jewish people. It's called Tisha B'Av or the Ninth of Av.

Lamentations is read on the night of this day, and appropriately so. Many disasters befell the Jews on the Ninth of Av, including the following:

- The destruction of the First Temple in Jerusalem by the Babylonians in 586 B.C.E. As a result, the Kingdom of Judah (comprised of the two tribes of Judah and Benjamin) lost its independence and the population was slaughtered or exiled.

- The destruction of the second Temple by the Romans in 70 C.E. Led by Titus (known as "the evil Titus"), the Romans killed innumerable Jews and exiled the survivors throughout the Roman Empire—where they were sold as slaves. This marked the end of Jewish sovereignty over their homeland for almost 2,000 years.

- In 135 C.E., the Bar Kochba revolt against the Romans was crushed and the city of Betar, the stronghold of the rebellion, was captured and destroyed. On Tisha B'Av of the following year, the Romans plowed under the Temple Mount, and Jerusalem was rebuilt as a pagan city to which entry was forbidden to Jews. As ironic torment, only on the Ninth of Av were the Jews permitted to visit Jerusalem and to mourn the destruction of their Temple and foreign occupation of their land.

- More disasters befell the Jews on Tisha B'Av when Pope Urban II declared the First Crusade, in which tens of thousands of Jews were killed, and many Jewish communities were destroyed.

- King Ferdinand of Spain issued the expulsion decree ordering all Jews to leave Spain, setting Tisha B'Av 1492 as the final date for them to leave.

- World War I broke out on Tisha B'Av, setting the stage for the Holocaust.

- During World War II, Deportation of the Jews from the Warsaw Ghetto began on that day.

Jews observe Tisha B'Av by abstaining from food and drink from sunset till sunset. Traditional mourning customs, such as refraining from wearing leather shoes, abstaining from marital relations, and refraining from bathing, are also observed.

In the evening of Tisha B'Av, the Book of Lamentations is read in the synagogue, with lights dimmed. Only candles illuminate certain synagogues on this night. Special dirges called Kinnot are recited both in the evening and the following morning. In Israel, restaurants and places of entertainment are closed. In Jerusalem, some have the custom to walk around the walls of the Old City on the evening of Tisha B'Av.

Jewish tradition believes that when the Messiah will come, Tisha B'Av will be transformed from a day of sorrow into a day of rejoicing.

The Least You Need to Know

- The Scroll of Lamentations was written by the prophet Jeremiah in the sixth century B.C.E.

- The scroll contains dirges or sad laments concerning the situation of the Jewish First Commonwealth and warnings by the prophet Jeremiah to mend their ways or suffer exile.

- The Book of Lamentations exhorts the people to take responsibility for their actions and recognize that punishment comes as a result of unrepentant sins.

- Jeremiah does not leave the people without hope. Many passages in the scroll contain both veiled and open hints to consolation and eventual redemption from exile.

- The Lamentations scroll is read on the night of Tisha B'Av, the Jewish national day of mourning.

Chapter 26

Fearing God: The Book of Ecclesiastes

In This Chapter

- ◆ A schizophrenic king?
- ◆ The profits of labor
- ◆ A time for everything
- ◆ The curse of money

The ancient sages wanted to suppress the Book of Ecclesiastes as it makes its author—the very wise King Solomon—seem almost schizophrenic. As an example, he introduces the book with "All is vanity"—which, for all intents and purposes, reads like an indictment against the endeavors of man. But in a later chapter, he seems to praise the pursuit of physical pleasures. In one place he praises the dead over the living; in another he does just the opposite.

What's more, Solomon proclaimed that the only reason we should fear God and do His bidding is because the world's pleasures are worthless. But what if the pleasures in the world were good? Would that be a reason not to do His bidding?

What lessons can be extracted from this most unusual work that contains so many paradoxical statements? You'll find out in this chapter.

Vanity of Vanities

As Lamentations is mournful and depressing, for the most part, *Ecclesiastes* is sobering and philosophical. King Solomon, who authored Ecclesiastes, repeatedly expressed how much he had experienced in this world and how worthless all its pleasures truly are.

Solomon introduces his somber work with the famous phrase, "Vanity of vanities, all is vanity" (Ecclesiastes 1:2), and repeats this theme throughout the scroll—seven times in the inaugural verse alone! It's almost too depressing to read. In the last chapter he concludes, "At the end of everything, when all is heard (the final verdict) fear God and keep His statutes, because this is all of man." (Ecclesiastes 12:13)

> **Tower of Babel**
>
> *Ecclesiastes,* the English title of this book, comes from the Greek *ekklesiastes,* which is derived from the word *ekklesia* (assembly, congregation, or church). The Hebrew title for Ecclesiastes is *Kohelet,* which is typically translated in non-Jewish circles as "preacher" or "teacher." Its Jewish meaning comes solely from the fact that Solomon would gather or "Mekahel" (related to Kohelet) people to hear his inspired wisdom. Both titles speak to Solomon introducing these teachings to the people who regularly gathered in Jerusalem to catch pearls of his wisdom.

In fact, the keyword in Ecclesiastes is vanity—the word "vanity" actually appears no less than 37 times. In today's world, we typically define vanity as meaning excessive pride. But in Solomon's world, vanity meant something else. To Solomon, vanity expressed the futile state of trying to live a fulfilling life apart from God. It also relates to the things that we cannot understand about life because we are not God.

Some versions of Ecclesiastes translate vanity as futility, which might make more sense in today's world. Either way, what Solomon is doing in this book is imparting his wisdom on the true meaning of life, which basically boils down to this: Pursuing earthly things means nothing unless God is part of it.

Ecclesiastes is publicly read in the synagogue on the Sabbath of the intermediate days of the holiday of Succot, the Feast of Booths (generally celebrated in October). One rationale behind this practice is that because feasting and celebration are associated with this festival, levity and frivolous behavior is likely to occur. Reading Solomon's somber prose is a reality check and tempers the joy and festivities with an aura of seriousness.

Giving Readers the Vapors

As mentioned, Solomon opens Ecclesiastes with a somber view of life as being futile and perplexing. Given everything that Solomon accomplished in his life, he was more than qualified to write a treatise on what it all means. His teachings are replete with what appears to be a relentless torrent of pessimism. Some might find life full of excitement and virtually endless potential. Not King Solomon. He spilled much ink—and made extensive use of metaphor—to tell his readers that life is rather flimsy and transient, much like a vaporous windswept cloud.

We certainly know where Solomon stands on the issue, but who wants to think of life as pointless and vain? Could there be another meaning here? According to the sages of the Talmud, there is.

Hevel, the Hebrew word for vanity, also translates as breath or vapor. Solomon uses hevel no less than seven times in the very first verse. The sages of the Talmud suggest that these repetitions correspond to seven stages of a person's development. Here's how it plays out:

1. We start out as kings. A baby demands a lot of attention and we are inclined to satisfy his every whim—just like a king.

2. Then we graduate to the stage of the pig. Anyone who has had close contact with a tot can testify to how appropriate this description can be. Of course, life does not end there.

3. As a child develops, he can be compared to a frisky goat skipping around with no cares or consequences for his actions.

4. As that person grows older, he becomes like a horse. Strutting his stuff, brash and proud—who can't relate to all the prancing around we engaged in as teenagers and young adults to pursue our careers and social development?

5. Upon marriage we enter the age of the donkey. Shouldering the burden and responsibilities of our expanded families makes this a most apropos metaphor.

6. Middle age brings in its wake increased financial responsibilities as families grow in size, thus we enter the age of the dog. The dog is viewed in Talmudic literature as the most bold and brazen of all four-legged creatures. Often, people lose all sense of dignity when in the pursuit of the hard cash they need to keep their creditors at bay!

7. The monkey epitomizes the final stage. In old age what is left of that noble king is but a shadow of his former glory and dignity.

The sages teach us that this outlook on life is only provisional, and that there is an alternative meaning behind the word hevel—it can also mean wind. Likewise, *ruach*, the word for spirit, can also mean wind.

When people devote their lives to spiritual pursuits, they truly become more alive. Although it is relatively easy to identify people who act as living examples of the futility inherent to each one of life's seven stages, it is far more difficult to find examples of those who do the opposite. Therefore, in these verses Solomon was hinting to humankind's natural tendency to incline toward the very materialistic side of these stages. He wanted us to be aware that by infusing them with just a little more religious consciousness we can transform that futility into spirituality.

Futility of Labor

"So I turned to despair of all that I had achieved by laboring beneath the sun. For there is a man who labored with wisdom, knowledge and skill, yet he must hand his portion to one who has not toiled for it. This, too, is futility and great evil." (Ecclesiastes 2:20–21)

As a pretty good indication of Solomon's disgust for even successful pursuit of one's goal, he indicated that there is an inevitable, yet concealed, consequence for all one's labor and toil—the fruits may not be realized in the laborer's lifetime! Life can become futile when self-denial of one's needs never allows them to benefit from their efforts, as they are amassing this wealth for others.

On the other hand, one chapter later, Solomon praised good old-fashioned hard work: "The sleep of a laborer is sweet, whether he eats little or much, but the abundance of a rich man permits him no sleep." (Ecclesiastes 3:12)

Solomon was suggesting that there is no better sleeping pill than a hard, honest day's work. Wealth brings with it baggage that tends to get in the way of a good night's sleep: anxiety concerning keeping the riches, investing wisely, worries about being robbed, and the like. Or as one wise man once put it, "Grandeur often pays a nightly penance for the triumph of the day."

Thus, if a person's labor leads him to the sentiment of "So I saw that there is nothing better for a man than to enjoy his work, because that is his lot" (Ecclesiastes 3:22), then Solomon would conclude that a man could be happy in life if he is truly able to "enjoy his work." That depends, for the most part, on being satisfied with one's portion, and not craving unlimited (and unattainable) wealth.

A Time for Everything

For contemporary readers of biblical Scripture, one of the most well-known chapters of Ecclesiastes is chapter 3. The first eight verses of the chapter, which speak to the theme of time, were the inspiration for "Turn, Turn, Turn," written by folk legend Pete Seeger and recorded by the '60s rock group The Byrds.

The lyrics are very similar to these memorable verses:

"Everything has a season, and there is a time for everything under heaven

A time for war and a time for peace

A time to plant and a time to uproot planting

A time to kill and a time to heal

A time to destroy and a time to build

A time to weep and a time to laugh

A time to wail and a time to dance

A time to scatter stones and a time to gather them up again …

A time to love and a time to hate

A time for war and a time for peace" (Ecclesiastes 3:1–8)

Seeger used King Solomon's words to compose his tune during the Vietnam War, and it was (and is) viewed as a song of protest against war. Solomon's words, however, are not viewed as such. According to the sages of Israel, he wrote them to describe various components of war and how they affect people. For instance, the stanza about "a time to plant and a time to uproot planting" is not speaking about conventional sowing and harvesting of grain. Instead, it speaks about the need to uproot plantings that are needed for the war effort (for example, to provide raw materials for a besieging army), and a time to plant, when the campaign is over and peace is restored.

Another interpretation of these stanzas is that they allude to events in Israelite history. "A time to gather stones together" (Ecclesiastes 3:5), is one example. The Talmud explains that this verse refers to two major events in Jewish history. The first is the splitting of the Red Sea. In the words of King David, "He caused Israel to pass through its [the Red Sea's] midst." (Psalms 136:14)

In this instance, the Jewish people, symbolized by stones, were gathered to safety by virtue of an open miracle. The second occasion Solomon is referring to is the giving of the Torah, when the people were gathered around Mount Sinai in accordance with God's instructions. Mount Sinai is a very rocky mountain.

Solomon's words conclude on a positive note; "A time for war and a time for peace." His reign as king for 40 years was a time of remarkable world peace in general, and specifically for the Jewish people. His father, King David, experienced exactly the opposite environment. He fought against Israel's enemies on many fronts for many years.

Perhaps King Solomon was immortalizing this contrast and hinting to the correct order of affairs—to achieve peace, one has to fight a just war. History has demonstrated that true peace often comes only after "a time for war." We might not like it, but that is the way of the world. True peace is a prize we bequeath to our children, as a reward for our vigilance in standing against tyranny and despotism. But it will not come, as Solomon is teaching, simply because we want it.

Still another take on these famous words, and one you'll typically find in Old Testament translations, is that God predetermines the events of life.

Money Matters

"He who loves money shall not be satisfied with money; nor he who loves abundance with gain [this also is vanity]." (Ecclesiastes 5:9)

Money—or, more specifically, wealth—is the main entity that Solomon picks on as vanity throughout Ecclesiastes. It's the proverbial root of all evil, and Solomon drives the point home repeatedly in verses like these: "There is a severe evil which I have seen under the sun: Riches kept for their owner to his detriment. But those riches perish through misfortune. When he begets a son, there is nothing in his hand. As he came from his mother's womb, naked shall he return, To go as he came; And he shall take nothing from his labor that he may carry away in his hand. And this also is a severe evil, that just exactly as he came, so shall he go. And what profit has he who has labored for the wind? All his days he also eats in darkness, and he has much sorrow and sickness and anger." (Ecclesiastes 5:13–16)

Solomon follows up these somber words with a little encouragement, as he does throughout Ecclesiastes:

"Here is what I have seen: It is good and fitting for one to eat and drink, and to enjoy the good of all his labor in which he toils under the sun all the days of his life which God gives him; for it is his heritage. As for every man to whom God has given riches and wealth, and given him power to eat of it, to receive his heritage and rejoice in his labor—this is the gift of God." (Ecclesiastes 5:17–19)

God Grants Ultimate Success

"Again I saw under the sun that the race is not won by the light-footed, and that the war is not won by the strong, and also that bread does not come to the wise, and also that wealth does not come to the intelligent, and also that favor does not come to the learned, for time and death occur to all of them." (Ecclesiastes 9:11)

Among the many moral lessons found in this scroll, King Solomon taught that even though it seems like it is usually the mighty who win wars, and the clever who are able to provide themselves with sustenance, and the highly intelligent who become wealthy, the truth is that vanquishing enemies, gaining sustenance, and becoming fabulously rich are not solely dependent on these features of the person. Rather, it is God who grants ultimate success and it's based on His unfathomable reasons. Put simply, wealth is not dependent on wisdom.

In the same chapter 9, speaking of God-guided success, a time-honored Jewish custom of both groom and bride wearing white at the wedding ceremony is hinted to in the verse "At all times your clothing should be white." (Ecclesiastes 9:8) This means that one should try to remain pure and not be stained and sullied by the temptations of the world. Therefore, when groom and bride are getting married they don white to remind themselves that even though they are currently entering a new exciting stage in their life, they must remember to keep their "clothing" white and pure—just as it was on their wedding day!

A Dead Lion or Live Dog?

As mentioned earlier, the sages of Israel initially expressed serious concerns over Solomon's writings in Ecclesiastes. Not only did he contradict himself, he also contradicted the great teachings of David, his father.

One of the first areas of contradiction was over the very creation of man. In the first chapter he praised those who have already died. However, in a later chapter he seemed to harbor just the opposite sentiment: "For to him that is joined with all the living there is hope; for a living dog is better than a dead lion. For the living know that they shall die: but the dead know not anything, neither have they any more a reward; for the memory of them is forgotten." (Ecclesiastes 9:4–6)

Some of the Talmudic sages believe Solomon wrote these passages about his noble father King David, who is likened to a lion, which is also the emblem and metaphoric symbol of his tribe—Judah. Once dead, however, even the great David could not accomplish anything more on this earth. However, even a scoundrel in David's court, of which there were many, likened to a dog, as long as he was still alive could still achieve more God consciousness and penitence. Hence a living dog (for example, a loathsome person) has an advantage over the most saintly deceased (a dead lion).

Another interpretation of Solomon's words here might simply be this: As long as the flame of the soul still flickers within a person, he or she can still accomplish great things. After it's extinguished, nothing more can be done.

The Least You Need to Know

- Ecclesiastes was written by King Solomon and speaks about the futility of man's material pursuits in this world.

- The sages of Israel initially wished to conceal the scroll, as it seemed to contradict itself as well as accepted scriptural concepts about life.

- Solomon chose colorful metaphors to illustrate his points.

- Throughout Ecclesiastes, Solomon challenges conventional thinking on how one attains wealth, wins wars, or succeeds in many endeavors, and what one does with it. He indicates that humankind's successes are all up to God.

Chapter **27**

Seeking God's Hand: The Book of Esther

In This Chapter

- ◆ Persian life
- ◆ Avuncular actions
- ◆ Royal intrigues
- ◆ A queen's plot for her people
- ◆ Joyous celebrations

A royal scandal brought about by a headstrong queen, a search for her replacement, and an evil plot hatched by a menacing court official. Sounds like the makings for a modern-day soap opera or a romance novel, doesn't it? It definitely could be, but all this, and more, was written about centuries ago in the Book of Esther.

This biblical book is a historical record of the miraculous deliverance of the Jewish people who lived in ancient Persia. It's also a great epic story that illustrates profound truths about God's providence and protection and the triumph of good over evil.

Exile and Redemption

The story of Esther takes place in ancient Persia during the first exile of the Jewish people, after the Babylonian emperor Nebuchadnezzar destroyed the Holy Temple of Jerusalem.

During this time of Diaspora, some Jews had resettled in Judea and had rebuilt the Jerusalem Wall. Most of the Jewish people, however, were scattered throughout the Persian Empire. Some established communities were in cities such as Susa, the capital of the Persian Empire and the setting for Esther.

Lord Knows

Interestingly, although the Book of Esther demonstrates profound truths about God's providence, it doesn't mention any of God's proper names. The name of this biblical book can also mean "revealing the hidden," as the root for the name Esther is "hester," which means hidden. Megillah means to reveal. The message? At certain times in history, God appears to be hiding his face and not supervising the affairs of man, specifically as they pertain to the Jewish people. This is one reason that the proper name of God was omitted.

No one knows who wrote the Book of Esther, but there's no dispute about its historical accuracy. It contains precise dates and accurate descriptions of both the Persian court and the customs of the time.

A Grand Feast

Esther begins with a flashback that sets the stage for the action that's to come. We're in the fifth century B.C.E., in the court of King Ahasuerus. Ahasuerus is married to the beautiful Vashti. Noted as a boisterous man of emotional extremes, he enjoyed a good time and had planned a royal celebration for the people of Susa. Besotted with his lovely wife, he planned to put her on public display so that others could admire her.

Ahasuerus threw a 180-day epicurean orgy for the men of his kingdom, including his Jewish subjects. He lavished his guests with every known pleasure; fattened calves, wine the same age as the person drinking it, opulent couches, and royal gardens for their aesthetic enjoyment. No worldly delight was withheld. Not to be outdone by her husband, Queen Vashti threw a similar bash for the women.

After some drunken revelry, Ahasuerus ordered his wife to appear before his guests, wearing nothing but the royal crown. But Vashti refused to come.

> ### It Is Written
>
> Talmudic writings reflect a couple of different takes on Vashti's refusal to appear nude in public. The first reflects a negotiation of sorts where Vashti offered a compromise—she'd appear in lingerie, like a harlot. But her husband's guests refused. They wanted the full show. The vainglorious Vashti, not one too prudish to shy away from such exhibitionism, then agreed to come without the crown, not wanting its beauty to overshadow her own. They objected to this as well. They wanted the queen and her crown.
>
> Another explanation is that she had a blemish on her face. Some commentaries describe it as leprosy. Others say it was a hallucination and no one could understand what Vashti was talking about.

Completely confused and unable to decide what to do with his wayward wife, Ahasuerus summoned his chief advisors for a spousal summit. Doing nothing to her would diminish the respect for the men folk by their wives. On the other hand, dealing harshly with the queen might eventually depress the drunken king when he sobered from his intoxication.

Jewish sages were also consulted. However, they recused themselves by asserting that ever since the Temple was destroyed, they lacked the keen insight required to deal with such an issue.

Vashti was executed that night.

A Royal Beauty Pageant

As his advisors predicted, Ahasuerus's anger over Vashti's impudence subsided rather quickly, and he was saddened over the execution of his queen. His young servants had the perfect remedy—a beauty pageant! They suggested their king gather all the beautiful young women from throughout the kingdom, and choose the one who pleased him most for Vashti's replacement.

The call for contestants reached the ears of a Jewish man named Mordechai. Mordechai lived in the capital city with his orphaned niece Esther, who he adopted when her father and mother died. (According to some sources, he married her.)

Esther was a good-looking and nubile young woman. Mordechai attempted to hide her from the search committee. As fate would have it, she, too, was "rounded up" and taken to the palace.

Esther found favor in the eyes of Hagai, the king's chamberlain. He placed her in the best quarters and provided seven maids to wait on her. Esther told no one of her origins, as Mordechai had instructed her not to reveal that she was a Jew. To make sure that all went well, Mordechai visited the palace gates every day to check on her welfare.

Why did Mordechai want Esther to keep her origins a secret, and go through such pains to make sure that she did? We don't know for sure. Talmudic commentators offer a few possible suggestions:

◆ So the king would think she was from a lowly stock and pass on her. This way, Mordechai would have Esther as his own.

◆ Mordechai had prophetic knowledge that keeping her identity secret would in some fashion position her to help save the Jewish people.

◆ So that the royal servants would not deliberately force her to violate Jewish laws.

Lord Knows

In the book that bears her name, Esther is introduced as "Hadassah, that is, Esther, his uncle's daughter." Why the double identity? Her real name was Esther but she was called Hadassah, which means myrtle branch. The name could have come from the color of her skin, which, legend has it, took on a greenish hue when she was incarcerated in the king's palace and had to eat a strictly vegetarian diet. Alternatively, in ancient times, righteous people were sometimes compared to the pleasantly scented myrtle tree.

The Book of Esther also provides an interesting behind-the-scenes peak regarding ancient beauty routines.

Each woman wishing to compete in the royal beauty pageant could only be brought before the king after a year's worth of mandatory preparations. These included six months of anointing with oil of myrrh and six months of perfuming and other preparations done "for beautifying women." (Esther 2:12)

When Esther's time came for going before the king, he "loved [her] more than all the women, and she found more favor and kindness before him than all the other maidens; so that he set the royal crown upon her head, and made her queen in place of Vashti." (Esther 2:17) We don't know how Esther felt about being named the new queen of Persia, but we do know that she continued to conceal her true identity and ethnic origin, as per uncle Mordechai's command.

The king was enthralled with Esther. He held a huge celebration in her honor for his officers and servants, declared a tax amnesty for his subjects, and bestowed gifts deemed "worthy of the king's hand." (Esther 2:18)

Through all this, Esther continued to keep her origins a secret. Mordechai continued to sit at the king's gate, keeping an eye on her and monitoring the goings on of the kingdom. In Mordechai's mind, Esther's elevation to queen was an auspicious sign that something big was brewing.

Royal Plots and Intrigue

As it turns out, Mordechai was right. Something big was brewing. While sitting at the king's gate, he overheard two of Ahasuerus's servants discussing a plot to assassinate the king. He told Esther, who wasted no time telling her new husband that his life was in danger. Ahasuerus investigated the matter and found Mordechai's accusation to be true. The servants were executed, and Mordechai's exemplary service was written in the king's court history. However, his efforts went unrewarded beyond this, and were quickly forgotten.

Soon after Mordechai's efforts on the king's behalf, Ahasuerus promoted a man named Haman to a superior position in his court.

 It Is Written _____

Identified as a descendant of Amalek, an archenemy of the Jewish people, Haman is the resident evildoer in the story of Esther. No friend of the Jews, the villainous Haman's desire was clearly genocidal, "to destroy, to slay, and to exterminate all the Jews, from young to old, children and women, in one day ..." (Esther 3:13)

Some commentaries say that Haman deified himself, claimed to be a god, and demanded that people bow down to him.

According to the king's decree, all the servants at the king's gate would now bow down before Haman. As one of the king's servants (if only by his good deed, as Ahasuerus has neglected to reward Mordechai), Mordechai refused to do so. Why? Haman had idols sewn into his clothes. This meant that anyone who bowed down to him was also bowing down to his idols. As a Jew, Mordechai refused to bow down to anyone but the one and true God.

My Lips Are Sealed

The other servants at the gate asked Mordechai why he was defying Haman, but Mordechai refused to answer them. They continued to ask, and Mordechai continued to ignore them. Finally, they decided to turn him in. Although the Bible doesn't go into detail about why Mordechai stonewalled them, it's implied that he did so because he was a Jew.

Mordechai's defiance enraged Haman. He decided it was not enough to just punish Mordechai for such insolence. The only remedy was to go after all Mordechai's people—that is, all the Jews in Persia.

Casting Out Lots

Haman schemed and plotted against Mordechai and the Jews for a solid year. During this time, he cast *purim*, which is Hebrew for lots, to determine the most auspicious day to carry out his plans. The most favorable lot fell on Adar, the twelfth month of the Jewish calendar. Haman was elated, for he knew that was the month in which Moses, the greatest Jew and leader of all time, died.

Ahasuerus, May I?

After he had his date, Haman asked for an audience with his king. He told Ahasuerus:

"There is certain people scattered abroad and dispersed among the peoples in all the provinces of your realm. Their laws are different from every other people's … they do not observe the king's laws … If it pleases the king, let it be recorded that they be destroyed …" (Esther 3:8–9)

Ahasuerus agreed with Haman that it was in his best interest to get rid of these people. He gave Haman his signet ring and told him he could do what he wished with these people. Oh, and go ahead and keep the money, too.

Ahasuerus summoned his scribes and dictated a royal decree, written exactly to Haman's specifications. It called for the slaughter of all the Jews, "young and old, women and children," on the thirteenth day of Nisan, the first month of the Jewish calendar. After all were killed, their property was to be turned over to the king.

Enter Esther

The decree came as a shock to the people of Susa, and especially to the Jews. They had lived among the Persians for some years without much strife. What had they done to merit such treatment?

When Mordechai heard the news, he immediately tore his garments and donned sackcloth with ashes. He then traveled about the city crying out "with a loud and bitter cry" (Esther 4:1), trying to rally the people to mend their ways and imploring the Almighty to intercede on their behalf.

Esther's maids and servants caught wind of Mordechai's behavior and told their queen about it. Mortified, she asked her uncle to give up his sackcloth and sent clothing to replace it, but he refused. Mordechai's decidedly odd behavior continued to worry her, and she asked one of her advisors to find out what was going on.

Mordechai told the man what had happened to him, and told him of Haman's plot to kill not just him, but all the Jews. He also gave the man a copy of the decree to show to Esther, and implored him to ask the queen to intercede with the king on behalf of her people.

Esther was reluctant to do so. Because the plot against Ahasuerus's life was revealed, the king had taken precautions against uninvited visitors. Even she couldn't approach the court without first being asked to do so: "All the king's servants and the people of the king's provinces know that any man or woman who approaches the king in the inner court, who is not summoned, his law is one—to be put to death; except for the one to whom the king shall extend the gold scepter so that he may live. Now I, I have not been summoned to come to the king for these [past] thirty days." (Esther 4:11)

At this point, Mordechai pulled rank. He reminded Esther of her ancestry and God's loyalty, and told her that she mustn't fear the consequences of entering unannounced to the chamber of this mortal king: "For if you persist in keeping silent at a time like this, relief and deliverance will come to the Jews from another place, while you and your father's house will perish. And who knows whether it was just for such a time as this that you attained the royal position!" (Esther 4:14)

Esther said yes, but not without some support from her people. She asked Mordechai to assemble all the Jews in Susa for a group fast.

The Queen's Scheme

During the three-day fast, Esther devised a scheme of her own. As part of her plot, she decided to ask the king and Haman to dinner.

On the third day of the fast, Esther went before Ahasuerus. Although her visit was unannounced, Ahasuerus was glad to see her. He extended his gold scepter to her, and she touched it.

Ahasuerus asked Esther what she wanted. Still very fond of his queen, he told her that he'd grant her anything, even "half of my kingdom." But no, her request was quite simple—just the presence of her husband and his most trusted advisor at her dinner table.

> **It Is Written**
>
> Why did Esther invite Haman to the banquet? Talmudic commentary suggests a number of plausible explanations. Perhaps an opportunity would arise to make Haman look really bad in front of the king. Maybe Esther wanted to make the king jealous of Haman, or to make other members of the court jealous so no one would protect him. Perhaps she didn't want Ahasuerus to suspect she was a Jew. Ahasuerus was a fickle man, known to change his mind frequently. Thus she wanted Haman available so that as soon as Ahasuerus decided to eliminate him, he would be able to do so without delay—before changing his mind. She wanted to keep Haman preoccupied so that he wouldn't rebel against Ahasuerus and make himself the king.

Playing in the Big Leagues

Ahasuerus immediately accepted, much to Haman's delight. He figured he was the big man now, perhaps even Ahasuerus's equal, at least in the queen's eyes. But his glee didn't last for long. As he left the palace, he saw Mordechai, who, as usual, refused to acknowledge him.

Newly incensed, Haman went home and shared his angst with his wife. Almost as wicked as he, she suggested he build a gallows on which to hang Mordechai.

The Big Turnabout

For some reason, Ahasuerus couldn't get to sleep the night before Esther's dinner party. As a calmative, he asked for the royal history book to be brought and read before him. Interestingly, the reading just happened to be about the assassination plot against the king. He asked what was done to reward Mordechai. His servants replied that no reward had been given.

Lord Knows
Some say that the reason for the king's insomnia was that he was suspicious of what appeared to be a strange relationship between Haman and Esther. Was Esther's ploy to invite the king to an exclusive banquet intended only to assassinate him? Why weren't his advisors coming forward with information? Thus the paranoid king couldn't sleep that night. But was it merely his own insecurities, or was the Master Planner orchestrating these events behind the scenes?

At this exact moment, Haman arrived at the palace to ask permission to kill Mordechai. Ahasuerus, of course, didn't know this, and took the opportunity to ask his trusted advisor what should be done for "a man whom the king wishes to honor?" (Esther 6:6)

Haman, being a supreme egoist, thought Ahasuerus was pondering a gift for him. He responded that an appropriate gift would include being "… dressed in the king's royal garment by one of the king's highest officers, placed upon the king's horse, and led through the streets of the city, and they shall cry out before him, 'Thus shall be done to the man whom the king wishes to honor!'" (Esther 6:7–8)

Can you imagine the shock to Haman's ego when the king then ordered Haman to hurry and do all these things for Mordechai? So commanded by the king, Haman hastened to carry out the king's orders. He dressed Mordechai in royal attire and led him through the city on a royal steed, crying out, "Thus shall be done to the man whom the king wishes to honor!" (Esther 6:11)

After this divine example of poetic justice was over, Mordechai returned to the king's gate. Haman rushed home with his tail between his legs. When Haman told his wife and friends what had happened, they gave him a taste of what was to come, telling him, "If Mordechai, before whom you have begun to fall, is a Jew, then you will not prevail over him, you will surely fall before him." (Esther 6:13)

Haman had little time to lick his wounds. As this conversation was taking place, the king's soldiers arrived to escort Haman to Esther's banquet.

A glorious feast was unveiled. During the second day, Ahasuerus again asked Esther what he could do for her. This time, she revealed her true origins and petitioned for the lives of her people.

"If I have found favor in your eyes, O king, and if it pleases the king, give me my life as my request, and my nation as my entreaty. For had my nation and I not been sold to be destroyed, killed, and wiped out. If we had only been sold as slaves and maid-servants I would have kept quiet. But our oppressor does not care about the loss to the king." (Esther 7:4)

Ahasuerus, incensed, asked, "Who is this? Where is this one who tries to do such a thing?" Esther responded, "A man who is a tormenter and adversary, this wicked Haman!"

The king decided to take a moment to cool off and left the table. Haman then seized the opportunity to beg Esther, of all people, for mercy. While doing so, he fell onto the couch where Esther was seated. When Ahasuerus returned from his stroll in Esther's gardens, he saw Haman prostrated on Esther's couch and leapt to the obvious conclusion (obvious for him, anyway). He accused Haman of trying to molest the queen while he (Ahasuerus) was in the house.

This spelled the end of Haman. He was executed on the very gallows that he had erected to hang Mordechai.

On that day, the king gave the estates of Haman to Esther. The king also met with Mordechai, because Esther had informed the king that Mordechai was related to her. The king gave to Mordechai his ring, the same ring that he had previously given to Haman. Esther appointed Mordechai over Haman's estate. The great turnabout was complete. But there was one more item of unfinished business.

Esther then approached Ahasuerus a second time, falling at his feet, crying and begging that he undo Haman's evil plot. She asked him to call back the scrolls that had been sent out by Haman ordering the extermination of the Jews. She told him that she could not bear to see her people suffer. King Ahasuerus told Mordechai and Esther that he had already given the estates of Haman to them and that he had executed Haman because of his attempt to harm the Jews.

Ahasuerus then gave them permission to issue a new decree that permitted the Jews to attack and destroy all their enemies on the thirteenth day of Adar, including Haman's 10 sons.

Near the end of the Megillah (revelation) we find Mordechai leaving the presence of the king dressed in royal finery, to the great delight of all the people of the city of Susa.

Lightness, Gladness, Joy, and Honor

The Jews have celebrated the feast of Purim ever since Haman's downfall. It falls sometime during the months of February and March. The day before Purim is a day of fasting, in memory of Esther's fast. The fast is then followed by two days of dancing, merrymaking, feasting, and gladness: "The Jews had light and gladness and joy and honor. And in every province, and in every city, every place where the king's word and his decree reached, the Jews had gladness and joy, a feast and a holiday … And these days should be remembered and celebrated by every generation, every family, every province, and every city; and these days of Purim should never cease among the Jews, nor shall their remembrance perish from their descendants." (Esther 8:16–17, 9:26–28)

As part of the Purim celebration, the Book of Esther is read aloud twice in the synagogue. It is traditional to sound noisemakers, or graggars, when Haman's name is mentioned.

Lord Knows

Sounding noisemakers when Haman's name is mentioned during the public reading of Esther is a long-established Jewish custom. It is a variation of an old practice that took on different forms through the generations. The earliest sources, about 1,000 years ago, speak of burning effigies of Haman on a bonfire. In medieval Europe, children would write Haman's name on stones or wood blocks, and bang them until the name was erased.

Particularly among German Jews, the institution of the "Purim-*shpiel*" was developed, a raucous play on the Megillah story (or other theme) traditionally performed on Purim. Borrowing from the German theatre as well as from Jewish exegesis, these productions took great liberties with plot and characterization, such that Mordechai might appear as a pathetic clown, Haman as a pitiful figure. Such mockery would be tolerated only at Purim time—as it is practiced today in many circles.

The Least You Need to Know

- The Scroll of Esther records the account of a great deliverance that occurred for the Jews of Persia after their first exile from the Land of Israel around 422 B.C.E.

- The main protagonists of the story are Mordechai and Esther, who were both prophets and leaders of the Jewish people. The antagonists are Ahasuerus, the King of Persia, and Haman the Amalekite, who was an archenemy of the Jewish people.

- Although the proper name of God doesn't appear anywhere in the Book of Esther, it bears testimony to his providence.

- The Book of Esther forms the basis for many time-honored customs that are practiced by Jews yearly to commemorate the great salvation by the "Hidden Hand of God," experienced by their ancestors more than 2,400 years ago. These observances include the public reading of the Scroll of Esther, feasting, gifts to the poor, food gifts to friends, and general rejoicing.

Part 7

Writings Part III: The End of Prophecy

The Historical Books (Daniel, Ezra/Nehemiah, and Chronicles) were the last to be completed and the last to be received as Scripture, although parts of them might be very ancient indeed. Coming as they do at the end of the Prophetic Era, these books contain significant messages concerning the imminent coming of the Messiah, along with apocalyptic descriptions of the tribulation that may transpire during that time.

28

The Visionary:
The Book of Daniel

In This Chapter

- ◆ Being a true believer
- ◆ Interpreting royal dreams
- ◆ Being in the lion's den
- ◆ Learning about the End of Days

The Book of Daniel contains some of the most entertaining stories in the Hebrew Bible, which makes it a favorite of children and adults alike. It also contains the author's visions for the future, which makes it very popular among students of prophecy.

Some believe that all the secrets of the world's history, past, and future, can be found in the Book of Daniel. Whether you agree or not, there's no denying that the book's stories of courage and commitment to one's faith offer many rich life lessons.

A Promising Young Man

Daniel, whose life and ministry covers the entire 70 years of the Jews' captivity in Babylon, was set on the path to becoming one of Israel's most influential leaders at a very young age. As a young teenager, he was hand-picked from Judah's nobility, deported to Babylon, and enrolled in a special school established to train advisors to the royal court of King Nebuchadnezzar.

Daniel, whose name in Hebrew means "God is my judge," would not only serve as a government official—eventually becoming chief of the governors over all Babylon's wise men—but also as God's mouthpiece. How he achieved that distinction is one of those amazing Jewish rags-to-riches stories, paralleling that of his distant cousin Joseph, the son of Jacob.

The Book of Daniel is divided into two parts. Chapters 1 through 6 are a collection of narratives about Daniel and his friends, and document historical events that took place while he served both the Babylonian and Persian empires. Chapters 7 through 12 are a collection of apocalyptic visions foreseeing the course of world history.

Remaining true to the religion of his ancestors, even when having to keep company with some rather violent and shady pagans, is one of Daniel's greatest deeds. He not only survived, he thrived and excelled to the point where he merited receiving prophecy in a foreign land. He served in this capacity until the time of the Persian monarch Darius, a period of more than 70 years.

The Sages Say

The sages teach that the Divine Presence of prophecy is only in the Land of Israel. One verse they base this on is: "A Land which … the eyes of the Lord, your God, are on from the beginning of the year until the end of the year." (Deuteronomy 11:12) The "eyes of the Lord" imply that the Land of Israel is the land of prophecy. Alternatively, Maimonides explained that there is no prophecy outside of Israel because there is no true joy outside of the Land, and prophecy only rests among entities with complete happiness. Rabbi Yitzchak Abarbanel, who we quoted earlier in this guide, explains that prophecy is part of the special characteristics of the Land of Israel.

Leadership Training, Babylonian Style

As mentioned, Daniel and three of his friends—Chananiah, Mishael, and Azariah—were all enrolled (among other youths) in a school established by Nebuchadnezzar to train future administrators for the Babylonian Empire. Tradition has it that they were 13 years old and descendants of King Hezekiah.

> ### Lord Knows
>
> Chananiah, Mishael, and Azariah were close colleagues of Daniel. Along with Ezra the Scribe, they were instrumental in leading the campaign of Jewish return to their Holy Land and rebuilding the Temple in Jerusalem. Scripture relates that when Chananiah, Mishael, and Azariah (identified as Shadrach, Meshach, and Abed Nego in Daniel 3:12) faced the choice to either bow before a 120-foot-tall image of Nebuchadnezzar or be thrown into a fiery furnace, they chose the latter. Miraculously, they went through the furnace unscathed and made quite an impression on the emperor, who publicly acknowledged the supreme power of God in these men. (Daniel 3:29)

While in the palace, Daniel and his friends resolved to remain faithful to God and refused to eat the royal cuisine or drink the royal wine because it was not kosher. He informed the school's chief official accordingly. This worried the man, who felt that an alternative diet might be to the detriment of his young charges, and that it wouldn't reflect well on him if this were to be the case: "I fear my lord the king, who has appointed your food and drink. For why should he see your faces looking worse than the young men who are your age? Then you would endanger my head before the king." (Daniel 1:10)

Daniel reassured the man that everything would be okay, and proposed a test to prove it. For 10 days, he said, he and his friends would eat only vegetables and drink only water. When the 10-day period was up, they would be examined and dealt with accordingly.

> ### Lord Knows
>
> Daniel and his group clearly prospered, but might not have made friends among their classmates. Scripture notes that the boys' good health resulted in a vegetarian diet for their classmates as well.

The administrator agreed, and Daniel and his friends embarked on the test. As noted in Scripture: "And at the end of the ten days their countenance appeared better and fatter in flesh than all the young men who ate the portion of the king's delicacies." (Daniel 1:17)

"And to these youths, the four of them, God gave knowledge and understanding in every script and wisdom, and Daniel understood all visions and dreams … And in all matters of wisdom and understanding about which the king examined them, he found them ten times better than all the magicians and astrologers who were in all his realm." (Daniel 1:20)

At the close of the three years of training, the four young men were brought before Nebuchadnezzar and put through their paces. They proved to be heads above their classmates, and were chosen to serve the king. Of them, Daniel was distinguished for his God-given proficiency in visions and dreams—the "wisdom" of the day.

Interpreting Royal Dreams

Daniel's first challenge as a government official came about as the result of a bad dream: "Now in the second year of Nebuchadnezzar's reign, Nebuchadnezzar dreamed dreams, and his spirit was deeply troubled, and his sleep was interrupted." (Daniel 2:1)

Nebuchadnezzar must have been really shaken up, because he wanted to have the dream interpreted. He called his magicians, his astrologers, his sorcerers, even the Chaldeans (who were noted soothsayers), to not only interpret the dream but to tell him what he dreamed. No one, not even the Chaldeans, were up to the task. In fact, the Chaldeans told the king that he was asking the impossible.

The Chaldeans replied before the king and said, "There is no man on the earth who can declare the king's word; because no great and powerful king has asked such a thing of any necromancer, astrologer, or Chaldean. And the matter that the king asks is difficult, and there is no other who can tell it before the king but the angels, whose dwelling is not with people." (Daniel 2:10–11)

This irritated the king to no end. He issued a decree to have all his wise men destroyed, including Daniel and his friends.

Scripture tells us that Daniel had the good sense to have a talk with the emperor's chief executioner, who revealed the exact nature of the decree. When Daniel heard what the real problem was, he took a chance and requested a few days to think of a response. He then returned to his three friends for a brainstorming session. As the following verses show, his deliberation, patience, and prudence paid off: "Then Daniel went home and let his colleagues, Hananiah, Mishael, and Azariah, know of the matter. And to pray and beg of the God of heaven about this secret, that Daniel and his colleagues should not perish with the remaining wise men of Babylon. Then the secret was revealed to Daniel in the vision of the night; then Daniel blessed the God of heaven." (Daniel 2:17–19)

Like Joseph before him, before Daniel revealed the dream and the interpretation, he humbled himself before his Creator and acknowledged the Almighty as the source of all wisdom: "Daniel answered the king and said, 'The secret that the king asks, no wise men, astrologers, necromancers, or soothsayers can tell the king. But there is a God in heaven Who reveals secrets, and He lets King Nebuchadnezzar know what will be at the end of days; that is your dream and the visions of your head on your bed.'" (Daniel 2:27–28)

The words "end of days," were a subtle (and historically accurate) hint that God would terminate Nebuchadnezzar's kingdom in a short while. Daniel then proceeded to reveal the king's dream: "O King, you were watching, and behold, one great image, an image which had a large base and with unusual splendor, was standing opposite you, and its form was frightening. That image had a head of fine gold, its breast and its arms were of silver, and its belly and thighs were of copper. Its legs were of iron, and its feet were partly of iron and partly of clay. You were watching until one stone was hewn without hands, and it struck the image on its feet of iron and clay and crumbled them. Then the iron, the clay, the copper, the silver, and the gold crumbled together, and they were like chaff from the threshing floors of the summer, and the wind carried them off, and no place was found for them, and the stone that struck the image became a huge mountain and filled the entire earth. This is the dream, and its interpretation we shall recite before the king." (Daniel 2:31–36)

He then tells the king what the dream means. "A head of fine gold," was a reference to the king himself, for his kingdom was strong and was presently in power and very prominent. The image of the four metals with feet of clay are interpreted as four great kingdoms:

♦ The head of gold, as Daniel explained, refers to Nebuchadnezzar and his Babylonian Empire.

♦ The breast and arms of silver signified the Persian Empire.

♦ The belly and thighs of copper signified the kingdom of Alexander of Macedonia.

♦ The legs of iron and feet of iron and clay signified the Roman Empire, which, during its pinnacle, did indeed crumble and flatten all its competition, and its influence (solid as iron) can be felt to this day.

Daniel ended his interpretation with a prediction of a fifth kingdom that would dominate all four previous ones: "And in the days of these kings, the God of heaven will set up a kingdom forever, it will not be destroyed, and the kingdom will not be left to another people; it will crumble and destroy all these kingdoms, and it will stand forever. Just as you saw that from the mountain a stone was hewn without hands, and it crumbled the iron, the copper, the clay, the silver, and the gold. The great God has let the king know what will be after this, and the dream is true, and its interpretation is reliable." (Daniel 2:44–45)

Nebuchadnezzar's response was quite astounding. Because Daniel had predicted his downfall, conventional wisdom would make us think the king would order his execution on the spot. Or at least banish him from his court. Yet the king did just the opposite: "Then King Nebuchadnezzar fell on his face and prostrated himself before Daniel, and he ordered to offer up a meal-offering and libations to bring him satisfaction (deifying Daniel). The king replied to Daniel and said, 'Truly, your God is the God of the gods and the Master of the kings, and He reveals secrets, being that you were able to reveal this secret.' Then the king elevated Daniel and gave him many great gifts and gave him dominion over all the capital cities of Babylon, and he was the chief prefect over all the wise men of Babylon." (Daniel 2:46–48)

The Writing on the Wall

After Daniel relayed his initial interpretation to the king, he recapped it by going back through and explaining the imagery a bit more clearly. As part of the recap, he mentioned that another king would rise after Nebuchadnezzar, and that this king would head an inferior kingdom. This was a prediction of the continuation of Nebuchadnezzar's kingdom under his son, Belshazzar. However, it would be short-lived.

When Belshazzar ascended to power, he threw a feast with his lords, drinking wine from the golden vessels of Solomon's Temple. Needless to say, the God of Israel, despite the exile of his children, was not pleased with such desecration of hollowed property.

At this banquet a man's hand was seen writing certain mysterious words on a wall. Frightened by the apparition, Belshazzar ordered his astrologers to explain the inscription, but they were unable to read it. Daniel was then summoned to the royal palace where the king promised him lavish gifts if he would decipher the inscription.

Daniel had no problem reading the Aramaic inscription, *Mene, mene, tekel, upharsin.* He explained it to mean that God had "numbered" (*Mene*) the kingdom of Belshazzar and brought it to an end; that the king had been weighed (*tekel*) and found wanting; and that his kingdom was divided (*upharsin*) and given over to the Medes and Persians. (Daniel 5:1–28)

The very next day, just as Daniel predicted, Belshazzar's empire crumbled, and he was assassinated in his own palace by Darius the Mede. His daughter Vashti (remember her from the Book of Esther?) was abducted and would later become the queen of the Per-sian Empire.

Daniel in the Lion's Den

Daniel's long career as advisor to foreign dignitaries marches right on through Darius. He retained his high position under the Median monarch until his fellow dignitaries, jealous of the successful Jew whom the king wished to appoint over his entire kingdom, induced the king to issue a decree forbidding anyone to ask anything of God, or of any man except the king, for 30 days.

Daniel, who already had shown no fear for Nebuchadnezzar, continued to pray three times a day at an open window looking toward Jerusalem. This act of defiance was not lost on the new king—who, ironically, sought to rescue Daniel by finding a loophole in his own decree.

The other advisors convinced Darius that he should make no exceptions to his royal edict and that action should be taken against all who defied it. Darius ran out of options and felt compelled to put Daniel (and his God) to the test: "Then the king commanded and they brought Daniel and threw him into the lion's pit. The king exclaimed to Daniel, 'Your God, Whom you serve continually, He will save you.' And a stone was brought and placed over the opening of the pit, and the king sealed it with his signet ring and with the signet ring of his ministers, so that his will regarding Daniel not be changed." (Daniel 6:17–18)

The king had a restless night, while, according to the historian Josephus, the beasts in the den received Daniel as "faithful dogs might receive

> **The Sages Say**
>
> The service of God that Darius attributed to Daniel was understood by the sages of Israel to be acts of loving-kindness. For instance, Daniel would frequently prepare dowries for brides and rejoice in their weddings, he gave charity to the poor, and of course, he prayed thrice daily!

their returning master, wagging their tails and licking him." The king arose before dawn and cried out to Daniel in the lion's den to see if a miracle had occurred: "Then Daniel spoke to the king, 'O king, live forever! My God sent His angel and shut the lions' mouths, and they did not wound me, for merit was found in me before Him, and also before you, O king, I have done no harm.'" (Daniel 6:22)

The king had his accusers and their wives and children thrown into the pit, but they didn't fare quite as well—as a matter of fact, "They did not even reach the bottom of the pit before the lions prevailed upon them and crushed all their bones." (Daniel 6:25) Daniel was thus praised and honored anew by the king. He retained his influence until the third year of Cyrus the Persian's reign over Babylon (circa 367 B.C.E.).

End of Days Prophecies

Jewish and Christian theologians alike have written extensively about the End of Days or apocalyptic prophecies attributed to Daniel's vision. It is impossible to offer a comprehensive look at what they are (and what they aren't) here. But we can take a quick look at some of the most intriguing.

Maimonides, the greatest Jewish philosopher and scholar of the last millennium, wrote that Daniel predicted a proliferation of false messiahs who would lead the masses astray and eventually be revealed as frauds: "And in those times … the children of the violent among your people shall lift themselves to establish the vision, but shall stumble." (Daniel 11:14)

This surely has happened in Jewish history. The first was the warrior-scholar Bar Kochbah (135 C.E.), who tried to save the Jewish people from the hands of the Roman Empire—but in the end, failed dismally. Then there was Shabtai Zvi (circa 1648 C.E.), who led many astray and disgraced his people by converting to Islam. He caused many Jewish people to lose their homes in Europe and Asia under false pretenses of proclaiming himself the anointed Messiah who would conquer Israel. Lastly, Jacob Frank (1726–1791 C.E.) founded a heretical Jewish sect professing to find the doctrine of Trinitarianism in the Kabbalah. He and his followers feigned conversion to Roman Catholicism in 1759. Nothing good came of this Messianic movement either.

Many religious writers claim that an actual date of the redemption of the world and restoration of the throne of David are also found in Daniel's writings. This notion is refuted by one verse: "But you, Daniel, close up the words and seal the book until the time of the end." (Daniel 12:4) Based on this verse, the sages of Israel actually issued a stern warning against anyone who would attempt to predict the date of the

Messiah's coming. They believed such occupation could incite false hopes and distract the people from their primary goal of Torah-observant Jews. They were right.

Nonetheless, it is undeniable that Daniel revealed that the period before the Final Redemption would be one of trials and tribulations. He warned, "And there shall be a time of trouble such as never existed since there were nations, until that time." (Daniel 12:1)

People of all faiths will be seriously challenged in "that time," according to Daniel. Opposing forces and camps will be formed between those who cling to faith in God and those who are inclined to do evil and partake in vices. Daniel commented on this quite emphatically: "Many shall purify and cleanse themselves (in those days to come), and be tried; but the wicked will act wickedly; and none of the wicked shall understand, but the wise (righteous) will understand." (Daniel 12:10)

Finally, Daniel described another element associated with the End of Days in the last chapter of his visions. He alluded to God's resurrection of the dead. This concept is a maxim of Judaism and bedrock component of its faith: "And many of them that sleep in the dust of the earth shall awake, some to everlasting life, and some to shame and everlasting contempt." (Daniel 12:2)

Lord Knows

Daniel is the only book in Hebrew Scriptures in which angels are actually identified by given names, such as Gabriel in 8:16 and 9:21 and Michael in 10:13, 10:21, and 12:1. Why is this so? There's no definitive answer, but one theory is that angels act entirely behind the scenes and under God's jurisdiction. Revealing their identity in writing might compromise their hidden and mysterious nature. Since the angels in Daniel are the only ones in Scripture to communicate and reveal specific information—including a timeline—about the end of days, Daniel must have felt it necessary to reveal their identity and specifically mention them by name to lend credibility and veracity to this message.

The Least You Need to Know

- The Book of Daniel contains historical information and serves as a rich repository for much End of Days material envisioned by Daniel.

- When Nebuchadnezzar, the Babylonian conqueror, laid siege to Jerusalem and led the Israelites into captivity, he chose certain youths from among the Jews to be groomed as his courtiers and advisors. Daniel was the best of them.

- Daniel quickly showed that he was imbued with the spirit of God, and established himself as a leader of his fellow expatriates in their exile.

- Like his predecessor, the patriarch Joseph, Daniel gained favor in the eyes of both Nebuchadnezzar and Darius the Mede as a fabulous interpreter of dreams.

29

A Spark of Greatness: The Books of Ezra/Nehemiah

In This Chapter

◆ A master of Scripture

◆ Foreign influences

◆ The Great Legislator/The Moses of His Day

◆ From Royal Courtier to Judean Pioneer

The two books of Ezra and Nehemiah are usually considered as one in the Jewish canon, as they were written by the same author—Ezra—and they cover the same subject matter—the Jews' return from captivity in Babylon.

The writings contained in these two books cover two pivotal figures in Jewish history. Both were instrumental in guiding the Jewish people through their 70-year exile in Babylon and in establishing the second Jewish Commonwealth. You learn more about what both prophets did for their people in this chapter.

Leading the Return

Ezra the Scribe was a great sage from the priestly *caste* and a direct descendant of Aaron the High Priest. Ezra was called the Scribe in recognition of his mastery of all Scripture and teaching of the sages up to his time. The Talmud describes him as being worthy of having received the Torah had Moses not come before him.

Tower of Babel

Caste is a social category in which membership is fixed at birth and usually unchangeable. This very aptly describes the status of a Cohen, or Priest, in Judaism.

Ezra was also the head of the legal body known as the Great Assembly, which consisted of 120 of Israel's wisest men. They enacted much communal legislation, decided the official canon of Jewish Scripture, and organized the text of the prayer book. Ezra himself was responsible for 10 very significant decrees, which are discussed in more detail later in this chapter. But leading the nation back to its homeland and helping restore the Holy Temple were his greatest contributions to his people.

The Book of Ezra is basically a record of the events that catalyzed the peoples' return. Like many other aspects of Jewish history, it happened quite miraculously: "Now in the first year of Cyrus king of Persia, that the word of God by the mouth of Jeremiah might be accomplished, God stirred up the spirit of Cyrus king of Persia, that he made a proclamation throughout all his kingdom, and put it also in writing, saying: 'Thus says Cyrus king of Persia: All the kingdoms of the earth has Lord, the God of heaven, given me; and He has charged me to build Him a house in Jerusalem, which is in Judah. Whosoever there is among you of all His people—his God be with him—let him go up to Jerusalem, which is in Judah, and build the house of the Lord, God of Israel, He is the God who is in Jerusalem. And whosoever is left, in any place where he sojourns, let the men of his place help him with silver, and with gold, and with goods, and with beasts, beside the freewill-offering for the house of God which is in Jerusalem.'" (Ezra 1:1–4)

In his opening words, Ezra is actually writing of an earlier event that involved his colleague Nehemiah. The Persian monarch Cyrus was "aroused from above" to initiate an ambitious building campaign. Nehemiah, his chief wine butler and a Jewish leader, was the one to whom this proclamation was being addressed. He hoped this would herald the end to the 70-year exile as predicted by the prophet Jeremiah.

It Is Written

The foundation for the Temple was laid in that first year under Cyrus, but foes of the Jews managed to suspend the building campaign for another 18 years. When Cyrus II, Cyrus's grandson (and the son of King Ahasuerus and Esther) came to power, he immediately ordered the resumption of this rebuilding project. As a result of his Jewish origins and power, it took only four more years to complete the Second Temple and to inaugurate the Second Commonwealth that would stand for some 420 years. The Romans under Titus would later destroy the Second Temple around 70 C.E.

Teaching the Laws

Five chapters and 20 years later (458 B.C.E.), we find Ezra asking King Cyrus II to send him to Jerusalem so he can teach Israel the statutes and ordinances of the Law of the Torah. The benevolent king granted Ezra's request.

What's more, he gave Ezra a considerable royal entourage and extensive funding to get the job done. So emphatic was Cyrus that Ezra succeed in his mission, that he issued an ultimatum against slackers: "And whosoever will not do the law of thy God, and the law of the king, let judgment be executed upon him with all diligence, whether it be unto death, or to banishment, or to confiscation of goods, or to imprisonment." (Ezra 7:26)

With such a mandate, Ezra soon persuaded a group of 1,496 men and their families to leave Babylonia for good and return to their homeland.

On the way, Ezra picked up several hundred more Jews who spontaneously responded to his call.

> ### Lord Knows
>
> It was not easy to leave the comforts of one's familiar surroundings, even if the motivation was the lofty ideal of restoring one's homeland. Less than 42,000 Jews picked themselves up from that first proclamation by Cyrus to reclaim their land and Temple. This number represented less than 10 percent of the estimated population of Jews in Babylonia.

The roads leading to Israel from Babylon were fraught with danger, and the trip would not be an easy one. In chapter 8, the prophet revealed a glimpse of his mindset and concerns over embarking on such an arduous journey: "Then I proclaimed a fast there, at the river Ahava, that we might humble ourselves before our God, to seek of Him a straight way, for us, and for our little ones, and for all our substance. For I was ashamed to ask of the king a band of soldiers and horsemen to help us against the enemy in the way; because we had spoken unto the king, saying: 'The hand of our God is upon all them that seek Him, for good; but His power and His wrath is against all them that forsake Him.' So we fasted and besought our God for this; and He was entreated of us." (Ezra 8:21–23)

Removing Foreign Wives

Upon his arrival in Judea, Ezra was disappointed to find a Jewish community that was heavily intermarried and assimilated into the morals and customs of the indigenous pagan population. This problem extended to the very leaders of Judea themselves: "Now when these things were done, the princes drew near unto me, saying: 'The people of Israel, and the priests and the Levites, have not separated themselves from the peoples of the lands, doing according to their abominations, even of the Canaanites, the Hittites, the Perizzites, the Jebusites, the Ammonites, the Moabites, the Egyptians, and the Amorites. For they have taken of their daughters for them-selves and for their sons; so that the holy seed have mingled themselves with the peoples of the lands; yea, the hand of the princes and rulers has been first in this faithlessness.'" (Ezra 9:1–2)

Ezra set about to remedy the situation by introducing far-reaching changes aimed at preserving the Jewish people's unique identity. He began by praying and confessing Israel's sins to God. His faithful gathered with him at the Temple. Shecaniah, a man who had brought 300 others with him out of Elam (the lowlands of western Iran), urged that the Israelites divorce their foreign wives and send them away with their children. Ezra liked the idea and told the priests, Levites, and all of Israel to divorce their foreign wives and send them away. Only four people refused to do so. As it was early in the winter rainy season, those who did send their wives away were given three months to do so. Dissenters were to leave Israel and abandon their property.

To the modern mind it might seem harsh to require those who had married foreign women to either leave the community of Israel or divorce them. In fact, it sounds outright racist. This is particularly enigmatic as the prophets and Rabbinic leaders were generally very welcoming of gentiles who were seeking God and Torah. It seems difficult to understand that these prophets who spoke of universalism just a few years prior were now coercing many people to divorce their loved ones. What's going on here?

Ezra was advocating sanctity, not segregation. He viewed the gentile spouses as idolaters, as they continued to practice idolatry. In urging his people to separate from them, he was saving them from their own destruction.

The Great Legislator

With mass assimilation and intermarriage during the exile, very few accurate Torah scrolls were to be had. With divine guidance, Ezra wrote a letter-perfect Torah scroll that would become the standard for all Torah scrolls that followed. This is another reason why he is called Ezra the Scribe.

The Talmud also records 10 special *takanot*—legal enactments that Ezra and his court initiated for the newly repatriated Jewish community. Several of these enactments seem to be directed at remedying the problems the community suffered from before he arrived. They included the following:

♦ Requiring merchants to travel throughout the Land of Israel offering cosmetics and jewelry to wives, thus endearing them more to their husbands and keeping the husbands away from illicit Canaanite women.

♦ The consumption of garlic on Friday nights. This was probably ordered as garlic was known to be an aphrodisiac and Friday nights were a traditional time for Jewish men to cohabit with their wives.

♦ Men were required to immerse in a Mikvah (ritual pool) following marital relations. This was a ritual observance, not a physical cleansing activity. A seminal emission rendered a man, in ancient times, ineligible to attend the Temple in any capacity, study Torah, or a number of other activities. The only remedy for this was immersion in a mikvah. Since a mikvah wasn't a structure found in every house, or even every neighborhood, it meant a man would have to show some restraint, unless he intended to dip in a mikvah every morning.

♦ To strengthen Torah observances, Ezra instituted the public reading of the Torah in all synagogues (even outside Israel) on Mondays, Thursdays, and Sabbath afternoons. With the exile, the Jewish community adopted the local languages and no one was able to speak a common language. Hebrew had been transformed into a concoction of incoherent mishmash. Public readings would insure the continuity of Torah study and regular contact with the text.

Ezra realized that the most significant way to link the dispersed Jews and revive a connection to the Temple was by creating a common language of prayer. Along these lines, he helped formulate the "Shemoneh Esrei," a series of 18 blessings covering spiritual and physical communal and individual needs. No matter where a Jew lived or what language he spoke, the words of prayer would anchor them to their God and nation.

Judaism's very survival and continued relevance is due in great part to this farsighted and dynamic leader.

From Royal Courtier to Judean Pioneer

Nehemiah, whose identity is somewhat of a mystery, supervised the many facets of the Jewish expatriates who wished to resettle the Land of Israel. He was among those taken into captivity from Judah, but had risen to prominence in the government of Persia as cupbearer to King Cyrus I. Although Nehemiah did not hold political or military office, he was in a position of highest personal trust.

Nehemiah was greatly moved when some men came from Judah and reported the poverty and affliction there, and that the golden city of Jerusalem had become a slum. He was crestfallen, and despite his elevated position, he mourned and poured his heart out to God.

As a hallmark of a true Jewish leader, Nehemiah confessed the sins of the sons of Israel as if they were his own. He recalled God's promise to scatter Israel when they disobeyed, but reminded his Lord, the Guardian of Israel, that He said He would gather the exiled of Israel when they repented: "If you trespass, I will scatter you abroad among the peoples: but if you return unto Me, and keep my commandments and do them, though your outcasts were in the uttermost part of the heavens, yet will I gather them from thence, and will bring them unto the place that I have chosen, to cause my name to dwell there. Now these are thy servants and thy people, whom thou have redeemed by thy great power, and by thy strong hand. O God, I beseech thee, let now thine ear be attentive to the prayer of thy servant, and to the prayer of thy servants, who delight to fear thy name;

> **Lord Knows**
>
> Nehemiah was King Cyrus's butler or cupbearer. The two most trusted positions in royal households were typically the baker, who prepared the food, and the butler, or cupbearer, who served the food and beverage. Thus, when Pharaoh of Egypt found something unseemly in his supply of food, both the butler and baker were jailed. (Genesis 40:1–3)

and prosper, I pray thee, thy servant this day, and grant him mercy in the sight of this man." (Nehemiah 1:8–11)

Some four months later, Nehemiah, whose sad countenance was a reflection of how he felt inside, caught the attention of his boss while he was serving him wine. Nehemiah recaps the ensuing dialogue with the king: "… 'Why is thy countenance sad, seeing thou art not sick? This is nothing else but sorrow of heart.' Then I was very sore afraid. And I said unto the king: 'Let the king live for ever: why should not my countenance be sad, when the city, the place of my fathers' sepulchers, lies in waste, and the gates thereof are consumed with fire?'" (Nehemiah 2:2–3)

Nehemiah then asked the king to release him from his duty. It must have come as quite a surprise to Cyrus, as sending a trustworthy close servant on a long, arduous journey was not normal protocol of the royal court of Persia, or any other, for that matter: "Then the king said unto me: 'For what dost thou make request?' So I prayed to the God of heaven. And I said unto the king: 'If it please the king, and if thy servant have found favor in thy sight, that thou would send me unto Judah, unto the city of my fathers' sepulchers, that I may build it.' And the king said unto me, the queen also sitting by him: 'For how long shall thy journey be? And when wilt thou return?' So it pleased the king to send me; and I set him a time. Moreover I said unto the

king: 'If it please the king, let letters be given me to the governors beyond the River, that they may let me pass through till I come unto Judah; and a letter unto Asaph the keeper of the king's park, that he may give me timber to make beams for the gates of the castle which appertained to the house, and for the wall of the city, and for the house that I shall enter into.' And the king granted me, according to the good hand of my God upon me." (Nehemiah 2:4–8)

> **It Is Written**
>
> Asaph, the keeper of the king's park, was the guardian of the royal forests or nature reserve of Cyrus, which was probably located in Judea. As a musician of some repute, his name also prefaces 12 psalms.

Facing Subversive Forces

All good things in life come with opposing forces. Notwithstanding Cyrus's influence and protection, Nehemiah's mission was not going to be a piece of cake. Sanballat was then governor of Samaria. He was a Moabite, and ineligible to enter the Temple, or into the fold of the Jewish people for that matter. As such, he was anything but a good Samaritan and perceived any assistance given to Jerusalem as a threat to his dominion over the region.

But here was Nehemiah, with authorization from the king himself and captains of his army. After the wall of Jerusalem began to be rebuilt, they ridiculed it and suggested they were rebelling against the king. But Nehemiah told Sanballat that they had no rights and privileges in Jerusalem: "But when Sanballat the Horonite, and Tobiah the servant, the Ammonite, and Geshem the Arabian, heard it, they laughed us to scorn, and despised us, and said: 'What is this thing that ye do? Will ye rebel against the king?' Then answered I them, and said unto them: 'The God of heaven, He will prosper us; therefore we His servants will arise and build; but ye have no portion, nor right, nor memorial, in Jerusalem.'" (Nehemiah 2:19–20)

Sanballat and his allies schemed to thwart the efforts of the Jews to rebuild, and amassed a significant army to intimidate the pioneers. Nehemiah steeled his nerves and rallied his people to stay the course. They did with one hand on the trowel and one hand on the spear: "So we wrought in the work; and half of them held the spears from the rising of the morning till the stars appeared. Likewise at the same time said I unto the people: 'Let every one with his servant lodge within Jerusalem, that in the night they may be a guard to us, and may labor in the day.' So neither I, nor my brethren, nor my servants, nor the men of the guard that followed me, none of us put off our clothes, every one that went to the water had his weapon." (Nehemiah 4:15–17)

Nehemiah demonstrated much courage and persistence in the face of tremendous opposition. Sanballat contrived many ruses to frustrate his holy efforts. Eventually, he sent an open letter accusing the Jews of rebelling and preparing to name Nehemiah their king. Nehemiah sent a return message, saying, "You made it up yourself." Sanballat and Tobiah then hired Shemaiah, a Jew, to appear fearful and urge Nehemiah to barricade himself inside the Temple from Sanballat. Nehemiah saw through that, too. Tobiah sent letters to put him in fear but he ignored them all. Because "the people had a mind to work," the wall was completed in just 52 days. By the next week, the 42,360 people of Judah were settled in their newly fortified homes.

It Is Written

Twenty days after the wall was completed, the eight-day Feast of Tabernacles (*Sukkoth*—booths) was kept for the first time since Joshua died 1,000 years before. Two days later the sons of Israel were fasting and confessing their sins, the Levites read aloud the Law of the Lord for three hours, and then they recounted for another three hours the Lord's protection from the time He called Abram out of Ur in Chaldea, to entrance into the Promised Land, and then the disobedience of Israel in the land for which they had been dispersed and impoverished. The people all made a covenant to be faithful, and 84 priests, Levites, and princes set their seal to it.

Nehemiah had other internal problems to contend with. The harvest had been meager that year so grain prices were high. Large families went into debt, mortgaging their farms, and even selling their children into bondage to the wealthier Jews: "We are mortgaging our fields, and our vineyards, and our houses; let us get corn, because of the dearth ... we bring into bondage our sons and our daughters to be servants." (Nehemiah 5:3)

The tenacious Nehemiah called them all together to tell the wealthy that he himself had previously bought back the Jewish slaves from the gentiles but had not held them in bondage to himself. In his 12 years as governor, Nehemiah took no taxes from the people for himself. (Nehemiah 5:14–18) Then the wealthy, faced with the multitude, agreed to release the children from bondage, give back the farms, and refund the 1 percent interest they had charged.

Cleaning House

Throughout the remainder of the book, Nehemiah relates that his enemies gave him no rest and he had to continuously "clean house." Tobiah and his son had each married Jewish women, so some of the Jews were on Tobiah's side. They even acted as spies for Tobiah against Nehemiah. After Nehemiah returned to Persia, the High Priest allied himself with Tobiah the Ammonite, took away the treasure room of the Levites, and converted it into spacious living quarters for Tobiah. Upon Nehemiah's return, he irately threw out Tobiah's furniture, restored the room for the Levites' tithe, recalled the Levites from their refuges, and appointed another priest, a scribe, and two Levites over the treasuries.

Although Nehemiah did not rebuild the actual Temple, his efforts to instill the people with greater religiosity and "kosher" living represented the foundation stone that Ezra, his successor, would build upon.

The Least You Need to Know

- The books of Ezra and Nehemiah are actually considered one as they were both authored by Ezra and chronicle the same period of Jewish history.

- Ezra led a contingent of pioneers who heeded his call to resettle Jerusalem and help rebuild the Temple with the generous support and authorization of Cyrus II, King of Persia.

- Ezra enacted many ordinances for his repatriated co-religionists that facilitated restoration of normative Jewish living in the Holy Land.

♦ Nehemiah was a close servant of Cyrus I, who, some 52 years after the destruction of Solomon's Temple, was given the nod to begin its restoration with the building of the walls around the old city of Jerusalem.

♦ Like his colleague Ezra several years later, Nehemiah was challenged with rebuking his people for intermarriage with pagan wives and instilling them with greater religious observance.

Chapter 30

The Kingdom of Messiah: The Book of Chronicles

In This Chapter

◆ Turning two books into one

◆ Learning more than just genealogy

◆ Revealing deeper truths

◆ Seeking the final redemption

Chronicles might very well be the most perplexing book in the Hebrew Bible. Open it to any chapter and you'll find pages full of nothing but names followed by more names: This person was the son of that father and in turn had these children of his own. Take a closer look, and nothing written there seems original—it's all a rehash of stories found elsewhere in Jewish Scripture, and particularly in Samuel and Kings.

But there's more to Chronicles than meets the eye. On one level it does seem to repeat the same material, but the perspective here is different. We take a closer look at the differences in this chapter.

Two Books or One?

In the original Hebrew canon, Chronicles consisted of a single book called *Divrei Hayamim*. They were divided into two in the Septuagint, the third-century B.C.E. Greek translation of the Hebrew Bible.

> **Tower of Babel**
>
> *Divrei Hayamim* literally translates as "Words of the Days," or "Matters of the Days." The closest English word to describe its contents is Chronicles.

Like the books of Samuel and Kings, Chronicles became two in printed editions even within the Jewish community. There is some justification for dividing the book, as the first nine chapters are a general chronicle of biblical history from Adam until David (pre-monarchy history), while the remainder of the book concentrates on the Kingdom of David and his great deeds and culminates in the destruction of the First Temple. Nonetheless, Jewish tradition holds that they are essentially a single work.

Chronicles can be thematically divided into four main parts:

♦ A list of genealogies in the line of Israel down to the time of King David. These are contained in the first nine chapters of Book I.

♦ The reign of David. This is contained in the remainder of Book I.

♦ The reign of King Solomon. This is contained in the first nine chapters of Book II.

♦ The history of the Kingdom of Judah to the time of the return from Babylonian exile. These are contained in the remaining chapters of Book II.

The Talmud relates that Chronicles, along with the books of Ezra and Nehemiah, were written by Ezra the Scribe with some help from Nehemiah, who completed the last 16 chapters.

It is believed that Ezra wrote Chronicles as a supplement to the books of Samuel and Kings, and that he used a collection of ancient genealogies of most of Israel's tribes to draft the text. Ezra actually alluded to such texts early in Chronicles, "… now these are ancient traditions." (I Chronicles 4:22)

For various reasons, Ezra found it necessary to provide Israel a detailed record of its origins and growth into a nation. The brilliance of his accomplishment was the ability to assemble and filter through these ancient records and lists. Naturally, such lists would contradict each other, lack information, or contain errors. But Ezra worked with what he had. According to the Jerusalem Talmud, he used three main sources. If two concurred against the third, he went with the majority.

The Sages Say

The rabbis of the Talmud taught that the Book of Chronicles (and Psalms) are comparable to the Five Books of Moses. How so? The Torah describes itself as being "... the account of the descendants of Adam." (Genesis 5:1) This account doesn't only cover 10 or 20 generations, but forms a backdrop for all human history. In a similar fashion, Ezra wrote Chronicles to tell the story of humankind through the eyes of its greatest leaders.

Deeper Meaning

Ezra's writing in Chronicles sometimes contradicts what he wrote in the books of Ezra and Nehemiah. Sometimes he abbreviates some of the genealogical lineages for no apparent reason. Was Ezra's writing more his own work than pure divine inspiration? If so, how did these books attain the holiness necessary to be included in the Hebrew canon?

One of the greatest Talmudic commentators of the medieval period seemed to be quoting Ezra himself in providing one answer: "Although I mentioned part of the genealogies, I have not mentioned them all. They are listed in the 'Books of Jewish Kings', however, those books are no longer extant among us, like the Book of Rectitude and the Book of Wars of God." (Moses alludes to this book in Numbers 21:14.) As for Ezra's writings contradicting what he previously wrote, it's believed that Ezra simply found different accounts—he wrote one in Chronicles, and cited the other in Nehemiah.

The original authors of Ezra's genealogical tables intended them to be merely birth records and political and military exploits. They had no idea they could serve as vessels for Godly instruction, which is what Ezra used them for.

Ezra came on the scene at a time of exile and depressed national pride. He analyzed these chronicles to transcend the factual nature of their authors. And herein lies the gist of these chapters of Chronicles—to capture the spiritual qualities of these personalities that shaped Jewish faith and culture that would inspire future generations.

From this collection of facts, Ezra extracted a deeper meaning and infused them with a divine quality that transformed them into sacred texts. Based on this assessment, the Jewish commentators all suggest that Chronicles cannot be understood by its simple meaning. To do so would be tantamount to looking upon a Rembrandt as merely a collage of nicely mixed paint. Instead, cloaked in Ezra's words are dimensions of the biblical personalities who shaped Jewish history that are not obvious to the naked eye.

Strange Names (and Outright Strangers)

At times, the very identities of these people are concealed with names unfamiliar to anyone who has read the other 23 books of Jewish Scripture. There are many instances in Chronicles where people are ascribed to families where they simply don't belong: "The sons of Shelah the son of Judah was Er the father of Lecha ... and Yokim and the people of Kozevah and Yoash and Saraph that married (Lit. became masters) of Moab ... now these are ancient traditions." (I Chronicles 4:21–22)

At first the chronicler is going all the way back to Judah (son of Jacob) whose third son was indeed Shelah. No problem here. But then he skips many generations to Yoash and Saraf who are identified only as they "became masters of Moab," meaning they took wives from the women of Moab. This is a clear allusion to events from the first chapter of Ruth (some 500 plus years after Shelah) where two descendants of Judah—Machlon and Kilyon—married Ruth and Oprah. But we never see them identified with the names Yoash and Saraf. What's going on?

According to the sages of the Talmud, many names found in Chronicles are not proper names but descriptive ones. They reflect the nature of these two people. The name Yoash is related to the Hebrew word "Ye'ush" which means despair. This indicates that Machlon despaired redemption for his fellow Judeans, who he perceived were doomed to remain in exile.

> **Lord Knows**
>
> One of the main biblical commentators suggests that the concept extracted from the verse "now these are ancient traditions" applies to all genealogical material found in Chronicles.

Saraf means "burning," for Kilyon as a leader of his people was deserving of being consumed by fire as punishment for abandoning his countryman during a famine.

The Book of Ruth is concerned with the actual history of the time and gives their proper names. Chronicles, on the other hand, avoids the obvious and reveals deeper truths.

The last words of the verse "now these are ancient traditions" also teach a significant lesson. Ezra is saying that the story of Machlon and Kilyon is generally not well known because it occurred many years earlier. And while it is not found in any of the scriptural books, it is based on a reliable tradition—in fact an ancient one that was handed down from generation to generation.

Other examples of strange names and outright strangers that appear in Chronicles include the following:

♦ Yokim, who crops up in King David's genealogy. The sages say his name is actually a reference to Joshua, as Yokim is a derivative of the Hebrew word *heikim*, which means "to establish." Joshua righteously upheld an oath to a Canaanite group in spite of their deceit. Furthermore, he established or set the stage for the eventual rule of David by conquering the Land of Israel.

♦ Batya, who is identified as the Egyptian princess who pulled Moses from the Nile. In Exodus she's simply the daughter of Pharaoh. Why the discrepancy? A possible explanation is that the events surrounding the birth of Israel's first savior and teacher were the focus of the earlier book. Accordingly, neither Batya nor any other personality is identified by proper name. However, in the extended Chronicles of Scripture, Batya receives her due recognition as Moses' adopted mother.

♦ Hatzleponi, Samson's mother. As a rule, males are listed in genealogies as the heads of families, but Hatzleponi is mentioned in I Chronicles 4:3 as a woman from the tribe of Judah. Curiously, her name doesn't appear in any form in the Book of Judges where Samson's name appears. Why is she identified at all in Chronicles? The translation of her name, which means "she saw (or turned) to an angel twice" might have something to do with it. Seeing angels wasn't an everyday occurrence, and Hatzleponi saw them twice.

These enigmatic names, and more, grace the Book of Chronicles making it one of the most fascinating and perplexing books of Scripture.

Twice-Told Tales

As mentioned, Chronicles often fills in or complements the narratives found in the books of Samuel and Kings. However, it also often clashes or contradicts details of these books. Let's take a look at one such discrepancy: "Then David said to Ornan:

'Give me the place of this threshing-floor, that I may build thereon an altar unto God; for the full price shalt thou give it me; that the plague may be stayed from the people.' And Ornan said unto David: 'Take it to thee, and let my lord the king do that which is good in his eyes; lo, I give thee the oxen for burnt-offerings, and the threshing-instruments for wood, and the wheat for the meal-offering; I give it all' And king David said to Ornan: 'Nay, but I will verily buy it for the full price; for I will not take that which is thine for God, nor offer a burnt-offering without cost.' So David gave to Ornan for the place six hundred shekels of gold by weight." (I Chronicles 21:22–25)

Here, as in the Book of Samuel, David is purchasing the threshing floor that will become the site of the Temple Mount. Though Ornan is gracious and wishes to grant this place, David refrains from using his influence and insists on paying full price in gold. However, the amount David pays in the Book of Samuel is only 50 shekels and the commodity is silver, not gold. Which is correct?

The commentators give a number of clever answers. The sages of the Talmud have a tradition that David collected the full amount of 600 gold shekels from the Twelve Tribes of Israel. Each contributed the amount of 50 shekels, however they gave its equivalent in silver—which they had in abundance. Alternatively, the sages suggest that the 50 shekels mentioned in Samuel were only for the area of the threshing floor that the altar would sit upon. Chronicles relates that David paid 600 shekels for the entire threshing floor—that measured 500×500 cubits—just for the record.

Lord Knows

Each one of the Twelve Tribes of Israel is given prominent mention in Chronicles, which painstakingly records each one's genealogy. Chronicles also teaches that each tribe had a specific banner or flag that distinguished it during its 40-year sojourn in the Sinai wilderness. As an example, the flag of the Tribe of Yissocher featured the sun, the moon, and the stars. The reason for this was because the Tribe of Yissocher possessed "men of understanding of the times." (I Chronicles 12:33) They mastered the astronomical sciences and served as consultants to the Sanhedrin for questions dealing with the calculation of the appearance of the new moon.

King David's Thirst

Chronicles does not give up its secrets easily. Ezra seems to have imbedded layer upon layer of meaning. One of the book's many passages about King David illustrates this point: "And David was then in the stronghold, and the garrison of the Philistines was then in Bethlehem. And David craved, and said: 'Oh that one would give me water to drink of the well of Bethlehem, which is by the gate!' And the three broke through the host of the Philistines, and drew water out of the well of Bethlehem, that was by the gate, and took it, and brought it to David; but David would not drink thereof, but poured it out unto God, and said: 'My God forbid it me, that I should do this; shall I drink the blood of these men that have put their lives in jeopardy? For with the jeopardy of their lives they brought it.' Therefore he would not drink it. These things did the three mighty men do." (I Chronicles 11:16–19)

There is a host of hostile Philistines teeming around Bethlehem and David has this sudden urge to drink from a well? Who would be so cavalier to risk his soldiers' lives on such a whim? Is David that capricious? What does this episode really mean?

It is known that David came from Bethlehem, and he probably craved the taste of the sweet cistern waters he remembered from his youth. Obviously, he did not literally expect his soldiers to risk their lives to fulfill his cravings, for he forbids himself the waters that were obtained at such a "price." Rather, he wistfully desired them and perhaps his thoughts about them now were an inspiration to vanquish the enemy Philistine troops who occupied the area.

The Sages Say

The fact that David identified a specific location, "which is by the gate," intrigued the sages of the Talmud and convinced them that David had something else in mind altogether. They teach that King David wasn't thirsting for water but for something metaphorically compared to water—Torah knowledge. (Isaiah 55:1) David was in need of some instruction here. Because the Sanhedrin was located in Bethlehem, three of David's soldiers courageously broke through the city's defenses, posed the problem, and relayed the response to the king. David was incensed at his men for risking their lives over something not required of them and rebuked them accordingly.

The Future and Final Redemption

Like other books of Scripture, there are passages in Chronicles that hint to a future Messianic Age. Rather than go into detail about them here, we'll end this guide with a general look at how traditional Judaism envisions this much-anticipated period of time.

Rabbi Elchanan Wasserman was a great religious leader who was martyred in the Holocaust. He used the following parable to explain world events during the apocalyptic period in which he lived.

A man wishes to learn about agriculture. So, he comes to a field filled with beautiful plants. After enjoying this breathtaking view, he observes the farmer digging and churning up this beautiful ground. If that is not enough, suddenly there are seeds spreading all over the ground, in enormous quantity—what a waste! To top it off, the new harvest again ruins the beautiful lush scenery.

After some time, this observer returns to taste a delicious piece of bread made from the grain of this field. Only then does he realize that it was a step-by-step process, not realizing what was taking place until the very end. As human beings, we are only given a partial picture of reality; the rest will only become clear to us at the time of the redemption.

That redemption period seems to be upon us. From Genesis to Chronicles and from Moses to Ezra, we have been given 22,000 divinely inspired verses of Scripture to glimpse and analyze this process as it unfurls. They relate humankind's fame and folly, their "best of times and the worst of times." Of course, they also contain profound directives that reveal how to live a righteous life and the significance of all historical events from the beginning of time. We only need the proper tools to access these secrets and realize the step-by-step process. They are all here.

Lord Knows

A personage no less than Sir Isaac Newton, among other great minds, has suspected that not only the past but also the future of mankind is encoded and hinted to within Scripture. The following are just a few examples of relatively modern-day events that many believe are to be found imbedded within its holy pages:

Both world wars

The Holocaust and Hiroshima

The Lincoln and Kennedy assassinations (among other world leaders)

Major earthquakes and moon landings

The Oklahoma City and World Trade Center bombings

Collapse of the financial markets and the New York Stock Exchange in 1929

Global terrorism

As we march to the epoch that the prophets allude to called *Achrit Hayamim* (End of Days), events are unfolding before our very eyes, often just as the prophets predicted. The Scripture was originally given only to the Jewish people; However, it is now accepted by multitudes of humankind as the focal point of civilization.

God, in His infinite wisdom, is using the Bible to galvanize the entire world to recognize genuine truth and bring the idealistic concept of a redeemed world into the hearts of all His creation.

When that glorious ideal is realized, the world will bear witness to the immortal words of Isaiah:

"The nations will beat their swords into plowshares,

and the wolf will lie down with the lamb.

… and the earth shall be filled with wisdom

as waters cover the ocean floor."

May it be very soon in all our lifetimes, sooner than anyone can imagine.

The Least You Need to Know

- Chronicles might very well be the most perplexing book of Jewish Scripture.

- Ezra the Scribe wrote most of Chronicles. The last 16 chapters are attributed to Nehemiah.

- Much of Chronicles retells narratives that are found throughout the other books of Scripture, primarily the books of Samuel and Kings.

- Chronicles relates the genealogies of humankind from Adam until the period of the destruction of the First Temple in Jerusalem.

- The simple meaning of the text is often anything but simple and can only be understood in context, allegorically, or homiletically.

- Chronicles contains passages that foresee a redeemed world that will be led by God's anointed Messiah.

Appendix A

Glossary

achrit hayamim   End of Days.

Adonai   The God of the Hebrews.

Baal worship   A generic term for the main idolatry practiced during the time of the Jewish Bible.

baale teshuva   "One of Return." Used to describe someone who either never observed Torah law, or left the fold and is now a penitent Jew.

bat kol   A heavenly voice, a subtle form of prophecy

Bereshith   The original Hebrew title of the Book of Genesis. It means "in the beginning."

brit milah   The covenant of circumcision. Usually referred to simply as a brit.

Daniel   Hebrew for "God is my judge." Is the name of a prophet.

Divrei Hayamim   The Hebrew name for the Book of Chronicles. Translates as "Words of the Days" or "Matters of the Days."

Eicha   "Alas" in Hebrew and the Hebrew title of the Book of Lamentations.

Genesis   Greek for "origin," "beginning," "source," or "generation." Name of the first book of the Jewish Bible.

Hebrew Bible   Another name for the Tanakh or Jewish Bible. This term is preferred by some scholars who wish to avoid sectarian bias.

kashrut   From the Hebrew kasher, meaning fit, proper, or approved. The more commonly known word "kosher" describes food that meets these standards, comes from the same root.

ketav   Hebrew for "writing." The plural is ketuvim, meaning "writings."

Kohelet   Hebrew for "to congregate." Named for Eclessiastes.

maaseh merkava   "Divine Chariot" in Hebrew. Derived from the word *maaseh*, meaning "action"; and *merkava*, a chariot or riding vehicle. Alludes to Kabbalistic teachings in general.

megillot   Scrolls.

mezuzot   Literally "doorposts," named for scrolls placed on the doors of Jewish homes and rooms.

Midrash   A body of Rabbinic literature containing commentary on biblical texts.

Mikra (plural Mikraot)   Readings. Used to describe the entire body of the Jewish Bible, especially before the term Tanakh was invented.

mikvah   Ritual pool.

mitzvah   Commandment. Based on the root word *tzav*, meaning "connection." Hence, mitzvah connotes a connection with God.

mizmor   One of the main forms of song found in Psalms, defined as "a musical out-pouring of the soul."

monotheism   The belief in one supreme God who is the sole source of all existence and upon whom everything remains totally dependent.

Moshe   The biblical name for Moses, derived from an Egyptian expression coined by Pharaoh's daughter that means "From the water he was drawn."

nazirite   From the Hebrew *nazir*, meaning "delineation" or "designation." Nazirites were individuals who vowed to dedicate themselves to special sacred service. The dedication could last for a limited period or a lifetime.

Ne'um HaMitvoth   "The Speech of the Commandments." Used to describe Moses' main speech in Deuteronomy.

Ne'viim Achronim   Hebrew for "Later Prophets." Also known as the Latter Prophets, these include Isaiah, Jeremiah, Ezekiel, and The Twelve.

Ne'viim Rishonim   Hebrew for "Early Prophets." They include Joshua, Judges, Samuel, and Kings.

pantheists   People who believe that God and the material world are one and the same, and that God is present in everything. As such, they believe in many deities.

pardes   Hebrew for "orchard." An acronym that developed in the Middle Ages to refer to four levels of biblical analysis or exploration.

Parshat HaShavua   In Hebrew, "portion of the week." The time-honored system of completing the Five Books of Moses annually by reading a part of the Pentateuch publicly in the synagogue each week of the Jewish calendar year.

parshiot   Paragraphs or breaks in the Torah.

Passover   The holiday that celebrates the liberation of the Jewish people from slavery in Egypt, a prelude to their standing at Mount Sinai.

Pentateuch   Hebrew for "five cases," referring to the sheaths or boxes in which the separate rolls or volumes of the ancient Bible are believed to have been originally stored.

Rosh Hoshana   The Jewish New Year.

Sefer HaYahsar   In Hebrew, "Book of the Upright," an alternate name for the Book of Genesis.

Sefer HaYuchasim   In Hebrew, "Book of Lineages," an alternate name for the Book of Chronicles.

Septuagint   The third-century B.C.E. Greek translation of the Hebrew Bible.

shekel   Ancient Jewish coin or unit of weight.

Shemoneh Esrei   A series of 18 blessings covering spiritual and physical communal and individual needs.

shir   One of the two main forms of song found in Psalms, defined as "song" and "poetry."

Shir Hashirim   The Hebrew title of Song of Songs, derived from the opening verse of Solomon—"The song of songs, which is Solomon's."

shoftim   Hebrew for "judges."

Shulamite   The term used to describe the bride in Song of Songs. Might have been derived from the town of Shunem, located southwest of the Sea of Galilee.

smicha   Derived from the Hebrew word *lismoch*, which means "to rest" or "to support." Name of ceremony for rabbinical ordination.

sotah   Hebrew for "to turn away," as in turning away from the proper way. Name for a ceremony conducted by High Priest in the Temple to examine the innocence or guilt of a wife suspected by here husband of infidelity.

Succot   A seven-day Jewish festival held in the fall to celebrate the harvest. In the Diaspora it is observed for eight days.

Takanot   Legal enactments, such as those that Ezra and his court initiated for the newly repatriated Jewish community.

Talmud   Another set of Jewish Scripture in which the great teachers of the Jewish faith explain how mitzvoth and tenets of Jewish customs are derived from verses in Scripture. It also contains worldly wisdom including health directives, science, astronomy, and business advice, as well as accounts of Jewish history, among other information.

Tanakh   An acronym for the Hebrew words Torah, Ne'viim, and Ketuvim. These translate as Torah = Five Books of Moses, Ne'viim = Prophets, and Ketuvim = Holy Writings.

Tefillin   Frontlets or phylacteries, derived from the word *tefilah*, meaning "prayer."

Torah   The first five books of the Bible. Also called the Pentateuch or the Five Books of Moses.

Trei-Assar   Hebrew for "The Twelve." Included in the grouping known as the Later Prophets.

trinitarianism   The belief in the Christian doctrine of the trinity.

Tzidduk HaDin   A service in which mourners for loved ones acknowledge the ultimate righteous judgment of God over their loss.

yetzer hara   Hebrew for "evil inclination."

Zephaniah   Hebrew for "hidden of God." Name of a prophet.

Zohar   One of the earliest Kabbalistic texts, written by the second century sage Rabbi Shimon bar Yochai.

zonah   Term often used in the Bible to describe a prostitute.

Resources

The resources listed in this appendix have been arranged according to books that will help further your studies in Hebrew Scripture and websites that help provide more information. Readers are invited to visit my website www.ravparry.com for more resources or questions you may have about the material in this book.

Books

Scherman, Nosson, and Meir Zlotovitz; General Editors. *The Stone Edition Chumash*. New York: Mesorah Publications Ltd., 1993.

A must read for all serious students of Jewish Scripture. The translation follows a distinctive Jewish traditional approach. The major commentators, especially Rashi, are found here. There are dozens of helpful charts and maps that help make the more enigmatic sections of the Five Books of Moses accessible and simplified. This text is possibly the most often referenced and read from in the Jewish religious community today.

Scherman, Nosson; Editor. *The Stone Edition Tanach*. New York: Mesorah Publications Ltd., 1998.

All 24 books of the Torah, Prophets, and Writings are found in this remarkable 2,200-page volume, as interpreted by the classic sages of Talmudic and Rabbinic literature. It enables everyone to obtain a basic knowledge of the entire Tanach and is an indispensable book for those interested in knowing about the People of the Book. Very clear introductions to each book of Tanakh, illuminated notes and comments, a full index of topics with several pages of explanatory charts, illustrations, and maps. This work is the benchmark for all other biblical works of this nature.

Herczeg, Yisrael, in collaboration with Rabbis Yoseph Kamenetsky, Yaakov Petroff, and Yaakov Blinder; edited by Rabbi Avie Gold. *The Sapirstein Edition Rashi*. New York: Mesorah Publications Ltd., 1997.

The father of all commentators, Rashi is the most stimulating and thought-provoking biblical commentator of them all. He leaves you with profound questions and answers that bring the text alive. Behind the deceptive simplicity of Rashi is a depth and clarity that has engaged the minds of great scholars for more than 800 years. This edition translates the actual text according to Rashi's understanding and thus provides one of the most Judaism-authentic translations available to the English-speaking public.

Scherman, Nosson. *The Rubin Edition of The Prophets (Joshua-Judges-Samuel)*. New York: Mesorah Publications Ltd., 2002.

This is a highly regarded new translation, firmly grounded in traditional sources such as Rashi, Ramban, Radak, Malbim, and so on. A very accurate Hebrew text and translation. Each volume has an overview of the prophets and explains the institution of prophecy in general. As with other works from Mesorah, this one contains introductions and explanations of difficult concepts and many maps and diagrams.

Miller, Avigdor. *Behold a People*. New York: 1968.

Rabbi Miller was a great Talmudist as well as historian. This volume covers the biblical history of the world from Creation until the prophet Jeremiah. It has a unique format and the author cites copious resources.

Hirsch, Samson Raphael; translated by Karin Paritzky. *From the Wisdom of Mishle (Proverbs)*. New York and Jerusalem: Feldheim Publishers, 1976.

Proverbs is an illumination of the unprecedented wisdom of King Solomon. Rabbi Hirsch, the great nineteenth-century German-Jewish scholar and philosopher, lucidly renders his timeless proverbs into practical guidance to help solve the social and ethical problems of contemporary living.

Kaplan, Aryeh. *The Living Torah*. New York and Jerusalem: Maznaim Publishers, 1981.

As with everything written by the master of modern translations, the late Rabbi Kaplan, a physicist by trade, elucidates the Torah text like no one else. This is another masterpiece of Jewish literary accomplishment where the author avoids literal translation in favor of teaching accurate tradition. The footnotes are extensive and there is a glossary of words in the back of this 1,400-page work that is second to none.

Kaplan, Aryeh. *The Handbook of Jewish Thought*. New York and Jerusalem: Maznaim Publications, 1979.

Rabbi Kaplan explains in two volumes "everything you ever wanted to know about Judaism." A college course could easily be taught from this brilliantly organized and clearly written work. The section on prophets and prophecy is particularly significant and a must for all who wish to explore the subject further.

Sokolovsky, Meir Simcha. *Prophecy and Providence*. Jerusalem and New York: Feldheim Publishers, 1991.

The author does a very commendable job in showing how the fulfillment of Scriptural prophecies in the course of Jewish and contemporary history has taken place.

Parry, Aaron. *The Complete Idiot's Guide to the Talmud*. Indianapolis: Alpha Books, 2004.

Much reference is made to the Talmud in this *Complete Idiot's Guide to Hebrew Scripture*. Readers might want to explore the origins of this ancient record of the Oral Law that is essential to understanding the origins of Jewish observance and tradition today.

Rosenberg, A. J. *The Judaica Press Books of the Bible Series*. New York: 1983.

The entire series was one of the first to translate all the books of Tanakh. It features a superb English digest of the major medieval commentators. Each volume contains the Hebrew text and all the classical commentaries. The facing page contains a modern English translation with extensive translation of the particular Scriptural text. The Judaica Press Series is an excellent tool for Torah study for students or teachers of Scripture.

Websites

www.ravparry.com. What can I say? Have questions about this book or my work on the Talmud? By all means, contact me here.

www.breslov.com/bible. One of the best websites out there that offers several valid Jewish translations of Jewish Scripture. The translations include Massoretic, Hebrew, Aramaic, Jewish Publication Society, and Kaplan.

www.torah.org. A truly stellar website with thousands of pages of information including contemporary scholars commenting on all books of Scripture.

www.messiahtruth.com. Serious scholarship here. Written with the main purpose of refuting Christian fundamentalist interpretations of Scripture, it has much more.

www.chabad.org/library/archive/LibraryArchive.asp?AID=63255. Here's the entire shebang with Rashi's complete commentary on Tanakh. This might be the only place on the web where you will find it.

www.jewishencyclopedia.com/index.jsp. The complete, unedited contents of the 12-volume Jewish Encyclopedia (as published in 1906), is found here with more than 15,000 articles and illustrations.

www.jewishstudies.org. Classic areas of Jewish studies in online courses, with contemporary references.

www.jewfaq.org/index.htm. Well-thought-out categories on almost anything with good internal links and background files: the FAQ is narrative in style and hosted on AOL.

www.ou.org/torah. This site contains tradition, online study and resources, audio library, publications, and e-lists.

www.davka.com. A veritable Jewish software superstore. You can get Bible, Talmud, Midrash, processors, programs to learn the Hebrew language, kid's educational games, utilities, Hebrew fonts, clip art, and much more.

Timeline of History in Jewish Scriptures

Event	Jewish Calendar	Gregorian Calendar (B.C.E.)
Creation	1	3760
Noah and the flood	1656	2104
Abraham (born Abram)	1948	1812
Isaac born	2048	1712
Jacob born		1652
Joseph sold into slavery		1544
Jacob and family go to Egypt	2238	1522
Israelites enslaved in Egypt		1428
Moses born		1392
The Exodus	2448	1312
Torah given at Mount Sinai		1312
Children of Israel enter the Land of Israel	2489	1272
David born	2854	906
Solomon born	2912	848
Solomon builds the Holy Temple	2935	825

Event	Jewish Calendar	Gregorian Calendar (B.C.E.)
Rebellion of the Ten Tribes; Kingdom is split into Israel (10 tribes) and Judah (2 tribes)	2964	796
Israel conquered by Shalmanesser; its people exiled to places unknown	3205	555
Holy Temple destroyed; Judah exiled to Babylon	3338	422
Holy Temple rebuilt; end of Era of Prophecy	3408	352
Second Holy Temple destroyed	3828	C.E. 68 or 70

Key Players

The men and woman of *Tanach* were real people, with complex personalities, moral dilemmas, and general human interaction. Although not exhaustive, this list includes a pretty comprehensive glimpse of the main characters of Scripture who had a major impact on Jewish religious thought, practice, and history.

Aaron—Moses' brother.

Abel—Adam and Eve's son.

Abram, Abraham—The great patriarch of Israel.

Adam—The first man (along with Eve—the first woman) to inhabit the Garden of Eden.

Ahab—The king of Israel who was led astray by his wife Jezebel, an idolater.

Amos—A prophet during the reign of King Uzziah of Judah and Yeravam ben Yoash.

Amram and Yocheved—Father and mother of Moses.

Azariah—Daniel's friend—along with Chananiah and Mishael. The three also are identified as Shadrach, Meshach, and Abed Nego.

Bathsheba—King David's second wife.

Beldad—Along with Eliphaz and Tzofer, they were Job's three friends.

Bithiah—The Pharaoh's daughter who found baby Moses.

Cain—Adam and Eve's son.

Chananiah—Daniel's friend along with Azariah and Mishael. The three also are identified as Shadrach, Meshach, and Abed Nego.

Cyrus—The Persian king who issued a decree allowing the Jews to return to their homeland and rebuild their temple.

Daniel—One of the last prophets. His ministry covered the entire 70 years of Jewish captivity in Babylon.

David—King Saul's successor and the second king of Israel.

Deborah—The sole female judge, and prophetess. She led Israel to victory over the Canaanites with Barak, her general.

Delilah—The naughty consort of Samson who cut his hair and robbed him of his strength.

Elijah—Along with Elisha, both were main prophets of their time. Elisha was Elijah's disciple.

Eliphaz—Along with Beldad and Tzofer, they were Job's three friends.

Elisha—Along with Elijah, they were the main prophets of their time. Elisha was Elijah's disciple.

Esau—The older son of Isaac and Rebecca and the twin brother of Jacob.

Esther—The Persian queen who helped deliver the Jewish people from Persia.

Eve—The first woman (along with Adam—the first man) to inhabit the Garden of Eden.

Ezekiel—The first prophet to receive his communications from God outside of Israel.

Ezra—One of the last prophets, he was instrumental in guiding the Jewish people through their exile in Babylon.

Habakkuk—A student of Isaiah, he prophesied between 612 B.C.E. and 606 B.C.E.

Hagar—The maid Sarah gave to Abraham as another wife.

Haggai—A prophet who prophesied during the reign of King Darius. He was instrumental in the rebuilding of the Second Temple.

Ham—One of Noah's three sons, along with Shem and Japheth. Ham is associated with the peoples of Africa.

Hezekiah—A king of Judah. He sought to unify his country with the kingdom of Israel.

Hosea—Often called the gentlest prophet, he communicated God's word for 90 years.

Isaac—The son of Abraham and Sarah.

Isaiah—The greatest of the Jewish prophets.

Ishmael—The son of Abraham and Hagar.

Jacob—A son of Isaac and Rebecca and the twin brother of Esau.

Japheth—One of Noah's three sons, along with Ham and Shem. Japheth's name is synonymous with beauty and represents the European-Asian people.

Jeremiah—A prophet who delivered his prophecies during the reign of King Josiah and continued through the reigns of three of Josiah's successors, Jehoiakim, Johoiachin, and Zedekiah.

Jesse—King David's father.

Job—The righteous man whose suffering is detailed in the book that bears his name.

Joel—A prophet who predicted the restoration of Judah and Jerusalem and the triumph of Israel over her enemies.

Johoiachin—The last of the kings of Israel.

Jonah—A prophet who prophesied during the reign of Jeroboam II.

Joseph—The son of Jacob and Rachel.

Joshua—Moses' successor who led the people of Israel into the Promised Land.

Josiah—One of Judah's few righteous kings. Credited with restoring the Temple service and eradicating Israel of idolatry.

Leah—Rachel's older sister and Jacob's first wife.

Lot—A nephew of Abraham.

Malachi—The last of the Minor Prophets, he prophesied after the Temple was rebuilt.

Micah—A prophet who lived at the same time as Isaiah and Hosea. Sometimes called the "prophet of the poor" as he might have belonged to the peasant class.

Miriam—Moses' and Aaron's sister.

Mishael—Daniel's friend—along with Chananiah and Azariah. The three also are identified as Shadrach, Meshach, and Abed Nego.

Mordechai—Esther's uncle.

Moses—Israel's first savior and major teacher.

Nahum—The prophet who predicted Nineveh's destruction.

Naomi—Ruth's mother-in-law.

Nebuchadnezzar—The Babylonian king who sacked Jerusalem and destroyed the First Temple.

Nehemiah—One of the last prophets, credited along with Ezra for helping to build the Second Temple.

Noah—The father of Shem, Ham, and Japheth, and the hero of the Great Flood.

Obadiah—The only converted Jew to have his prophecy included in the official canon.

Rachel—Jacob's wife and the daughter of Rebecca's brother Laban.

Rahab—The woman who harbored Joshua's spies as they scouted out Jericho.

Rebecca—Isaac's wife and the mother of Esau and Jacob.

Rehavam—Solomon's son, he succeeded his father to the throne of the kingdom of Israel.

Ruth—The Moabite princess who converted to Judaism, motivated by her love for and dedication to her mother-in-law Naomi. By marriage, she also became King David's great-grandmother.

Samson—The twelfth and last judge of Israel.

Samuel—One of Israel's last judges, and major prophet, he led the nation as it transitioned into a monarchy.

Sarai, Sarah—The great matriarch of Israel.

Saul—The first king of Israel.

Shem—One of Noah's three sons, along with Ham and Japheth. Shem represents the Semitic people.

Solomon—King David's son by Bathsheba. Also a king of Israel, noted as the wisest man of all.

Tzofer—Along with Beldad and Eliphaz, they were Job's three friends.

Zechariah—A prophet whose teachings focused on persuading the tribe of Judah to complete the Second Temple.

Zephaniah—A prophet who prophesied during the time of King Josiah.

Index

R